Teaching
for Critical
Thinking

Teaching for Critical Thinking

Tools and Techniques to Help Students Question Their Assumptions

Stephen D. Brookfield

JOSSEY-BASS
A Wiley Imprint
www.josseybass.com

Published by Jossey-Bass

A Wiley Imprint

One Montgomery Street, Suite 1200, San Francisco, CA 94104-4594—www.josseybass.com

Jossey-Bass books and products are available through most bookstores. To contact Jossey-Bass directly call our Customer Care Department within the U.S. at 800-956-7739, outside the U.S. at 317-572-3986, or fax 317-572-4002.

Wiley also publishes its books in a variety of electronic formats and by print-on-demand. Not all content that is available in standard print versions of this book may appear or be packaged in all book formats. If you have purchased a version of this book that did not include media that is referenced by or accompanies a standard print version, you may request this media by visiting http://booksupport.wiley.com. For more information about Wiley products, visit us at www.wiley.com.

Library of Congress Cataloging-in-Publication Data

Brookfield, Stephen.
  Teaching for critical thinking : tools and techniques to help students question their assumptions / Stephen D. Brookfield. – 1st ed.
    p. cm. – (The Jossey-Bass Higher and adult education series)
  Includes bibliographical references and index.
  ISBN 978-0-470-88934-3 (hardback)
  ISBN 978-1-118-14670-5 (ebk.)
  ISBN 978-1-118-14671-2 (ebk.)
  ISBN 978-1-118-14672-9 (ebk.)
  1. Critical thinking.   2. Critical thinking–Study and teaching.   3. Psychology, Applied.   I. Title.
  BF441.B7915 2012
  153.4'2–dc23
                                                    2011030030

Printed in the United States of America
FIRST EDITION
HB Printing   10 9 8 7 6 5 4 3

Contents

Preface

For the last 30 years or so I have run numerous workshops at colleges and universities across the world on how to teach students to think more critically. At every campus I visit I hear many of the same laments. One is that students' attention span has become so compressed in the digital age that the cognitive stamina needed to stick with an argument until you understand it from the inside, and the intellectual rigor needed to analyze its validity in a critical way, has all but disappeared. I hear that students don't read books any more, that they don't go to the library (or even know where it is on campus), that they're gullible consumers of any conspiracy theory that gains traction on the Web, that they're celebrity-obsessed, and that they refuse to pay attention in class unless the professor makes the class as "fun" as playing a computer game.

This is a pretty low estimate of students' abilities. And I'm sure that in some cases it's right. But it just doesn't jive with the students I see organizing community projects, marching against the unilateral invasion of countries, or moving into long and heated arguments on Facebook. Neither does it compute with the fact that for many middle and high school students in the last decade, the biggest event in their year was the publication of a book. For many of my generation (I'm now in my 60s) a major early adolescent moment was a TV event—The Beatles on the *Ed Sullivan Show*. (I should point out that this was no big deal to me, since I had grown up in Liverpool and gone to the original Cavern Club as a kid.) For my own children's generation, however, it was the publication of whatever was the latest installment in the *Harry Potter* series that was the moment of high significance. Now I know Harry Potter isn't a text on macroeconomics or an explication of Heidegger, but it was astonishing to me to see pre-teens and adolescents, who supposedly couldn't sit still to read much more than a sentence before lunging for a game controller, line up for hours to buy a book as soon as it was published, and then disappear for a day or two as they immersed themselves in it.

So if we are finding it difficult to get students to think critically, I think we need to look elsewhere than some supposed change in young people's DNA whereby the gene determining intellectual rigor and stamina has apparently been supplanted by the need to purchase the latest game controller. Instead, we need to take a long, hard look at how critical thinking is explained and taught. Having worked with students at widely varying stages of educational preparedness—from adult nonreaders to precollege developmental students with a very poor grasp of reading and writing, right up to doctoral students at Harvard University—I have been struck by what is similar across these contexts in terms of how people learn to think critically, rather than with what is different. Differences exist, to be sure, in the level of materials that can be used, but the essential dynamics of how you sequence curricula incrementally to support the development of critical thinking remain the same. So, too, do the dynamics of teaching it; for example, a group of precollege, developmental students struggling to understand the simplest passage in a college orientation handbook, or a group of doctoral students struggling to comprehend Foucault, both look to their teachers to model a critical engagement with a text and to show how they also sometimes struggle to understand what an author is saying.

In *Teaching for Critical Thinking* I build on my last three decades of experience running workshops and courses on critical thinking to explore how students learn to think this way, and what teachers can do to help students develop this capacity. In writing the book I'm very aware (as I outline in Chapter Two) that notions of exactly what constitutes critical thinking vary significantly across disciplines. Of the different intellectual traditions informing this idea, it is the critical theory tradition that has had the biggest influence on me, followed by the tradition of American pragmatism. But I didn't want to write a book that explored only how critical theory conceived of critical thinking. If you're interested in reading my work in that area, *The Power of Critical Theory: Liberating Adult Learning and Teaching* (2004) and *Radicalizing Learning: Adult Education for a Just World* (coauthored with John D. Holst, 2010) both explore this territory.

I wrote this book as if the readership were the same as the typical group of faculty who show up to workshops I run at most campuses I visit. I usually have instructors attending from every disciplinary area and department represented in the school. Biologists are next to theologians, mechanical engineers next to women's studies instructors, mathematicians next to romance language teachers, business educators next to art historians, and so on. In such an environment I have to be able to talk to people in a language that is generic enough to foster a shared understanding of critical thinking, and in a way that helps them adapt general principles to specific disciplinary contexts. There's little point in running a workshop on critical thinking if no one can actually agree on what constitutes that kind of thinking, and if only a segment of the faculty thinks the workshop has any relevance for their discipline. So much of the early part of this book tries to establish some general protocols of what critical thinking is, and how it can be taught, that make sense across widely varying disciplinary areas.

I've tried to write this book in a personal, relaxed, conversational style. I've used contractions, written in the first person, and as much as possible I've tried to keep extensive bibliographic references to a minimum. Essentially, I've tried to write the book in the same tone that I would speak to a group of colleagues. As I wrote I tried to imagine I was having lunch or coffee with a group of college teachers from different disciplines, and I was trying to answer the questions they had about how to get their students to think critically. So if you want a book written in a third person manner in which the author's biases and experiences are held in check and each point is extensively referenced, this is not the book for you. There are plenty of other texts out there that will be much more along the lines you seek. But if you want a text in which the author is engaged in a personal conversation with you, and academic jargon is put on the backburner and only used when absolutely necessary, then I hope this will meet that description.

Whenever I go to any professional development activity, I always feel my time has been well spent if I've learned something new I can try with my students. That's the spirit in which this book is written. I've tried to cram into its pages as many practical activities, exercises, protocols, techniques, and specific suggestions as I could. My assumption is that anyone who reads this will want to walk away with some new ideas about what they could do differently in their classrooms, or with some additional items in their pedagogic tool kit or back pack that they can try out the next time they meet with their students. If you see anything in here that might be helpful to you, please feel no compunction at all about stealing it and changing it so it makes better sense in your own classroom. The best teachers are good burglars, contextually attuned plunderers—they are always on the lookout for something they haven't tried before that, with a few adaptations, will work with their students. If this book gives you a few ideas you can steal and adapt then it will have been worth the effort in writing.

In the spirit of creative, contextually informed plundering let me also draw your attention to my home page: http://www.stephenbrookfield.com/Dr._Stephen_D._Brookfield/Home.html.

I've put pretty much all my classroom exercises up online for free download on that home page. Just go to the *Workshop Materials* link and scroll down the various PDF files and PowerPoint presentations and you'll find any number of exercises and activities contained there. If you see something that looks helpful—grab it with my blessing! That's why I've put it up there.

Overview of the Book

The book opens with an attempt in Chapter One to outline a basic protocol of critical thinking as a learning process that focuses on uncovering and checking assumptions, exploring alternative perspectives, and taking informed actions as a result. I explain three different categories of assumptions—paradigmatic, prescriptive, and causal—and I argue that assumptions are rarely universally right or wrong, but that they are more or less contextually appropriate. Throughout the chapter I try to draw on my own experience of using critical thinking to help me deal with clinical depression as a way of concretizing what can sometimes be an abstract idea.

Chapter Two then looks more closely at the different intellectual traditions informing the idea of critical thinking. One of the problems in holding conversations with colleagues about how to get students to think more critically is that different conceptions of what critical thinking looks like are held by teachers in different disciplines. I explore five different interpretations of this idea framed by, in turn, analytic philosophy and logic, the hypothetical-deductive method in the natural sciences, pragmatism, psychoanalysis, and critical theory. Where possible, I try to show connections between these traditions and to argue that aspects of the basic protocol outlined in Chapter One can be found in all of them.

Attention turns in Chapter Three to a crucial question: what do students say are the teaching methods and approaches that most help them learn to think critically? Drawing on thousands of student testimonies, many of which have been documented in students' Critical Incident Questionnaires (CIQ), I identify five major themes that seem to hold true across different contexts for learning. These are (1) that critical thinking is best experienced as a social learning process, (2) that it is important for teachers to model the process for students, (3) that critical thinking is best understood when grounded in very specific events or experiences, (4) that some of the most effective triggers to critical thinking are having to deal with an unexpected event (or disorienting dilemma, as it is sometimes called), and (5) that learning critical thinking needs to be incrementally sequenced. Students like to learn to apply the process to relatively impersonal situations or data and then, slowly over time, bring the process to bear more and more on their own direct thinking.

What the opening steps of a critical thinking course or program might look like is outlined in Chapter Four. I look at when teaching critical thinking should be a focus, how to build a case for critical thinking to students who are skeptical about it, the use of clickers and hand held devices, and how to use the Scenario Analysis approach as a beginning exercise that can be adapted across disciplines. Chapter Five then looks at how to move to more complex critical thinking protocols such as Crisis Decision Simulation, Critical Debate, Exemplars and Flaws, and Quotes to Affirm and Challenge. It ends with a description of a highly complex exercise, the Critical Conversation Protocol.

In Chapter Six the focus shifts to how to encourage critical reading and writing. I try to dispel some common misconceptions about what it means to read critically, and then review what should be the basic components of a critical review of a text. These components are that (1) the student understands the text in the terms the author sets for it, (2) the student can conduct a critical analysis of it, and (3) the student can take a position regarding its relative merit in a field of inquiry. Each of these three components is then broken down to its constituent elements. The chapter then turns to how to teach students to write more critically. I explain how to give highly specific feedback to students, including the use of Color Coded Critical Feedback, the Hatful of Quotes exercise, the Peer Writing Protocol, and the role of faculty modeling. The chapter ends with me doing a critical appraisal of a couple of passages from one of my own books—*Becoming a Critically Reflective Teacher* (1995)—to model for readers the same approach I am describing in the classroom.

One of the problems with making critical thinking a generic student behavior is that its implementation is spotty, varying from unit to unit, department to department, and school to school. In Chapter Seven I explore how to embed a general protocol of critical thinking across an institution. I begin by suggesting how a general definition of critical thinking can be crafted, and then examine what a Freshman Seminar on critical thinking might look like. I then return to the problem of how to build a case for critical thinking that was visited in Chapter Four, and this time I go into more depth about how this might be accomplished. I then look at how critical thinking can be incorporated into specific course assignments, how to introduce it in the syllabus, how to create connections between subject matter content and this kind of thinking, how to embed Critical Thinking Audits into assignments, and how to make such thinking part of the capstone experience.

Chapter Eight revisits in more depth the ways in which critical thinking is a social learning process, and it reviews ways in which typical classroom discussions can be conducted with a more critical edge. I outline what a critical discussion looks like and then look at some specific activities that can be crafted for critical thinking. These are the Circle of Voices, Circular Response, Chalk Talk, Spot the Error, Structured Silence, the Inferential Ladder, and the Appreciative Pause. The chapter ends with examples of discussion questions that encourage critical thinking, questions that uncover evidence, and questions that generate multiple perspectives.

The penultimate Chapter Nine pauses to review some of the most common misunderstandings of critical thinking, some challenges that have been issued to it, and some of the risks students experience when they try to learn it. Common misunderstandings are that being critical is the same as tearing something down or finding fault, that thinking critically leads to the paralysis of analysis, that it always involves fundamental change, that it's the same as problem solving, and that it always has a clear outcome. Challenges I explore are those posed by a gender analysis where critical thinking is seen as a masculine doubting game, by cultural analysis that identifies the Eurocentric rationality preeminent in critical thinking, and by postmodern analysis that critiques the notion of using critical thinking to come to greater self-awareness. The risks students face are those of impostorship, cultural suicide, lost innocence, and road running, and each of these is reviewed. The chapter ends with another affirmation of the importance of peer learning communities to critical thinking.

In the final chapter (Chapter Ten) I return to a deeper examination of a theme that surfaces regularly through the book, the importance of teachers modeling for students their own engagement in critical thinking. I explore how this can be accomplished through the use of appropriate autobiographical examples, how criticality can be modeled for colleagues, what modeling looks like in an online environment, and the risks associated with modeling.

Audience

The chief audience for this book is teachers in a wide range of higher and adult education institutions—community colleges, four-year colleges, universities, vocational institutes, proprietary schools, online institutions—who are trying to get their students to think critically. I hope I have written in such a way that teachers in GED classrooms or in community colleges can find as much in here as teachers in elite private Ivy League institutions. I also think that trainers in a wide range of corporate and nonprofit organizations and professional developers in different workplace settings (the military, hospitals, churches, social work, early childhood development, community health) will be able to do some good creative adaptations of the exercises and activities described throughout the book. So really anyone who thinks that for part of their work they're trying to get others to think critically about something should find something of interest in the book.

Acknowledgments

There are so many people who make a book what it is, and there's no way I can thank them all. But first, I'd like to acknowledge the thousands of teachers and other human service professionals who've attended my workshops across the world and been gracious enough to fill out the Critical Incident Questionnaires I peppered them with, as well as asking such wonderfully unanswerable questions and recounting such wonderfully different experiences. In trying to respond to you I learned a great deal about teaching for critical thinking. I hope this book doesn't embarrass you. Thanks, too, to the University of St. Thomas, and to Dr. Sue Huber in particular, for supporting me with the sabbatical time to write the bulk of this manuscript. There is nothing like waking up in the morning and knowing that the only thing you have to do that day is try and get your thoughts in order and then put them down on paper. For me it's a luxury I always appreciate. The fact that I was able to be relaxed and conversational in this book is down to David Brightman at Jossey-Bass, an editor who always encouraged me to write personally to practitioners, rather than to impress fellow academics. And thanks to Suzanne Copenhagen for skillful copyediting that zipped the manuscript along.

More personal thanks are due to my various band mates in The 99ers (the world's best punk/pop/rockabilly/surf band) over the period the book was written. The 99ers is my main creative outlet outside of academe, and if you're ever in the Twin Cities you should stop by to see us play a gig. There's nothing like smashing a power A-chord to make you forget about the complexities of critical thinking! So thanks to Molly Holley, Colin Selhurst, Chris Cave, Erik John, and Derek Kosky for giving me so many nights of pure musical fun. Finally, as always, thanks to the Rochester girl, Kim Miller, for being a partner through my life.

Stephen Brookfield
St. Paul, Minnesota

About the Author

The father of Molly and Colin, and the husband of Kim, Stephen D. Brookfield is currently Distinguished University Professor at the University of St. Thomas in Minneapolis-St. Paul, Minnesota. He received his B.A. degree (1970) from Lanchester College of Technology (Coventry, UK) in modern studies, his M.A. degree (1974) from the University of Reading (UK) in sociology, and his Ph.D. degree (1980) from the University of Leicester (UK) in adult education. He also holds a postgraduate diploma (1971) from the University of London, Chelsea College (UK), in modern social and cultural studies and a postgraduate diploma (1977) from the University of Nottingham (UK) in adult education. In 1991 he was awarded an honorary doctor of letters degree from the University System of New Hampshire for his contributions to understanding adult learning. In 2003 he was awarded an honorary doctorate of letters from Concordia University for his contributions to adult education. In 2010 Muhlenberg College awarded him an honorary doctorate of letters for educational leadership in the scholarship of teaching.

Stephen began his teaching career in 1970 and has held appointments at colleges of further, technical, adult, and higher education in the United Kingdom, and at universities in Canada (University of British Columbia) and the United States (Columbia University, Teachers College and the University of St. Thomas). In 1989 he was Visiting Fellow at the Institute for Technical and

Adult Teacher Education in what is now the University of Technology, Sydney, Australia. In 2002 he was Visiting Professor at Harvard University Graduate School of Education. During 2003–2004 he was the Helen Le Baron Hilton Chair at Iowa State University. He has run numerous workshops on teaching, adult learning, and critical thinking around the world and delivered many keynote addresses at regional, national, and international education conferences.

In 2001 he received the Leadership Award from the Association for Continuing Higher Education (ACHE) for "extraordinary contributions to the general field of continuing education on a national and international level." In 2008 he received the University of St. Thomas John Ireland Presidential Award for Outstanding Achievement as a Teacher/Scholar, and also the University of St. Thomas Diversity Leadership Teaching and Research Award. Also in 2008 he was awarded the Morris T. Keeton Medal by the Council on Adult and Experiential Learning for "outstanding contributions to adult and experiential learning." In 2009 he was inducted into the International Adult Education Hall of Fame.

He is a four-time winner of the Cyril O. Houle World Award for Literature in Adult Education: in 1986 for his book *Understanding and Facilitating Adult Learning: A Comprehensive Analysis of Principles and Effective Practices* (1986), in 1989 for *Developing Critical Thinkers: Challenging Adults to Explore Alternative Ways of Thinking and Acting* (1987), in 1996 for *Becoming a Critically Reflective Teacher* (1995), and in 2005 for *The Power of Critical Theory: Liberating Adult Learning and Teaching* (2004). *Understanding and Facilitating Adult Learning* also won the 1986 Imogene E. Okes Award for Outstanding Research in Adult Education. These awards were all presented by the American Association for Adult and Continuing Education. The first edition of *Discussion as a Way of Teaching: Tools and Techniques for Democratic Classrooms* (2nd ed., 2005), which he coauthored with Stephen Preskill, was a 1999 Critics Choice of the Educational Studies Association. His other books are *Adult Learners, Adult Education, and the Community* (1984), *Self-Directed Learning: From Theory to Practice* (1985), *Learning Democracy: Eduard Lindeman on Adult Education and Social Change* (1987), *Training Educators of Adults: The Theory and Practice of Graduate Adult Education* (1988), *The Skillful Teacher: On Technique, Trust, and Responsiveness in the Classroom* (2nd ed., 2006), *Teaching Reflectively in Theological Contexts: Promises and Contradictions* (coedited with Mary Hess, 2008), *Learning as a Way of Leading: Lessons from the Struggle for Social Justice* (coauthored with Stephen Preskill, 2008), *Handbook of Race and Adult Education* (coedited with Vanessa Sheared, Scipio Colin III, Elizabeth Peterson, and Juanita Johnson, 2010), and *Radicalizing Learning: Adult Education for a Just World* (coauthored with John D. Holst, 2010).

Teaching
for Critical
Thinking

1

What Is Critical Thinking?

As a reader and a working classroom teacher I always appreciate a chapter, or even a book, that starts by telling me what I'm going to be reading in the next few pages. That way, if it's of no interest to me I can skip it and spend my time doing something more useful or pleasurable (hopefully both). So let me begin this introduction by saying that in this chapter I want to introduce what I understand as the basic process of critical thinking. This entails (1) identifying the assumptions that frame our thinking and determine our actions, (2) checking out the degree to which these assumptions are accurate and valid, (3) looking at our ideas and decisions (intellectual, organizational, and personal) from several different perspectives, and (4) on the basis of all this, taking informed actions. I also propose a basic typology of different kinds of assumptions that critical thinking unearths and scrutinizes—paradigmatic, prescriptive, and causal.

I'm also using this chapter to make some strong claims about critical thinking. I argue that if you can't think critically your survival is in peril because you risk living a life that—without your being aware of it—hurts you and serves the interests of those who wish you harm. If you can't think critically you have no chance of recognizing, let alone pushing back on, those times you are being manipulated. And if you can't think critically you will behave in ways that have less chance of achieving the results you want. So critical thinking is not just an academic process that leads to good scores on SATs, elegantly argued essays, or experimental hypotheses that can stand the toughest scrutiny. It is a way of living that helps you stay intact when any number of organizations (corporate, political, educational, and cultural) are trying to get you to think and act in ways that serve their purposes.

How Critical Thinking Saved My Life

As a way of leading into these ideas I want to begin on a personal note by showing how critical thinking saved my life. A few years ago I was at rock bottom emotionally. I was one of the 20 million Americans diagnosed with clinical depression and anxiety, convinced most days that I was on the verge of death and feeling worthless and ashamed about my inability to control my state of mind. I spent a great deal of energy hiding my depression as best I could from family, friends, and colleagues, and steadfastly refused to seek medical help. Since, objectively, I had nothing to be depressed about (I had a job I loved and a loving family) my response to my depression was to tell myself to snap out of it. I believed the way to beat depression was to reason my way through it, to tell myself that since there was no earthly reason I should be depressed, I ought to just stop being that way. My depression's persistence and debilitating effect were heightened dramatically because I wasn't thinking critically about it. Once I started to do this, things improved dramatically. So, I begin this chapter with a bold statement; the ability to think critically about one's assumptions, beliefs, and actions is a survival necessity.

I've written about this period of depression in much greater detail elsewhere (Brookfield, 2011) and this may be entirely too much information about me for you to digest so early! If that's the case, then skip this introductory section and go to the next section, Hunting Assumptions. If you're still with me I want to focus on just one point—what was getting in the way of my dealing with my depression was my inability to think critically about it. What

I mean by that is that I refused to consider the possibility that any of my assumptions regarding my depression were wrong. For example, I assumed that the right way to deal with depression was to think your way out of it. I assumed that depression was a sign of weakness, unless external circumstances (such as divorce, being fired, or the death of a loved one) warranted it. Because I assumed I was weak, I assumed I needed to hide my condition from peers and colleagues. More fundamentally, I assumed that if I was a real man I would be able just to stare this condition down and force myself out of it by an act of will. I assumed it was up to me to "dig deep" (as the sports cliché has it) and dredge up the mental strength to beat it.

Some of the assumptions I've just outlined were on the surface and were reasonably easy to identify. These mostly had to do with how I understand cause and effect. For example, I reasoned that depression was caused by external circumstances and therefore, since my circumstances were good, it was a mistake to be depressed. The assumption that by engaging in intentional self-talk ("come on now, don't be ridiculous, it's all in your head, you are in great shape, there's no reason at all to feel the way you do") I could move beyond depression was also causal. Causal assumptions can always be stated as cause and effect linkages, as in "if I do A, then B will happen." Hence, they are both explanatory and predictive. They explain why the past happened by establishing the causes of particular events. They predict the future by positing what will be the consequences and effects of certain decisions.

Some of the assumptions about depression I reviewed were more about how good professionals (which is how I thought of myself) are supposed to behave. These were prescriptive assumptions. Prescriptive assumptions are assumptions we hold about what are desirable ways of thinking or acting. They can usually be recognized by their inclusion of the word *should*, as in "a good professional should be able to respond to cultural diversity," or "a good marriage is one in which partners can be totally honest with each other." Prescriptive assumptions state what a good friendship or relationship looks like, what should be the characteristics of a truly democratic decision, or how social resources should be allocated. I held a prescriptive assumption that a normal, fully functioning person copes well with life and doesn't get depressed. I believed that good professionals don't let irrational feelings of depression, worthlessness, or shame dominate their lives.

The third type of assumptions I held about depression was harder for me to uncover and challenge. These assumptions lay deeper within my mental structures and were not immediately apparent to me. They were so much a part of my outlook, and so central to my self-identity, that when they were pointed out to me as being assumptions I was tempted to reply, "that's not an assumption, that's reality." Specifically, I assumed that a fully functioning man is logical, clear-headed, and determined, a sort of steely-jawed, no nonsense mental equivalent of an early Clint Eastwood character, or Howard Roark in Ayn Rand's *The Fountainhead*. Although I would have strenuously denied it at the time, I had assumed that the ideology of patriarchy—the belief that men are governed by reason, women by emotion, and therefore that men's powers of rationality equip them to be natural leaders—was correct. As I say, this was *not* an assumption I held consciously. It was much more subtle than that; it had wormed its way into my consciousness, so to speak. I call this kind of assumption a paradigmatic assumption.

Paradigmatic assumptions are the deeply held assumptions that frame the whole way we look at the world. When we discover paradigmatic assumptions it often comes as a shock. In the case of depression I had no real awareness of just how strongly I had successfully internalized the assumptions of patriarchy. Patriarchy views men as natural leaders and decision makers because they are guided by reason and logic, unlike women who are regarded as being guided by irrational emotion. Patriarchy says that a "real" man has no need for drugs to fight depression and, moreover, that a real man doesn't suffer from depression in the first place. Because men are deemed to be naturally strong and in command they assume that if they simply tell themselves not to be depressed that will take care of the problem.

I had been well socialized over five decades into accepting the ideology of patriarchy, and it was so much a part of me that it was very difficult for me to see just how powerfully that ideology was shaping my behavior. But I'm convinced that one reason I didn't seek help until after years of misery was because I believed that if I was a "proper man," a "real man," I wouldn't need a psychiatrist, or drugs, to help me deal with depression. All I would need was manly inner fortitude. "I'm a man, I'm supposed to be ruled by reason, I should be able to keep my feelings under control" was the inner voice that rumbled beneath my more conscious conversations. To take drugs to deal with a problem was something that would be OK if I was a woman, but was surely a sign of weakness for a man. So month after month, year after year, I refused to consider any suggestion of medication. This refusal was underscored by the fact that the only people I knew who were taking medication for mental problems were all women. There was no male I was aware of under meds for depression.

One thing I learned about overcoming shame was that for me, a man, it required a process of ideological detoxification. I had to understand just how deeply and powerfully the ideology of patriarchy had been implanted in me over my five decades on the planet. And I had to understand, too, that stopping it from determining how I thought about, and responded to, my own depression would be a long haul. Even today, despite having written books on critical theory (Brookfield, 2004) and radicalizing learning (Brookfield and Holst, 2010)—both of which explore how to resist ideological manipulation—I still feel there's an unseemly lack of manliness, or grit, in my suffering from and disclosing my depression.

A second paradigmatic assumption I had to uncover had to do with the etiology of depression. I assumed that people feel depressed because something bad has happened to them. So the fact that depression had settled on me seemingly out of the blue was completely puzzling. Yes, 9/11 had happened a few months before, and yes, I had nursed my mother during her last weeks of cancer a year earlier, and yes, some test results I had received had been worrying—but none of those seemed to account for the overwhelming anxiety and depression that gripped me. The paradigmatic assumption that depression was rationally caused, and therefore treated by the application of reason, took me years to unearth, challenge, and discard. I had always considered myself a sentimental person, given to emotional reactions to people, compassion, sport, music, and film, and had no idea of just how deeply the epistemology of European rationality was assimilated within me. Challenging and changing my unquestioning belief in rationality with the assumption that depression was the result of chemical imbalances in the brain was enormously difficult. I was so fixated on my inability to reason myself out of feeling depressed that I was unable to consider any other way of understanding how depression was caused.

Once this second paradigmatic assumption was challenged then many of my causal and prescriptive assumptions started to totter. Having managed to reframe my assumptions about the etiology of depression, it became much easier to keep the debilitating effects of shame under control. If depression is linked to chemical imbalances in the brain, I could tell myself, then part of its treatment has to be pharmaceutical. Suddenly, drugs didn't seem a sign of weakness, an indication that I was a pathetic excuse as a human being. After all, my psychiatrist told me, you're fine with taking drugs for bodily imbalances such as high cholesterol, high blood pressure, acid reflux—why should taking drugs to redress chemical imbalances in the brain be any different? Instead of assuming that depression was always caused by the existence of depressing external circumstances that a real man should be able to transcend, I started to see it as a medical condition like asthma, diabetes, or high blood pressure. Once I started to view depression as caused by a chemical imbalance in my brain and not by the external circumstances of life, I opened myself up to the possibility that it might be appropriate to treat my condition with pharmaceuticals.

All this is by way of illustration of how critical thinking saved my life. Because I identified and challenged several assumptions I held about the nature, cause, and treatment of depression I was able to seek psychiatric help and eventually settle on a combination of medications that kept me emotionally stable. Instead of being plagued by permanent feelings of shame and worthlessness, and feeling suicidal on some days, I returned to my old self. That's not to say I don't have days when I feel down, get fed up with things, or feel anxious about situations. But because I was able to think critically about it, depression doesn't rule my life as it did. Had I not been able to think critically about it, the depression would still be overwhelming me.

Hunting Assumptions

The core process described in the example I've just given in the opening section of this chapter—as it is in all critical thinking—is hunting assumptions. Trying to discover what our assumptions are, and then trying to judge when, and how far, these are accurate, is something that happens every time critical thinking occurs. You cannot think critically without hunting assumptions; that is, without trying to uncover assumptions and then trying to assess their accuracy and validity, their fit with life.

Assumptions are guides to truth embedded in our mental outlooks. They are the daily rules that frame how we make decisions and take actions. Everyday communications are subject to a continuous and ever-present set of assumptions. We make assumptions about the meaning behind the words we, and others, use, about the meaning of certain gestures, expressions, or pauses, or about how to respond to a comment. Assumptions inform our judgments about whether or not someone is telling the truth, or how to recognize when we are being manipulated.

As we move through each hour of each day our actions are always based in assumptions, most of which have been confirmed by repeated experience. I brush my teeth assuming that doing so will prevent tooth decay and cut down on the expense and pain of dental procedures. I choose my food for the day based on assumptions about how healthy, or how pleasurable, eating those foods will be. I set the thermostat and choose clothes based on assumptions I'm making drawn from the weather report. As I drive to an appointment I fill the gas tank, lock the back door, follow traffic lights, and rely on street signs on the assumption that doing all these things will get me where I want to go in the speediest and safest way possible. All the assumptions I've mentioned are held because experience has shown them to be accurate. When I want to get to Fridley, Minnesota, I follow the AAA map and the interstate road signs, and set the GPS, because doing this in the past for other destinations has been successful. So I assume that it will be equally successful this time around.

Assumptions as instinctive guides to truth operate at much deeper levels than that of daily routine, however. In the example of depression, a host of assumptions were present about what it meant to be a man. Some of these were highly personal and context specific, but others were linked to dominant ideologies such as patriarchy and what critical theorists call the instrumentalization of reason (Brookfield, 2004). This is a fearsome sounding piece of academic jargon that actually is pretty easy to understand. Instrumentalized reasoning is described by Horkheimer and Adorno (1972) and Marcuse (1964) as the kind of thinking that is most valued in contemporary life. Basically, you reason instrumentally whenever you try to fix a problem without ever questioning whether or not the problem is the one that needs fixing. You reason instrumentally when you tinker with a system—for example, how to assess whether students are learning correctly—so as to improve it, to make it more effective. You don't ask whose interests are served by solving the problem, because you're so focused on being a good fix-it kind of person.

When people think critically they question the fundamental assumptions behind how problems are defined. They ask the big questions of life—what constitutes learning? How do we organize organizations and communities to encourage compassion or fairness? What is the fundamental purpose of teaching? What does it mean to work authentically? Needless to say, in an instrumentalized culture asking these questions is usually seen as either Utopian, impractical, or idealistic, something we grow out of and come to regard as an annoying waste of time.

Assumptions that spring from dominant ideologies are particularly hard to uncover, precisely because these ideologies are everywhere, so common as to be thought blindingly obvious and therefore not worthy of being the object of sustained questioning. These are the paradigmatic assumptions described earlier. Ideologies are the sets of beliefs and practices that are accepted by the majority as commonsense ways of organizing the world. Some of them operate at macro-levels, such as the assumption that majority vote democracy is the decision-making system that most fairly meets the most important needs of the majority. Others operate at micro-levels, such as the assumption that a secret vote gives the most accurate result, or that an action supported by a majority vote has the greatest legitimacy and is therefore the one that should be followed.

Along with democracy, free-market capitalism is another ideology that exercises enormous influence. On a macro-level capitalism holds that the less you regulate economic activity, the more you encourage individual entrepreneurship. Capitalism further assumes that individual economic enterprise and political liberty are inextricably intertwined, so that if you want to safeguard a free democracy you must defend capitalism. Consequently, socialism, communism, even social democracy are viewed as inherently undemocratic. After all, if capitalism is viewed as the economic arrangement that best guarantees individual freedom, then any noncapitalist alternatives must be regarded as threatening freedom to various degrees.

Capitalism and democracy are two dominant ideologies that are highly public. We learn them in school, from the media, in our families, at our workplaces, and through the organizations of civil society such as the church or local political associations. Much harder to identify but equally influential are ideologies that are submerged, such as White supremacy, patriarchy, or heterosexism. These ideologies all hold that leadership is best exercised by Whites and males and heterosexuals, because these are deemed to be smarter, more stable, and more accomplished. Civil rights legislation has ensured that these beliefs are rarely spoken. But ideology is learned not just through the spoken or written word, but also through behavior (what critical theorists call practices). When we go through life seeing leadership positions filled by Whites, particularly White men, and when no one remarks on this fact, we are learning dominant ideology. When a person of color, or a woman, or an "out" Gay or Lesbian attains a position of prominence or influence, and this fact is highlighted as an example of democracy and liberty in action, dominant ideology is in action. After all, when a heterosexual White male attains the some position, his race, gender, or sexuality is rarely mentioned. This is because Whiteness, maleness, and heterosexuality are the leadership norms that we observe everywhere and that we internalize without being aware of it. Paradoxically, an event that seems to disrupt and challenge dominant ideology—such as the election of a biracial president, or the appointment of an African American woman as secretary of state—actually confirms it, at least in the short term. The very fact that these are exceptions, and celebrated as such, actually confirms the enduring influence of the norm.

So Exactly What Is Critical Thinking?

Let's begin answering this question by dispensing a few misconceptions. Here's what critical thinking is *not*. It's *not* something that only people with a college degree can do. It's *not* the same as being logical, solving problems, or being creative—though aspects of some or all of these are sometimes present when we think critically. It's *not* something you do only if you've studied philosophy. It's *not* necessarily the same thing as being critical of something, as in when we tear apart a film, or criticize a partner's, friend's, or colleague's behavior, for their shortcomings. It's *not* something that only happens when you reach a certain age. It's *not* something that can only be pursued when you have the time to sit and reflect on an idea or a situation. And, finally, it's *not* correlated to IQ, personality, or other measures of intelligence. So whether or not you've been to college, how you score on intelligence tests, whether you're an extrovert or introvert, how busy or leisurely your life is, or what subjects you did best in at school are all irrelevant when considering how well you do critical thinking.

So what is it? Well, my best way of describing it is to say that critical thinking happens when we do four things . . .

Hunting Assumptions

Critical thinking happens first when we try to discover the assumptions that influence the way we think and act. Pretty much every action we take is based on assumptions that we have accepted, sometimes unthinkingly, as accurate. Critical thinking involves deliberately trying to find out what these assumptions are.

Checking Assumptions

When we become aware of the assumptions that are guiding our actions and ways of thinking, we begin to check out whether those assumptions are as accurate as we think they are. This is the second element of critical thinking—trying to assess whether or not our assumptions are valid and reliable guides for action. Here we're engaged in a process of appraisal—trying to see when assumptions make sense, and when they don't, what assumptions cover lots of situations and what assumptions are specific to very particular events. Key to this process is identifying and assessing what we regard as convincing evidence for our assumptions. Sometimes this evidence is experiential (the things that have happened to us), sometimes it's authoritative (what people we trust have told us is the truth), and sometimes it's derived from disciplined research and inquiry we've conducted.

Seeing Things from Different Viewpoints

One of the best ways to decide whether or not an assumption is accurate—or under what conditions it does or doesn't make sense—is to try and see our assumptions and actions from multiple, and different, points of view. In the different roles I play in life—partner, parent, teacher, scholar, bandleader—I usually act assuming that people around me are reading into my actions the same meanings I intend them to pick up. Experience has taught me that this broad—some would say meta—assumption is often seriously flawed. Often my words and actions have been understood in ways that are completely different from the ways I intended them to be understood. So one way to find out how accurate our assumptions are is to try and see ourselves as others see us.

Taking Informed Action

The whole point of critical thinking is to take informed action. The reason I'll do the first three things I've just described is so that I don't waste energy acting in ways that I think are good for me, and that I believe will have the effects I want, only to find out that the opposite is true. Life is too short, and too dangerous, to waste a lot of time acting in uncritical ways. Let me emphasize this point again. The main reason we need to think critically is so we can take informed actions. In shorthand terms, we think critically not just to survive, but also to live and love well. And a life in which our actions are based on what we feel are accurate understandings of our situations is likely to be experienced as much more satisfactory than a life in which our actions are haphazard and arbitrary.

But what exactly *is* an informed action? Well, it's an action that is based on thought and analysis, which means there is some evidence we take seriously as supporting such an action. To use a trite example, as a bandleader I sequence the sets our band plays based on the evidence of previous audience's reactions. The more I do this, the more I realize that audiences are different. Songs and jokes that go down well when we play the last set at a dive bar may bomb when we play a bowling alley full of families. So an informed action is one that is supported by evidence we find convincing. If someone asks us why we're acting the way we are, we can explain our choices and decisions in ways that allow our questioner to see that they're based on evidence.

Of course, the evidence we're basing our actions on can be nonsensical. For example, plenty of people act on evidence solely because of the source of that evidence. "If so and so says it's true," this reasoning goes, "then it must be true because I trust their insight." I'm no different. I often listen to music, read literature, or watch TV shows or films solely because someone whose taste and opinions I trust tells me they're good. This is how what has been called groupthink (Janis, 1982), automaton conformity (Fromm, 1941), or hegemony (Gramsci, 1971) develops. These three concepts all describe the easy way we fall unthinkingly into assuming that certain things are obviously true, a matter of common sense. The trouble with habitually relying on people with authority or credibility to tell us what to think is that sometimes these people are, at worst, evil and manipulative, at best, prejudiced or unreliable. After all, people have been willing to commit genocide because someone they believe to be superior in some way has convinced them of the filthy ideology that a person's race, ethnicity, creed, or culture means that person is less than fully human.

So to act based on evidence is itself no guarantee that critical thinking is happening. We also need to know that our actions are having the effects we wish them to have. In this sense an informed action is one that plays out the way we want it to—it has the results we want it to have. When the set list I have constructed for a particular club brings down the house, I usually conclude it's because I've scanned my previous experiences playing this, or similar bars, and chosen a sequence of songs that will have this result.

Why Should We Think Critically?

Up to now, I've presented critical thinking as the habit of making sure our assumptions are accurate and that our actions have the results we want them to have. Understood this way, critical thinking is uncontroversial, something that seems so obviously good that no reasonable person could object to it. This conception of critical thinking appears neutral, simply a question of checking and citing evidence. And it's this conception—drawn largely from the tradition of analytic philosophy—that is the most widespread one in American elementary, secondary, and higher education. When my two children went through the St. Paul, Minnesota, public school system, their annual report cards assessed their ability to think critically. Teachers explained this to me as assessing whether or not my kids could give reasons for their opinions and quote the evidence for their conclusions. Nothing controversial or contentious there.

However, as soon as you understand critical thinking to be linked to action you enter the realm of values, because you have to ask the questions, "Action for what?" and "Whose actions do we want to support?" Sometimes actions serve the ends of the actor, and if the actor is trying to hoodwink, manipulate, harm, or brutalize another, then those actions surely are questionable. After all, a skilled advertiser can think critically about which emotions to tap into and examine research on how to do this, all with the purpose of selling a product and improving stockholder dividends. Political spin-doctors think critically about how best to disguise the errors of their clients and how to present these as successes. Demagogues and racists examine the evidence of how best to whip up racial hatred and use potent narratives and symbols to play on people's insecurities to keep a racist system intact.

At other times the actions we think are in our best interests are actually harmful to us, even when we're not aware of that fact. This is how I connect the concept of hegemony (drawn from critical theory) to critical thinking. Hegemony is in place when people behave in ways that they think are good for them, not realizing that they are being harmed and colluding in their own misery. People suffering from anorexia assume that by not eating they make themselves more beautiful and less unsightly, closer to the idealized body images they see in advertising. People who assume that good workers need to be available 24/7 to serve the ends of their employers think ill health and exhaustion are natural. I know of what I speak here. Three times at work I have collapsed—once in my office, once at an airport on the way to give a speech, and once in my car driving home from a workshop I had given—each time to be rushed to the emergency room, hospitalized overnight, only to find out that there was nothing wrong with me other than exhaustion. All the time I was exhausted, I was congratulating myself on how well I was fulfilling my vocation as an educator. The more burned out I felt, the more professional and committed I told myself I was being. Instead of fighting against an insane situation I was a willing victim, feeling perversely proud of myself the more tired I became.

So part of critical thinking is making sure that the actions that flow from our assumptions are justifiable according to some notion of goodness or desirability. This is where things start to get complicated, and where questions of power arise. What if you and I disagree about the right response to a situation? How do we decide which is the better, more critical response? For example, if I think capitalism rewards those who already have and secures permanent inequity, and you think it ensures that the spirit of individual entrepreneurship stays vigorous and therefore is essential for the functioning of a healthy democracy, how do we assess who is thinking more correctly? Each of us can cite evidence, scan experience, and produce credible, authoritative individuals who support our respective point of view. But ultimately, each of us has arrived at our position from a mixture of analyzing our experiences, thinking in the most critical way we can about them, and then allying our analysis with our vision of what the world looks like when it's working properly.

Critical thinking can't be analyzed as a discrete process of mental actions that can be separated from our object of analysis, from exactly *what* it is that we're thinking critically about. If critical thinking is understood only as a process of analyzing information so we can take actions that produce desired results, then some of the most vicious acts of human behavior could be defined as critical thinking. Serial killers presumably analyze how best to take steps to avoid detection by examining their assumptions about how to stalk victims, hide evidence, and dispose of bodies. Religious cult leaders think critically about how to disassociate new recruits from their past lives and allegiances, and how then to create an identification with the new leader. Spousal abusers can think critically about how to beat up a partner in a way that hides bruises and overt signs of injury, while making partners feel that they deserved the abuse and that the abuser was doing it for their own good.

Josef Goebbels' use of propaganda is an example of critical thinking if we restrict our understanding of it solely to the mental process of how it happens. After all, he worked from paradigmatic and prescriptive assumptions about Jewish impurity, and the need for genocide to rid Germany of Jewish people and culture, that he felt were philosophically justified and empirically correct. He then developed carefully analyzed causal assumptions to decide that the best way to do this was to use propaganda—in particular moving and still visual images of Jews and the Führer—to bolster the official Nazi line that it was Jews' presence that was sabotaging Germany and preventing it from being the world power it was destined to be. This was also the thinking behind the Nazi adoption of Sorel's *Big Lie* theory—the notion that if a lie is repeated frequently and vociferously enough it becomes accepted as truth. Goebbels' critical thinking was successful in the terms set for it—to create a cultural atmosphere where extreme anti-Semitism became accepted as so obviously true that untold numbers of ordinary Germans became complicit in the mechanics of genocide.

This is one of the limits we should acknowledge about critical thinking. It can't be considered separately from values and commitments, whether they be moral or political. Neither can it account for spirituality. One can think critically about one's own spiritual belief or religious commitments, or about the practice of religious tenets, but you can't *think* your way to enlightenment, Satori, rapture, or salvation. Those states of being are realized through other means than the process of rational analysis.

What Are the Different Kinds of Assumptions We Think Critically About?

I've already partially answered this question in the discussion up to this point. But let me return to it and say a little more about the three kinds of assumptions people need to be alert to—paradigmatic, prescriptive, and causal.

Paradigmatic assumptions are the hardest of all assumptions to uncover. They are the structuring assumptions we use to order the world into fundamental categories. Usually we don't even recognize them as assumptions, even after they've been pointed out to us. Instead we insist that they're objectively valid renderings of reality, the facts as we know them to be true. Some paradigmatic assumptions I have held at different stages of my life as a teacher are that adults are self-directed learners, that critical thinking is an intellectual function only characteristic of adult life, that good adult educational processes are inherently democratic, and that education always has a political dimension. Paradigmatic assumptions are examined critically only after a great deal of resistance to doing this, and it takes a considerable amount of contrary evidence and disconfirming experiences to change them. But when they are challenged and changed, the consequences for our lives are explosive. The example I gave earlier of my assumptions about the causes and treatment of depression were paradigmatic in that they underlay everything I thought about how best to understand and deal with depression. Either they were obviously true to me, or they were so embedded in my consciousness (patriarchy) that I didn't even realize how much sway they held over my decisions.

Prescriptive assumptions are assumptions about what we think ought to be happening in a particular situation. They are the assumptions that are surfaced as we examine how we think we, or others, should behave, what good learning and educational processes should look like, and what obligations students and teachers owe to each other. Inevitably they are grounded in, and extensions of, our paradigmatic assumptions. For example, if you believe that adults are self-directed learners then you assume that the best teaching is that which encourages students to take control over designing, conducting, and evaluating their own learning. If you believe that depression is only caused by external circumstances, then you believe that if your external circumstances are fine, you shouldn't be depressed. You also then believe that the best way to respond to depression is to tell yourself you have no reason to be depressed.

Causal assumptions are assumptions about how different parts of the world work and about the conditions under which these can be changed. Of all the assumptions we hold, causal ones are the easiest to uncover. In workshops and classes I have taught on critical thinking over the past 30 years these assumptions are the ones that are by far the most common. At a rough estimate, I'd say that maybe 80% of assumptions covered in any one conversation, class, course, or workshop will be causal ones.

Causal assumptions are usually stated in two ways, the first of which is when those assumptions govern future behavior. This kind of causal assumption is usually expressed predictively, such as "if I do a, then b will happen". For example, my first year of teaching I was told "start off strict, show the kids who's boss, then you can ease off." I often tell beginning teachers "model everything you want students to do before asking them to do it." I also tell colleagues in courses I'm teaching, "We need to demonstrate what respectful disagreement looks like to students before asking them to do it." When bringing up a contentious issue such as racism I always tell myself I need to talk about my own racism before asking anyone else to start looking at theirs. These are all predictive causal assumptions; I'm assuming that if I follow them certain consequences will occur.

The second way causal assumptions are stated is retroactively, or historically. This is where we very explicitly draw on past experience and use that as a guide for future conduct. For example, I'm a guitarist, writer, and singer in a punk-rockabilly band, The 99ers (http://the99ersband.com) that regularly plays shows in bars, clubs, and festivals. When I construct a set list (the order of songs we're going to play live) for the evening I work on a number of causal assumptions, all of which are derived from noticing audiences' reactions to previous shows. I often start with a cover song, one the audience might recognize and like, to get their attention. We follow that with two quick tempo songs that segue straight into each other so as to create a feeling of energy. We then switch who is the lead singer on the next song to keep the audience's interest, follow that with another cover so they hear something they like and recognize, and on and on. All the assumptions I base a set list on (start with a cover because people will recognize and like it and therefore pay attention to it, follow with a fast two-song block to keep their attention and create energy, switch vocalists to give variety, follow with another cover to regain any wandering attention) are causal. They are also all retroactive, developed after playing many different kinds of venues and seeking what consistently works best.

Here's another example drawn this time from teaching. When I teach content-heavy courses on critical theory, in which students have to read material translated from German, French, and Italian that in English is dense, jargon-ridden, and almost impenetrable at times, I often disclose to students how hard critical theory is for me to understand and how much I struggle when I read it. I'll tell them I often read and reread a paragraph for 15 minutes and that at the end of that time I have absolutely no idea of what I've just read. I do this quite deliberately because I assume many of them will have the same response to the reading that I'm describing, and I want them to know that this is normal and predictable and that it doesn't mean they're not smart or academic enough for the course. I want them to know this work is sometimes a struggle. My assumption is that if they know that I also struggle with this material then they won't be so quick to give up when they hit a rough spot. This assumption has been confirmed for me by thousands of anonymous student evaluations over the past 30 years where students specifically mention how reassuring it was for them to hear me say how I also struggled with the material.

But although this assumption is accurate for me and over the years has apparently worked to ease my students' anxieties regarding their own struggles the first time they encounter critical theory, it only works because students know that at some level they trust I *know* this stuff, I know what I'm talking about. They tell me I know my stuff for two reasons. First, because when I use examples drawn from everyday life and explain ideas in everyday language it really helps them understand an idea that otherwise seems elusive. I assume the fact that I can do this shows I really understand the material inside and out. I also assume that my ability to give appropriate everyday examples that are a bridge between a difficult idea expressed opaquely and the students' own experiences and language means students trust in my teaching expertise. Second, they point to the articles and books I've published (such as *The Power of Critical Theory*) that have won international awards and that, to them, clearly signify I know what I'm talking about.

This is all by way of saying that my assumption is conditional; it works because certain conditions are in place (principally the fact that students trust in my basic command of the subject). If this condition did not exist, if I had published nothing on critical theory and found it very difficult to give meaningful everyday examples that illustrated difficult and opaque concepts, then telling students I really struggled to understand the material and often spent 15 minutes reading a paragraph and being no clearer at the end of it than at the beginning would create a very different result. Students might wonder why they were being taught by an incompetent, they may find out whether someone else was teaching another section or the same course, or they might just decide to drop out and take the course in a future semester when they could study with a different professor. This leads us to another important element in understanding critical thinking, particularly when it focuses on hunting and researching assumptions—contextuality.

Assumptions Are Rarely Right or Wrong—They Are Contextually Appropriate

Contextually appropriate—sounds like a $50 academic term designed to impress people at academic receptions or the dean's sherry party! I use this two-word term as a shorthand way of describing a situation that takes a little longer to explain. Most of the causal assumptions that critical thinking uncovers are not always right or always wrong in some absolute or universal sense.

It is not even that they are right at some times and wrong at others. No, most causal assumptions are more or less appropriate depending on the situation that exists at any particular time. For example, starting off a 99ers gig by playing a cover song to draw in the audience only works if the audience is of an age to recognize the song or if the genre of the song is one that matches the audience's taste or if the way we play the song is either recognizable or good! A badly played cover song that people know can actually drive an audience away.

This is all by way of saying that an important element of critical thinking is doing our best to understand the conditions that are in place when we are deciding which assumptions are more or less accurate. The only chance we have of making an informed judgment about the accuracy of any particular assumption is if we have the fullest possible information about the conditions surrounding its use. Often we assume that an assumption we follow has a much broader range of accuracy than is actually the case. Let me give an example of an assumption that anyone in a leadership role has probably followed at some time:

ASSUMPTION—*Giving praise for work well done motivates the person receiving the praise to work hard in the future*

This is an assumption you hear a lot in leadership workshops. It is grounded in the theory of behavioral reinforcement, the notion that you shape behavior best by rewarding the behaviors you like to see, rather than punishing the behaviors you wish to eliminate. It has always seemed an assumption to me that had a wide range of generality so I've followed it when I've been in a lot of leadership roles—as a parent trying to shape the behavior of my own young children, as a teacher trying to encourage students to undertake the risky business of thinking critically and to ask critical questions of me, and as a leader in multiple contexts (football

team captain, band leader, department head, community orga-
nizer) trying to make sure people who were under my direction felt
acknowledged and appreciated.

But this assumption that I have a lot of confidence in, and that
I've followed many times over the years, is rendered either irrelevant or actually harmful in the following situations:

- If the praise isn't recognized as praise—to some in
  leadership positions not tearing a subordinate's work to
  pieces and publicly humiliating them is equivalent to
  giving praise. To the subordinate, however, this may be
  interpreted as one of those lucky days in which the
  leader forgot to notice what you were doing.

- If the praise given is *too* public—for people who grow
  up in collectivist cultures, where individual identity is
  inextricably bound up with membership of the
  collective, being singled out for praise is excruciatingly
  embarrassing. If this is the case then receiving
  individual public praise for doing something well will
  make you resolve not to do that in the future.

- If the praise is not passed on by the team leader—
  sometimes a leader gives praise to a team leader and
  asks that it be passed on to individual members. Unless
  the team leader follows through and tells each person
  how well he has done, team members are none the
  wiser and there'll be no desire to repeat the behavior
  in the future.

- If the praise is contradicted by other actions—if a
  leader tells team members how much she liked it when
  they made an independent decision but then punishes
  that action the next time it happens, the initial praise

is forgotten. If a team leader praises members for trying something new and taking risks but penalizes them for making mistakes when doing so, this kills the likelihood of risk-full experimentation in the future.

Summary

At the end of this opening chapter I hope you have understood the following:

1. Critical thinking is a process of hunting assumptions—discovering what assumptions we and others hold, and then checking to see how much sense those assumptions make.

2. One way we can assess the accuracy of assumptions is by trying to look at them from multiple viewpoints.

3. We do critical thinking so we can take informed actions—actions that are grounded in evidence, can be explained to others, and stand a good chance of achieving the results we desire.

4. Critical thinking can't be understood just as a process of mental analysis; it is always done for some wider purpose. So we always need to be clear what values inform critical thinking, why it's being done, and how such thinking will improve a situation.

5. The most difficult assumptions to identify and question are those embedded in dominant ideologies such as democracy, capitalism, White supremacy, patriarchy, and heterosexism.

6. Assumptions are not all the same. Three important types of assumptions are paradigmatic assumptions (assumptions that frame how we view the world), prescriptive assumptions (assumptions about how we think the world should work and

how people should behave), and causal assumptions (assumptions we have about why things happen the way they do).

7. Assumptions are rarely right are wrong; they are best thought of as more or less contextually appropriate. How accurate an assumption is will depend on the conditions that are in place when that assumption is followed.

2

Critical Thinking Across the Disciplines

In the first chapter I presented what might be called a generic model of critical thinking that focused on uncovering the assumptions that frame how we think and act, and checking these for their accuracy and validity, often by seeing them from multiple perspectives. The point of doing this, I argued, was to help us take informed actions. In this chapter I want to look critically at this model (as is appropriate in a book on critical thinking!) and ask how it changes from discipline to discipline, field to field, subject to subject. So I open the chapter with a discussion of how accurate it is to view critical thinking as a generic intellectual skill. I then look at how the term *critical thinking* is used in different disciplines, and I distinguish five broad intellectual traditions that inform it. These five traditions are analytic philosophy and logic, natural science, pragmatism, psychoanalysis, and critical theory. If, as a reader, you are anxious to get to the practicalities of how to teach critical thinking you can skip straight to Chapter Three. But sooner or later you'll realize that although critical thinking is a term thrown around with great abandon in academe, how it's understood differs greatly from discipline to discipline.

What's Common About Critical Thinking Across Disciplines

When working with teachers across the disciplines on how to teach critical thinking to their students I start from the point that there is something they can all agree on. My argument is that whatever discipline one teaches in—from statistics to theology, physics to romance languages—the point of getting students to think critically is to get them to recognize, and question, the assumptions that determine how knowledge in that discipline is recognized as legitimate. Sometimes the emphasis is on ferreting out the assumptions behind the arguments of experts in the field, sometimes on students themselves making clear the assumptions they operate under. But no matter what the discipline, all areas of academic study are constructed on assumptions regarding what scholars in those disciplines regard as legitimate knowledge.

A helpful concept to explain this is what R. S. Peters (1973), the late British philosopher, called the grammar of a subject. The grammar of a subject comprises both content and epistemology. A subject's *content grammar* is the building blocks of knowledge that every student of that subject needs to know in order to be regarded as well versed in it. In physics this might be the law of gravity or the law of relativity, or Boyle's law determining the relationship between pressure and volume. In a branch of literature this might be a familiarity with the canon of whatever is regarded as great works. Hence, growing up in England I was required to study Shakespeare, Chaucer, and D. H. Lawrence. Of course this content grammar is the result of the politics of academic inquiry, of certain people in academic gatekeeper positions deciding that some knowledge is legitimate because of the way it has been established, and other knowledge is not. For example, in academic medicine holistic healing was, until recently (and still is in some circles), regarded as fraudulent. So what counts as content grammar is determined by scholars and institutions and often codified by professional associations in standards and lists of best practices.

The *epistemological grammar* of a subject refers not to any specific content, but to the processes by which we determine that certain disciplinary content is true. In the natural sciences the hypothetico-deductive method that can be traced back to Francis

Bacon was for a long time the gold standard. This is the method whereby a hypothesis is tested and proved or refuted. In experimental psychology it is the control group/experimental group method. In biblical study it is hermeneutics. All these processes are humanly constructed and, hence, all rest on assumptions regarding the establishment of truth that some person or group, at some point in history, has managed to convince the majority members of a scholarly community was correct. Of course, as Thomas Kuhn famously argued in *The Structure of Scientific Revolutions* (1962), scholars change their epistemologies, or their paradigms of legitimate knowledge, over time.

The late French cultural theorist Michel Foucault (1980) addressed this issue of how disciplines create what counts as legitimate knowledge in his concept of "regime of truth." He wrote . . .

> Each society has its regime of truth, its "general politics" of truth; that is, the types of discourse which it accepts and makes function as true; the mechanisms and instances which enable one to distinguish true and false statements, the means by which each is sanctioned; the techniques and procedures accorded value in the acquisition of truth; the status of those who are charged with saying what counts as true. (1980, p. 133)

Of course, when Foucault uses the term "truth" it is not to describe ideas or knowledge that exhibit some inherent universal accuracy or undeniable empirical correctness. *Truth* is a term that describes the system that decides that certain forms of discourse should be allowed. Hence, truth is "a system of ordered procedures for the production, regulation, distribution, circulation and operation of statements" (p. 133). Foucault points out that regimes of truth are often highly contextual, particular to a specific group. The rockabilly community in Minneapolis-St. Paul has its own regime of truth regarding which artists are authentically rockabilly, what tattoos are acceptable, how hair should be combed, the correct way to play slap back bass, and so on. The editorial boards of the six journals on which I serve as consulting editor similarly establish procedures for judging which articles are acceptable, which methodologies are allowed, what writing styles are permitted, and so on. In their procedures for establishing their regimes of truth there is considerable similarity between these two very different groups.

Five Critical Intellectual Traditions

Although I've been using the term *critical thinking* to refer to the general process of hunting and checking assumptions, it is not an unequivocal concept, understood in the same way by all who speak or write the term. In fact it is a contested idea. How the term is used reflects the ideology of the user and her disciplinary background. As an example of this, consider the different ways people define critical thinking at the workplace. Following the work of Argyris (2010), workplace critical thinking can be represented by executives' use of brainstorming strategies and double loop learning methods. Here the purpose of critical thinking is to examine the assumptions that govern business decisions, to check whether or not these decisions were grounded in an accurately assessed view of market realities, and to make sure that those assumptions that are followed lead to maximum profits. Inferential ladders are scrutinized for the false rungs that lead business teams into, for example, a disastrous choice regarding the way in which a brand image upsets a certain group of potential customers. The point of all this critical thinking is to take informed actions—actions that lead to an increase in profits and productivity and a decrease in industrial sabotage and worker absenteeism. This kind of critical thinking draws heavily on the analytic philosophy and logic tradition, which, as we shall see, is mostly concerned with how arguments are constructed.

For others, critical thinking in a business setting takes a very different form. This group argues that workplace critical thinking always entails a vigorous and explicit critique of capitalism (Allman, 2000, 2001). This kind of critical thinking at the workplace questions the morality of relocating plants to Mexico, China, or Honduras, where pollution controls are much looser and labor is much cheaper. It challenges the demonizing of union members as corrupt Stalinist obstructionists engaged in a consistent misuse of power. It investigates the ways in which profits are distributed, and the conditions under which those profits are generated. It points out and queries the legitimation of capitalist ideology through changes in language; for example, the creeping and ever more widespread use of phrases such as "buying into" or "creating ownership" of an idea, the description of students as "customers," or the use of euphemisms such as "downsizing" or worse, "rightsizing" (with its implication that firing people restores some sort of natural balance to the market) to soften and make palatable the reality of people losing their livelihoods, homes, marriages, self-respect, and hope. This kind of critical thinking draws heavily on the critical theory tradition, which, as we shall see, is mostly concerned with investigating power relationships with a view to creating democratic socialism (Brookfield, 2004; Brookfield and Holst, 2010).

In fact there are at least five distinct intellectual traditions shaping understandings of critical thinking, and these differ substantially—perhaps explaining why so many efforts to teach critical thinking across the curriculum fail so dismally. I have been on task forces to teach critical thinking, and in conference sessions that examine how to assess whether students are thinking critically, only to realize very quickly that although all in the room seem to be talking about the same thing—critical thinking—we actually mean very different things by that term. This is not so much a symptom of the failed logocentrism that postmodernists talk of—the fact that the meaning of words is always opaque and slippery and totally dependent on what the hearer brings to their interpretation—but more a reflection of the prominence of these five traditions.

What are these five traditions? Well, in rough order of their prominence in the discourse of critical thinking they are (1) analytic philosophy and logic, (2) natural science, (3) pragmatism, (4) psychoanalysis, and (5) critical theory. In the next section I outline each of these traditions and explore how differently each of them conceives of critical thinking.

Critical Tradition # 1. Analytic Philosophy and Logic: Detecting Language Tricks

This is by far the most influential intellectual tradition informing how critical thinking is understood and taught in North America. Here thinking critically describes the process by which students become more skillful in constructing and deconstructing arguments. When my children went through the St. Paul school system they were continually assessed according to their exercise of critical thinking. Boiled down to its simplest level they were required to give reasons for any opinions, conclusions, or statements they made, whether these were in calculus, social studies, or science. Furthermore, these reasons were judged to be more or less valid according to the evidence adduced in support of them. A common classroom activity in social studies was to read a paragraph from a local paper and to distinguish between factual statements and statements of opinion. In mathematics, the focus was on learning to demonstrate the reasoning that led to a particular answer, rather than just submitting the correct answer.

The great majority of texts currently published that have the words "critical thinking" in their title spring from this tradition. They focus on things such as recognizing logical fallacies, distinguishing between bias and fact, opinion and evidence, judgment and valid inference, and becoming skilled at using different forms of reasoning (inductive, deductive, formal, informal, analogical, and so on). In Wittgenstein's (2009) terms, social relations are understood as word games and social understanding is equivalent to being able to unpack the multiple meanings and uses of language. Social action is understood as participating in speech acts (Searle, 1995). The 21 mini guides published by the Foundation for Critical Thinking in California illustrate the preeminence of this tradition with individual titles on analytic thinking (Elder and Paul, 2010), Socratic questioning (Paul and Elder, 2007a), detecting mental trickery (Paul and Elder, 2006a), how to read a paragraph (Paul and Elder, 2008), how to write a paragraph (Paul and Elder, 2007b), how to study a discipline (Paul and Elder, 2007c), and the art of asking questions (Elder and Paul, 2006).

Although the analytic philosophy and logic tradition may seem to be primarily technical, concerned with the mechanics of putting arguments together and taking them apart, it is often linked to a moral purpose. Diestler (2009) argues that the reason for assessing the validity of arguments is so that one can spot manipulative, false reasoning and protect oneself against it. She and others, such as Bassham, Irwin, Nardone, and Wallace (2007), maintain that a familiarity with language games helps one understand how language can be powerful and potentially misleading, derailing effective critical thinking. The analytic philosophy tradition argues that if one can understand how bias and prejudice masquerade as empirical fact or objective interpretation, one is better placed to know what to believe and what to do. In his analysis of how we judge the claims people make, Vaughn (2009) argues that if we can comprehend better where our beliefs come from, we can judge whether or not those beliefs are worth having. One of the Paul and Elder (2006b) "mini guides" to critical thinking deals with detecting media bias and propaganda.

I believe that critical thinking in this tradition is potentially as political as the most critical elements of critical theory. George Orwell's essay "The Politics of the English Language" (1946), which is the most anthologized piece of writing in English, makes this point supremely well. Propagandists and demagogues understand that language tricks are powerful tools in securing the consent of people to situations that are actually against their best interests. This is what hegemony is—thinking something, and acting enthusiastically on that thought as if it were the most obvious, commonsense thing in the world, all the while being unaware that your actions benefit those who wish to keep you uninformed. Getting people willingly to agree to, even support, a situation that is hurting them is difficult and cannot be done with force, since outright and overt coercion is easily identified. But control how people think and how they perceive the world—particularly through the use of language and its juxtaposition with images— and you are well on the way to getting people to agree to things that will end up harming them.

Some of the most common language tricks used in this effort are as follows:

- Attaching an abstract argument to a highly personal, dramatic narrative so people associate the argument with an easily remembered personal story

- Repeating a distorted argument often enough so that it becomes fact and gains legitimacy through frequent repetition

- Taking one part of an opponent's argument out of context, changing its meaning, and highlighting it in such a way that it is presented as the main element in an opponent's platform

- Attaching powerful positive symbols and myths (democracy, patriotism, openness) to one's arguments and powerful negative symbols (communist, dishonest, unpatriotic) to one's opponent's arguments

- Representing one's argument as the will of the majority, as in prefacing a comment by saying "The American people will not stand for. . . . " or "What the American people really want is. . . . "

- Making inferences that are presented as indisputable truth rather than hypothetical predictions, as in "this policy is bound to lead the country into bankruptcy"

- Choosing one example from a general category ("I know this Republican who . . . ," "I have this English friend that . . . ") and making an unwarranted generalization—portraying the specifics of their behavior as the behavior of the whole

- Using a revered authority as the justification for one's argument, as in "The Bible clearly tells us . . . " or "In the Constitution the founding fathers clearly believed that . . . "

- Stereotyping a whole class of phenomena such as people (Whites, Blacks, Asians, Arabs), situations (undemocratic Unions, inflexible management, corrupt politicians, mendacious communists), or artistic creations (French films, heavy metal music, Restoration drama)

- Constructing an inaccurate analogy to discredit an opponent's argument, as in "Banning smoking is the first step to Nazism"

One could argue, in fact, that teaching people to recognize these language tricks is actually the most politically explosive thing a school can do. If students grasp how arguments are put together to persuade others of the inherent, objective rightness of a particular point of view, or how they are developed to achieve certain ends at the expense of others, then they are better placed to recognize when this is happening and to make an independent judgment whether or not these arguments should be accepted. The analytic philosophy and logic tradition is usually not attached to any particular political viewpoint, so is both claimed by, and on occasion attacked by, different political orientations. Neither does it escape the value-basis identified in Chapter One. After all, what is one person's unfair distortion is another's empirical accuracy; what one person views as an inaccurate inference another regards as historical inevitability. So even though it is not usually thought of as political, the analytic philosophy tradition can actually be argued as having great relevance for democracy.

Critical Tradition # 2. Natural Sciences: The Hypothetico-Deductive Method

In 1620 Francis Bacon published his *Novum Organum* in which he laid out the philosophical basis for inquiry across all branches of knowledge. Bacon argued that in seeking cause and effect relationships the surest road to truth was to find the one variable that was present when a phenomenon occurred differently; that is, the factor that was absent from all other instances of the same phenomenon. So, for example, if my band plays the same set, in exactly the same way, to the same people who are in exactly the same mood on two consecutive nights, except that on the second night we add one song to the set, then any different crowd reaction we receive on the second night must be because of the new song. Bacon believed that careful observation and experimentation were the basis of sound thinking, a philosophical conviction that led to the hypothetico-deductive method.

The hypothetico-deductive method begins with the careful observation Bacon stressed. First, one develops a plausible explanation for how a set of phenomena connect to each other. This initial phase is not coldly logical; in fact it is often distinguished by high imagination, by flashes of insight, or by "thinking out of the box," as it is often referred to. After studying a phenomenon a researcher posits a hypothesis—a possible cause and effect explanation—of the thing studied. She then creates an experiment to test whether or not the expected result of the experiment materializes and, on the basis of the result, either corroborates or falsifies the hypothesis. If the hypothesis is falsified then a new one is devised that incorporates information from the first experiment and the process is repeated again. An important adjustment to this approach was Karl Popper's *The Logic of Scientific Discovery* (2002/1959), which proposed the principle of falsifiability. For Popper a truly scientific theorem is one that is falsifiable, in other words one that experimental testing could ultimately disprove. Popper argued that what we come to regard as truth is what is left after we have done our best to disprove it.

Interestingly, for Popper, there was a natural correspondence between the scientific method and a politically open democracy in which new explanations for human behavior, and new possibilities for intellectual and social evolution, are always present. This was because any society that was run according to principles drawn from a set of theoretical formulations was by definition closed to new knowledge. Marxism, Fascism, or any kind of religious fundamentalism—all of which held that human history could be predicted in advance and would unfold in a set way—were, in Popper's terms, examples of systems closed to genuine inquiry. They all suffered from what he termed as historicism. In *The Poverty of Historicism* (Popper, 2002/1957) he argued that all such deterministic philosophical systems inevitably led to the suppression of dissent from the party line of revealed truth and the closure of new intellectual horizons. Historicism, and the closing of avenues for inquiry, was one of the chief enemies of the open society (Popper, 1971a,b).

Popper's work connecting the adoption of the principle of falsifiability to political openness has important ramifications for critical thinking. Something that crosses all five of the intellectual traditions underlying criticality is an attitude, a disposition, to intellectual openness. A critical thinker is, by definition, one who is always open to reformulating hypotheses—in my terms to questioning assumptions—and accepts as axiomatic the proposition that no matter how strongly she believes something, future events might prove her wrong. This does not mean that convictions are not held with passionate intensity; after all, a certain degree of passionate intensity is necessary to fuel the flame that ignites all serious social change. But it does mean that even the most passionately held convictions are open to being revised, or even abandoned, in the face of evidence (including personal experience) that they are wrong.

The natural science tradition of hypothesis formulation and testing has been hugely influential and, despite quantum mechanics, chaos theory, and the theory of probability, it is still what most people consider the apex of scientific reasoning. It has informed other traditions of critical thinking by stressing the importance of observation and evidence gathering. The only way that hypotheses are proved, or theorems falsified, is by the careful collection of evidence. So every time in this book I argue that checking assumptions requires us to check the evidence we have that underlies these assumptions, I am drawing on the natural science tradition.

This tradition also informs the conviction espoused by many who consider themselves to be critical thinkers that self-criticism is a necessary element of truly critical thought. Generally speaking, even the most politically driven critical theorist admits to the possibility that she might be wrong. Hence, Antonio Gramsci, founding member of the Italian Communist Party and a convinced Marxist, observed that Marxism "tends to become an ideology in the worst sense of the word, that is to say a dogmatic system of eternal and absolute truths" (1971, p. 407). In a 1918 article in *Il Grido del Popolo* (The People's Cry), Gramsci warned that Marx "is not a Messiah who left a string of parables laden with categorical imperatives, with absolute unquestionable norms beyond the categories of time and space" (1988, p. 36). He believed that the value of Marxist ideas was always a provisional value and that changing circumstances made it necessary to undertake a continuing critical assessment of their utility.

This focus on the provisional nature of all knowledge, particularly of theories that explain how the world is supposed to work, is something that pervades notions of criticality. Indeed, when it comes to teaching students to think critically, a major problem is to prepare students for this disposition of openness. As cognitive and developmental theorists since Piaget document (Sinnott, 2010), the move from fixed, dualistic modes of thinking (there is always a right or wrong, correct or incorrect answer) to relativistic or multiplistic modes (the answer depends on a lot of different variables and could change as those variables change) is challenging. This is why teachers of critical thinking constantly need to study how students are experiencing the onset of ambiguity endemic to critical thinking. When you answer a question with the response that "it depends" you can often expect an expression of frustration from students who feel your job is to dispense reliable answers and provide certitude, particularly if they've gone into serious debt to enroll in college to learn your truth.

Critical Tradition # 3. Pragmatism: The Experimental Pursuit of Beautiful Consequences

A third tradition woven into discussions of critical thinking is that of American pragmatism. Pragmatism emphasizes the importance of continuous experimentation to bring about better (in pragmatist terms, more beautiful) social forms. It argues that in building a democratic society we experiment, change, and tinker constantly to make democracy work better. Part and parcel of this effort is discovering our own, and others', fallibility. Pragmatists hold that the way to become more knowledgeable about how to make democracy work better is through three strategies: (1) constant experimentation, (2) learning from mistakes, and (3) deliberately seeking out new information and possibilities. Democracy is the political form embraced by pragmatism, since it fosters experimentation with diversity. Cherryholmes (1999) writes that "pragmatism requires democracy," since "social openness, inclusiveness, tolerance, and experimentation generate more outcomes than closed, exclusive, and intolerant deliberations" (p. 39).

Unfortunately, colloquial usage has completely altered how most people understand the term *pragmatism*, to the point where being "pragmatic" is to be highly opportunistic, ready to pursue one's selfish ends by any means necessary. This is wholly antithetical to original conceptions of pragmatism from Charles Sanders Pierce, Ralph Waldo Emerson, William James, and later John Dewey, in which pragmatism was always linked to the pursuit of desirable, beautiful consequences. Pragmatism places aesthetic considerations as primary, so the point of experimental action is to increase the amount of beauty in the world. The adult educator Eduard Lindeman, himself heavily influenced by Dewey, regarded a well-lived life as a beautiful and creative construction (Lindeman, 1961/1926).

In a conversation with bell hooks, Cornel West says that "to talk about America is to talk about improvisation and experimentation" (hooks and West, 1991, p. 34), themes at the core of pragmatism. Pragmatism "tries to deploy thought as a weapon to enable more effective action" (West, 1993, p. 82), particularly action taken to promote "the flowering and flourishing of individuality under conditions of democracy" (p. 32). Pragmatism does not support action for action's sake. Although it puts "a premium on human will, human power and human action" (p. 37), it is neither vulgar practicality nor unprincipled opportunism. West sees pragmatism as "preoccupied with . . . the democratic way of life" (p. 31) that comprises "unique selves acting in and through participatory communities (in) an open, risk-ridden future" (p. 43).

Its self-critical strain is a second argument West adduces in support of his advocacy of pragmatism. He particularly admires

Dewey's belief that philosophizing requires the constant critical analysis of assumptions. Thus, a pragmatic orientation "constantly questions the tacit assumptions of earlier interpretations of the past. It scrutinizes the norms these interpretations endorse, the solutions they offer, and the self-images they foster" (West, 1982, p. 20). To pragmatists "norms, premises and procedures . . . are never immune to revision" (p. 20). Pragmatism is defined by its "calling into question any form of dogmatism" and its belief in a form of fallibilism in which "every claim is open to revision" (West, 1993, p. 43). It is not to be confused with an anti-theoretical stance, or with the idea that anything goes depending on the context. Instead, "it subtly incorporates an experimental temper within theory-laden descriptions of problematic situations (for instance, social and cultural crises)" (p. 137).

If analytic philosophy and logic, and later the scientific method, are European traditions, pragmatism is most decidedly American. However, there is a direct intellectual thread running between the Popperian notion of falsifiability discussed in the last section on the scientific method, and pragmatism's emphasis on constant experimentation. Pragmatism also clearly finds a home in critical theory's concern with politics and social action, where the focus is on taking action to achieve the best possible results. Critical theory focuses on socialism, pragmatism on democracy, but there are multiple intersections between the two, as seen particularly in Jurgen Habermas's (1987) work. The same emphasis we find in Popper's work on science's need for open democratic societies to foster inquiry is found in pragmatism's veneration of democracy. Pragmatists believe democracy is the most beautiful social form because it allows for the widest possible range of ideas and contributions to be made by the greatest number of people, with no politics functioning to exclude some voices or regard others as inherently more legitimate.

This emphasis on opening inquiry up to the widest range of voices is where pragmatism makes its most distinctive contribution to conceptions of critical thinking. Whereas the scientific method is generally held to be the province of trained scientists, pragmatism places ordinary, everyday experience as the subject of serious inquiry. A classically pragmatic approach to solving a problem is to consult all those currently affected by the problem, those who have dealt with the problem in the past, and those with any kind of specialist information, and then to ask them to search their experiences together for useful insights about the causes and resolution of the problem. So when teachers ask students to think critically about the link between their everyday experiences and their assumptions, they are drawing on the pragmatic tradition. From a pragmatic point of view, the heart of critical thinking is being able to understand one's assumptions more accurately by seeing them from multiple points of view.

This may ring a bell with you. At the start of Chapter One I outlined critical thinking as the uncovering and analysis of assumptions and argued that this happened most productively when these assumptions, and the practices they led to, could be viewed from multiple vantage points. Both critical thinking and pragmatism have the understanding of daily experience as a central concern. Both also value the widest possible array of interpretations. And both view inquiry as a constant process of experimenting with new approaches and incorporating new insights. Hence, to analyze personal experience critically is to subject it to the widest possible array of different interpretations. Calderon (2011) argues that the ability to see things from a different perspective is the most important disposition needed in a democracy, which is why Reason (2011) believes that learning to do this should be at the heart of the college experience.

Critical thinking informed solely by analytic philosophy and logic can sometimes feel too abstract for students, a participation in ultimately meaningless intellectual games. Critical thinking informed solely by the scientific method can sometimes seem too intimidating, particularly to nonscientists. Critical thinking informed by pragmatism, however, has the advantage of being felt as more real, as having a point, as leading to decisions that influence everyday life. This is why undergraduate curricula that teach critical thinking to help students make better, more informed decisions in their lives owe a large debt to pragmatism. Whether or not this debt is acknowledged, it is pragmatism that is the dominant intellectual tradition at play in these courses.

On a personal note, my own discipline of adult education has been strongly influenced by pragmatism. The point of adult education is often described as helping adults analyze their experiences, particularly to help them discover solutions to problems that plague their lives. The field also privileges active learning and experiential methods that engage students actively in discussion, rather than having them listen to lectures. This is tied directly to the work of influential early theorists such as Eduard Lindeman (1961/1926), who incorporated many of Dewey's ideas into the field. In Myles Horton's (2003) renowned work at Highlander, a largely pragmatist emphasis was adopted in using conversation circles to help activists realize that their own experience—properly analyzed in a collaborative but critical way—could be an invaluable resource in their fight for social justice. Paulo Freire's (2005) problem-posing and conscientization work also used everyday experience, particularly the study of everyday words, as the focus of a critical deconstruction that would help peasants realize the political inequities their lives represented.

So, to sum up, pragmatism probably undergirds the majority of the teaching activities currently used to teach critical thinking in higher education. It makes students' own dilemmas, problems, and experiences a central focus of the curriculum. A typical workshop on critical thinking will cover a range of situations that students are currently grappling with, rather than covering a body of abstract material. Teachers of critical thinking who constantly experiment with different activities and resources to make their classes more relevant and engaging to students are also inspired by a pragmatist ethic. When teachers emphasize the point of learning from mistakes and stress how important it is to understand how earlier assumptions and perspectives are flawed, they are working pragmatically. When students consult each other for perspectives that have been missed in an analysis of a situation, they are acting as pragmatists.

Critical Tradition #4. Psychoanalysis: Living an Integrated, Authentic Life

The fourth tradition informing how critical thinking is understood and taught is probably one that most teachers would recoil at being associated with. This is the tradition of psychoanalysis and psychotherapy. Teachers would recoil not because these disciplines are suspect or intellectually dishonest. No, the recoil would be because teachers would argue, quite appropriately, that untrained practitioners dabbling in these areas risk causing great harm to students by exploring aspects of their psyche that are far too complex (and potentially much too dangerous) for ordinary teachers to understand. How on earth could a biology teacher be expected to help students unearth unresolved problems encountered in childhood that block their full development as adults? Taking a critical approach to photosynthesis—OK. Uncovering the effects of a domineering father—no thank you!

The influence of this psychoanalytically and psychotherapeutically inclined tradition is more restricted to the sorts of courses that make students' personal experiences the focus of curriculum. It is strong in the social sciences, in human services, and in applied fields such as social work, nursing, or education. In clinical psychology, of course, this is a central curriculum focus. But how does it manifest itself in associated fields where students are not being trained as therapists?

The answer lies in an axiomatic assumption embedded in this tradition. Put briefly, this tradition believes that each of us has a core, authentic personality that waits to be released and realized.

This personality is one that has a structural integrity; in other words, building on Anthony Storr's *The Integrity of the Personality* (1992/1961), a personality formed when we live a life that achieves a close, and psychologically healthy, correspondence between our own inner nature and our outer work and relationships. This central idea is reflected in recent educational works such as Parker Palmer's *A Hidden Wholeness* (2008), the subtitle of which—*The Journey Toward an Undivided Life*—perfectly encapsulates the central idea of the psychoanalytic and psychotherapeutic tradition. Palmer argues that modern life forces us to live divided lives in which our strivings for success and happiness are in direct opposition to what it means to live in a soulful way. Through participating in small and long-lasting groups that he calls "circles of trust," he believes we can heal our soul and hear it speak to us.

Parker's work posits an authentic soul, in Storr's terms, a personality with integrity, in which inner yearnings are in harmony with outer actions. How do we reach such a connected state? Through something remarkably close to what others call critical thinking. Jack Mezirow (1991, 2000), the major theorist of transformative learning, writes of "the emancipatory process of becoming critically aware of how and why the structure of psycho-cultural assumptions has come to constrain the way we see ourselves and our relationships" (1981, p. 6). Using the framework of transformative learning, theorists like Gould (1990) emphasize critical thinking as the process whereby adults come to realize how childhood inhibitions serve to frustrate them from realizing their full development as persons. This realization is the first step to slaying these demons, laying them to rest, and living in a more integrated, authentic manner.

Different theorists emphasize differently the extent to which the development of new social structures is a precondition of a newly constituted, integrated personality. Carl Rogers (1961), for example, sees significant personal learning and personal development as occurring through individual and group therapy, but he does not address wider political factors—an omission he regretted in his last book *A Way of Being* (Rogers, 1980). Others, such as Erich Fromm (1941) and Ronald Laing (1960), argue that personality is socially and politically sculpted. For them schizophrenia or madness is a socially produced phenomena representing the internal contradictions of capitalism as they play themselves out in personal relationships. A movie version of this is Ken Loach's *Family Life* (1971), in which a young woman's schizophrenic breakdown is portrayed as the confluence of mental health policy (shock treatment for personality disorder) and dominant ideology (parents who force her to get an abortion to avoid the stigma of unwed motherhood). To radical psychologists such as Laing and neo-Marxists such as Fromm, individual and social transformation cannot be separated. For the personality to be reconstituted, insane and inhumane social forms need to be replaced by congenial structures and the contradictions of capitalism reconciled. In *Marx's Concept of Man* (1961) Fromm argues that the young Marx was convinced that the chief benefit of socialist revolution would be the transformation of the personality, the creation of a new kind of humanitarian citizen.

We may seem to be straying from critical thinking here so let me reiterate why the psychoanalytic and psychotherapeutic tradition is important to notions of critical thinking. The tradition argues that through critical analysis of our experiences we can identify assumptions we hold that are preventing us from realizing our inner potentialities. Critical thinking is thus employed to restore the connection between one's inner yearning and one's outer work and love commitments. The central process employed to do this is intense talk-therapy, in which the assumptions that govern our lives, frame our actions, and inform our most important personal choices are looked at critically.

I myself am a consumer of psychotherapy and psychoanalysis for the depression I mentioned earlier. In this therapeutic situation two processes are stressed. First, I am encouraged to become aware of the assumptions I operate under regarding the causes and treatment of depression and what the dynamics of a healthy personality development look like. Second, I am introduced to a perspective on my depression that is different from the one I carry around in my head. In regard to depression I am encouraged to treat this as caused by a chemical imbalance or complication in brain chemistry, and to regard it in much the same way as I'd regard high blood pressure or acid reflux (both of which I also receive treatment for).

Uncovering and challenging assumptions that frame behavior, and seeing familiar actions and ideas from a radically different perspective—both these processes are endemic to psychotherapy and to the generic model of critical thinking I outlined in the opening chapter. Both assume that critical analysis leads to an improved life through the making of informed decisions, creation of healthy communication in relationships, or realization of one's true personality. In this regard, critical thinking is highly modernist, assuming that a core personality exists that is waiting to be uncovered and realized. As we shall see in Chapter Nine postmodernism rakes this idea across the coals of its own skepticism. But although the psychoanalytic and psychotherapeutic tradition is generally less influential than analytic philosophy, the scientific method, or pragmatism, its emphasis on coming to understand ourselves more clearly by uncovering influential assumptions, and on seeing things from others' points of view, means it must be considered as a tradition informing critical thinking.

Critical Tradition # 5. Critical Theory: Speaking Truth to Power

Of all the traditions influencing how critical thinking is understood the fifth one I examine, critical theory, is the most overtly political. Although pragmatism holds that democracy is the political arrangement that best guarantees the intellectual openness necessary for the advancement of knowledge, critical theory's debt to Marxism, and its connection to democratic socialism, makes it a much more politically "in your face" critical tradition. Here critical thinking is explicitly tied to promoting a conception of social justice and to uncovering and redressing power inequities. An example of critical thinking in this tradition is being able to detect and resist ideological manipulation and to lay bare the abuses of power.

Critical theory is a term associated with thinkers from the Frankfurt School of Critical Social Theory, such as Horkheimer and Adorno (1972), Marcuse (1964), and Habermas (1987). The theory describes the process by which people learn to recognize how unjust dominant ideologies are embedded in everyday situations and practices. These ideologies shape behavior and keep an unequal system intact by making it appear normal. As a body of work critical theory is grounded in three core assumptions regarding the way the world is organized: (1) that apparently open, Western democracies are actually highly unequal societies in which economic inequity, racism, and class discrimination are empirical realities, (2) that the way this state of affairs is reproduced as seeming to be normal, natural, and inevitable (thereby heading off potential challenges to the system) is through the dissemination of dominant ideology, and (3) that critical theory attempts to understand this state of affairs as a prelude to changing it.

Dominant ideology comprises the set of broadly accepted beliefs and practices that frame how people make sense of their experiences and live their lives. When it works effectively it ensures that an economically unequal, racist, homophobic, and sexist society is able to reproduce itself with minimal opposition. Its chief function is to convince people that the world is organized the way it is for the best of all reasons and that society works in the best interests of all. Critical theory regards dominant ideology as inherently manipulative and duplicitous. From the perspective of critical theory, a critical person is one who can identify this manipulation and discern how the ethic of capitalism, and the logic of bureaucratic rationality, pushes people into ways of living that perpetuate economic, racial, and gender oppression. Teaching critical thinking, therefore, involves teaching people to see behind the apparently normal façade of daily life to realize how ideological manipulation works to keep people quiet and in line.

An important element in this tradition is the thought of Antonio Gramsci (1971), whose concept of hegemony explains the way in which people are convinced to embrace ways of thinking and acting that they believe are in their own best interests, when they are, in fact, harmful to them. In addition, and crucially, critical theory views a critical person as one who takes action to create more democratic, collectivist, economic, and social forms. Some in the tradition (for example, Cornel West) link social change to democratic socialism, others (for example, Erich Fromm) to socialist humanism. The critical theory tradition thus informs courses that have as their intent preparing students to engage in some form of social or environmental activism. As with the psychoanalytic and psychotherapeutic tradition, the critical theory tradition is most strongly evident in the social sciences. However, upper level science courses that consider the social function of science, the scientist's moral responsibility, or the place of ethics in scientific decision making could be said to be at least partly informed by this perspective.

In the same way that pragmatism places an objective value on democracy, the critical theory perspective also believes that critical thinking's purpose is to help bring about democracy. But unlike pragmatism, critical theory places as much emphasis on economic democracy—removing structured inequity associated with class, race, or gender—as it does on its political form; hence its concern with socialism. This perspective also defines a clear enemy to critical thought—the existence of dominant ideologies such as capitalism, White supremacy, patriarchy, heterosexism, and the concurrent process of ideological manipulation that ensures that the majority accept these ideologies unquestioningly. Those working within this paradigm are the most likely to be regarded as troublemakers who see power, race, class, sexism, ableism, and homophobia everywhere, even when it's not. To some degree, anyone who practices critical questioning runs the risk of being perceived as awkward. Anytime in a meeting you ask the question, "What assumptions are we operating on here?" you can be regarded as time wasting or as needlessly and unproductively rocking the boat. But because critical thinking informed by critical theory always zeroes in on abuses of power and the way systems and structures deliberately exclude certain groups, it is always explosive.

Teaching critical thinking informed by this tradition entails helping students to develop what C. W. Mills (1959) called a structural worldview, in which individual troubles are always analyzed as political phenomena. So, for example, layoffs are related to the workings of capitalism that seek to develop new markets, maximize profits, and cut labor costs. The progression of an individual illness and its treatment (or lack thereof) is explained by the way pharmaceutical companies and insurance companies structure and ration health care. A divorce is linked to the stress placed on a relationship by working three jobs to pay for education, health care, and so on. In this paradigm learning to think critically is a sort of ideological detoxification, in which the ideology of individualism—the belief that we all make our own destiny, are captains of our own souls—is revealed as a tool of false consciousness. False consciousness is the state of being duped by dominant ideology so that you think inequality is a normal consequence of Darwin's law of the survival of the fittest, and that prosperity has come to those who deserve it because of their extraordinary talents or the fact that they work harder than everyone else.

One of the chief criticisms of the critical theory paradigm of critical thinking is that it too readily fixes on who are the good guys (critical theorists) and the bad guys (racist capitalists). It also is criticized for having a preconceived end point—democratic socialism—toward which it is working. This is in contrast to some of the other traditions, where a condition of critical thinking is always to be open to new possibilities and not to predetermine the end point of your critique. There is certainly some truth to this argument. Critical theorists are much more likely to call out what they see as an abuse of power, and they do regard certain ideologies (capitalism, White supremacy) as damaging, and certain enacters of those ideologies (bosses, managers, boards of directors) as agents of harm and destruction.

But the critical paradigm also has a self-critical strain within it; after all, the theory itself began as an attempt to reformulate Marxist thought in conditions Marx had not foreseen. The working class across the industrial world had not followed the Bolshevik revolution in Russia and overthrown capitalism. Indeed, they often seemed to be striving to become the bourgeoisie. Neither had Marx foreseen the rise of mass communications and the role that mass media played in carrying dominant ideology. As Bronner and Kellner (1989) observe, "inspired by the dialectical tradition of Hegel and Marx, critical theory is intrinsically open to development and revision" (p. 2). Books such as C.W. Mills' *The Marxists* (1962), Eagleton's *Ideology* (2007), and Bronner's *Critical Theory* (2011) all accept, provisionally, the basic accuracy and utility of explanatory frameworks drawn from the critical theory tradition, while doing their best to challenge these. So, in Marcuse's words, "critical theory is, last but not least, critical of itself and of the social forces that make up its own basis" (1989, p. 72).

Summary

In this chapter I began by arguing that critical thinking across the disciplines shared a common objective of helping students become aware of the ways that knowledge in those disciplines became regarded as legitimate. A central concept I used in this effort was R. S. Peters' notion of the grammar of a subject. I then outlined what I regard as the five most important intellectual traditions informing how critical thinking is understood and taught within

North America. I don't believe any of these are mutually exclusive; indeed, many work best when they inform each other. For example, learning to discern how media messages present false arguments and ensure compliance to dominant ideology is helped immeasurably if you have learned some of the tools of argument construction and deconstruction from analytic philosophy. Trying to displace power and build democracy in organizations and communities where it has not existed before is much easier if you are open to the kind of experimentation and learning from mistakes urged by pragmatism.

In the next chapter I move away from the kind of intellectual survey conducted in this chapter and turn to the realm of experience, particularly to the experiences of students. Working in a manner informed by pragmatism I am always seeking to ground my methodology for teaching critical thinking in a thorough understanding of how students learn it. Chapter Three summarizes the chief features of how students learn critical thinking and begins to consider what these mean for how we work as teachers.

3

How Critical Thinking Is Learned

In this chapter I want to go to the coalface of critical thinking—how students experience it viscerally and cognitively. Instead of beginning with studies of how critical thinking *should* happen, I want to explore how it actually takes place in students' heads and bodies. There is a legion of books written to help students understand what critical thinking is and how it should be applied to their studies. These focus on the intellectual processes that constitute critical thinking, and the kinds of exercises that can be developed to foster these. The majority of these texts focus on how to detect when arguments are sound or erroneous (Thomson, 2008; Fisher, 2001; Andolina, 2002; Waller, 2004; Barnet and Bedau, 2005; Chaffee, 2006; Ruggerio, 2008; Nosich, 2009). They draw strongly on the analytic philosophy and logic tradition to help students think straight (Flew, 1998), ask the right questions (Browne and Keeley, 2007), think logically (McInerny, 2005), and judge the claims of pseudo-science and superstition (Schick and Vaughn, 2002). Others explore how to apply critical thinking to moral problems (Wall, 2003), to profound ideas like freedom, justice, morality, and spirituality (Chaffee, 2008), and to questions of faith (Conrad, 2008). Still more instruct readers on how critical thinking is connected to writing (Barnet and Bedau, 2005; Cooper and Patton, 2009) and to developing good study skills (McWhorter, 2008). And some are texts of personal application, helping readers place critical thinking in the contexts of their own personal or work lives (Andolina, 2000; Paul and Elder, 2005).

In this chapter, however, I want to put aside the question of how students should practice and apply critical thinking processes and instead look at how they do it in reality. More specifically, I want to examine what students say about the kinds of activities and approaches that they feel are most useful in helping them learn to do this. My observations are derived from over 1,500 Critical Incident Questionnaires completed by students in courses and workshops on critical thinking taught over the past 30 years at my home institution, the University of St. Thomas (Minneapolis-St. Paul), as well as at two other institutions where I have done full time or adjunct teaching—Columbia University (New York), where I worked full time from 1982 to 1992, and National Louis University (Chicago), where I have served as occasional adjunct faculty since 1992.

The Critical Incident Questionnaire (CIQ) is a classroom evaluation tool I use in all my teaching. It is a five-item instrument that asks students to review their learning in class for any particular week and to answer five questions about that experience:

- At what moment were you most engaged as a learner?

- At what moment were you most distanced as a learner?

- What action that anyone took in class did you find most helpful?

- What action that anyone took in class did you find most confusing?

- What surprised you most about the class?

This instrument can be downloaded at my home page (www .stephenbrookfield.com), where you will also find case study examples of its use (Adams, 2001; Glowacki-Dudka and Barnett, 2007; Keefer, 2009). In a traditional semester-long course it is completed once a week. The last five minutes of the last class of any particular week are allocated for students to fill out their responses to the five questions. All CIQs are anonymously completed and no names are placed on the forms. A student collects them and hands them to me and I review them before the first class meeting of the following week. I make a note of the main themes that emerge, and begin the next class by sharing with the students a brief report of what the forms contain. For a more detailed review of how I use this instrument you can read chapter six of *Becoming a Critically Reflective Teacher* (Brookfield, 1995).

Five themes repeatedly emerge from these CIQs regarding how students learn critical thinking. First, they say that it is best developed in small groups where peers serve as critical mirrors shedding light on assumptions that have never been checked and introducing new perspectives that have not been previously considered. It seems that students experience critical thinking primarily as a social learning process. Second, they like it when teachers model the process and draw students' attention to how that's happening. Third, they find it helpful to ground critical thinking in concrete experiences through case studies, critical incidents, simulations, and scenarios. Fourth, they stress that the most significant moments in critical thinking happen when some kind of unexpected event or idea jolts them out of their comfort zone, what theorists of transformative learning such as Mezirow (1991, 2000) call a disorienting dilemma. Finally, they view the trajectory of how they learned critical thinking as developmental. They prefer starting with multiple opportunities to practice critical protocols in settings that are relatively nonthreatening, before gradually applying this process to their own life and experiences. The rest of this chapter reviews these findings in detail.

Critical Thinking Is a Social Learning Process

Overwhelmingly, students pick out participating in small group activities as the most engaging moments in learning to think critically. This is the theme that always attracts the most

comments on CIQ surveys, with approximately 80% of participants declaring that the most helpful moments and actions
were when something in a small group activity really hit home.
It seems that students discover assumptions and new perspectives
most meaningfully when a peer brings it to their attention. They
write vividly of how helpful it is to have peers ask them questions
that they had not considered before. They say how much they
learned from the observations peers made about their ideas, or
the suggestions they offered on how to think differently about
problems they were facing. This finding is remarkable in both its
predictability and its frequency. Course after course, workshop
after workshop, year after year, students say that it is through
peer exchange in small groups that the sometimes abstract activity of thinking critically is given a level of detail that drives the
process home. Some of the specific peer group activities students
find helpful are described in detail in Chapters Four, Five, and
Six, so I won't go into them in the current chapter. What I do
want to do here is look at why learning from peers is important,
and how social learning activities can be structured to be most
helpful.

Discovering that critical thinking is a social learning process is
hardly surprising if we consider how difficult it is to learn about
our motives, assumptions, and worldviews simply by deciding we
will do some deep self-examination. Becoming aware of our assumptions is a puzzling and contradictory task. Very few of us can get
very far doing this on our own. No matter how much we may think
we have an accurate sense of ourselves, we are stymied by the fact
that we're using our own interpretive filters to become aware of
our own interpretive filters! This is the equivalent of a dog trying
to catch its tail, or of trying to see the back of your head while
looking in the bathroom mirror. To some extent we are all prison-
ers trapped within the perceptual frameworks that determine how
we view our experiences. A self-confirming cycle often develops
whereby our uncritically accepted assumptions shape actions that

then serve to confirm the truth of those assumptions. It's enormously difficult to stand outside yourself and look back at your life to discover how some of your most deeply held values and beliefs have led you into wrong choices. To become aware of our assumptions we need to find some lenses that reflect back to us a stark and differently highlighted picture of who we are and what we do. Our most influential assumptions are too close to us to be seen clearly by an act of self-will.

One of the problems of using friends and colleagues to help you become aware of your assumptions, however, is that the people you find to serve as mirrors often share your assumptions. In this situation your conversation with them becomes an unproductive loop in which the same prejudices and stereotypes are constantly reaffirmed. Just as we tend to read authors we already agree with, or have some affinity for, so we tend to seek out peers whom we know are sympathetic to, and familiar with, our orientations. Rare indeed are the people who deliberately seek out books, conversations, and practices that they know will challenge or even undercut much of what they find to be comfortable and familiar. So one of the things it's important to do as a teacher when setting up small groups for critical thinking is to make sure that the activities you design deliberately throw up information, dilemmas, and perspectives that take people by surprise.

The whole idea of systematically searching out assumptions is often deliberately avoided for fear of where it might lead. No one likes to discover that ideas they have lived by for much of their life are distorted and invalid. But the process becomes more tolerable when it's a shared one, particularly if you can see that others are struggling just like you to discover their assumptions and consider new perspectives. Generally students say that when they hear questions from a peer, or when peers contribute a variety of different responses to a problem, this is easier to live with than hearing a question, or considering a new idea, from a teacher. There are two reasons usually given for this. The first is that a peer is more likely to ask a question, or to suggest a different perspective on a problem, by using language and examples closer to students' experiences. Hence, the question or perspective is put more helpfully, and understood more accurately, when framed in familiar language that students use. As someone in his fifth decade as a teacher it is increasingly difficult for me to use examples and language my students understand easily. If I'm 60 and my student is 18 it would be very surprising if our daily lives were the same, if we watched the same TV shows, liked the same music, or used social media the same way.

But students also find it easier to hear questions and consider new perspectives when they come from peers because the power dynamic is very different from the one in place when those questions or perspectives emanate from the teacher. This is not to deny that power dynamics are also important in student–student dynamics—they obviously are. Differences of race, class, and gender play themselves out in student groups, just as they do in any other situation. And every student runs into group members who try to take over the group either because they are enthusiastic about the topic or because they are egomaniacs who love the sound of their own voices. But a teacher's calling your assumption into question, telling you about an important perspective you've overlooked, or informing you about a piece of information whose significance you've missed is far more threatening than hearing those same things from the most egomaniacal, blowhard student. The teacher holds your fate in her hand; she wields the power of the grade over you. So in a strange way, when you hear a radical idea that challenges your thinking expressed by another student, it is more likely to be considered seriously than when it's the teacher who expresses it.

I want to end this section by stressing how important it is that small group activities be carefully structured. When I say that students report critical thinking to be a social learning process it is with one major qualification. The activities that students say they find to be most productive are the ones in which ground rules are clearly stated and understood, and in which the focus is on criticality. Social learning is not chatting comfortably and letting the conversation flow whichever way chance takes it. No, social learning for critical thinking focuses on students listening carefully to each other, asking questions of each other that uncover assumptions, and offering new perspectives or ideas.

Two structured social learning processes that could easily be the bookends to a critical thinking sequence may illustrate what I mean—scenario analysis and the critical conversation protocol. Scenario Analysis (explained more fully in the next chapter) asks students to read a brief fictional vignette in which a character is making a choice. Students are given three tasks to accomplish in groups. Having each read the scenario individually they share (1) the implicit and explicit assumptions each of them thinks the character in the scenario is operating under, and whether those assumptions are causal, prescriptive, or paradigmatic, (2) the different ways they think the character in the scenario could check out her assumptions, and (3) suggestions they have for different interpretations of the scenario—ways of interpreting it that are different to the interpretation the character in the scenario places on it. These three tasks correspond to the first three phases described in the generic model of critical thinking outlined in Chapter One. This introductory exercise is short and nonthreatening, since it focuses on a fictional situation and a made up character.

A much more intense version of a structured social learning process designed to elicit critical thinking is the Critical Conversation Protocol. This is described much more fully in Chapter Five. In this exercise the student brings a situation she is struggling with, and which she'd like to understand better, to a group of peers. The student describes the situation and then responds to questions about it from peers. There are careful ground rules to determine the way questions are asked, so that questions are heard as helpful requests for information, not as accusatory put-downs (as in "Are you seriously telling me that . . . ? Or "Why on earth didn't you . . . ?). The peers then inform the student of the assumptions they think she brings to her understanding of the situation. How these assumptions are reported is determined by ground rules designed to ensure the student does not feel attacked. The peers then suggest to the student different ways of understanding the situation, again following ground rules. Finally, peers tell the student directly what they think she should do and everybody does an audit of what they've learned from the exercise.

The Scenario Analysis and Critical Conversational Protocol exercises are both social learning activities in which the same critical thinking protocol is applied—hunting assumptions, considering how these might be checked, and generating different perspectives on a situation. Both benefit from the diversity of responses suggested by participants and both involve lively exchanges. But both are also clearly kept within the boundaries of the same critical thinking protocol. The intensity of the two exercises is clearly different, since there is far more at stake when a student brings a problem she is experiencing to a group with the intent of receiving critical feedback about her assumptions and interpretations. But this latter, more intense exercise is structured with ground rules designed to keep the focus on a nonjudgmental approach to giving critical feedback.

How to Model Critical Thinking

Of the five themes that emerge from students' responses on what most helps them learn to think critically, this is the one that surprises me the most. At the beginning of my career I believed I could measure my success as a teacher by how much my students noticed me; or rather, how much they forgot I was there. If they were learning without me saying or doing very much, and if they ignored my presence, then I felt I was teaching in the best way possible. I still believe this is very valid in many situations and that, in Finkel's terms, you can be very effective when you teach with your mouth shut (Finkel, 2000). But when it comes to students' learning how to practice critical thinking, it seems they constantly look to us to see what the process looks like. Furthermore, given the difficulties of this process, it's important that we earn the right to ask them to do it themselves by first modeling how we try to unearth and research our own assumptions.

The modeling that students appreciate from us takes different forms. Most important, it seems that the more personal examples we give of how we try to think critically, the more students appreciate this. A teacher's early disclosure of a critical thinking experience can set a tone of openness that significantly influences students' readiness to delve into their own assumptions. In a way, my disclosure at the beginning of Chapter One of how critical thinking helps me cope with my own depression is an example of this dynamic in action. My assumption in making this personal disclosure early in the book was that it would grab your attention, provide an example of how the process looks, and set the right tone for a book that would interweave personal examples with generalized advice and references to research.

Students also report that they find it helpful when we explain why we're doing what we're doing. Students say that when it comes to a threatening activity like being asked to think critically about their long-held assumptions, it inspires confidence when they see that teachers clearly have a plan for doing this, a set of reasons informing their actions. Speaking out loud about why you are introducing a particular classroom activity, why you're changing learning modalities, why you've chosen certain readings, how you decide to put students in certain groups, or why you're moving from a small group activity into a mini-lecture—all these public disclosures demonstrate to students that you are a thoughtful teacher. Knowing that they are in the hands of such a teacher builds students' confidence. No one likes to think that the person leading him or her in an activity is making it up as she goes along with no forethought, reasoning, or previous experience. This is particularly the case when the teacher is asking students to engage in a risk-filled learning activity, as is the case with critical thinking.

I would venture that it is almost impossible to talk your practice out loud too much. In thousands of Critical Incident Questionnaires collected over the years in many different courses, this is an amazingly consistent theme. Students really appreciate knowing why the teacher is doing what she is doing. They say this helps them learn whatever is being taught and also gives them the sense that they are in the hands of a trusted guide. To know why doctors wish us to take particular medications is an important element in our trusting that the doctor has our best interests at heart and that she knows what she is doing. To know why an auto-mechanic is suggesting that a certain part needs to be replaced is crucial to our trusting that we are not being conned. The same holds true for teachers. If students are to have confidence in our abilities they need to know, and trust, that there is a rationale behind our actions and choices.

Having discussed two general elements in modeling critical thinking—using personal examples and explaining the reasoning behind your actions—let me review some specific examples that students have picked out over the years as being helpful. All of these are designed to demonstrate either how to uncover and check assumptions or how to view knowledge and skills from multiple perspectives.

Speaking in Tongues

This activity is designed to show students how the same idea, facts, skills, or content can be interpreted in different ways. You begin by posting signs around the classroom corresponding to the number of different viewpoints you wish to consider. So, for example, if I was teaching a lesson on the intellectual traditions informing critical thinking I might post five signs—analytic philosophy and logic, scientific method, pragmatism, psychoanalysis and psychotherapy, and critical theory. The activity starts with you standing in the center of the classroom and reviewing the content in the way it's generally understood. Hence, I might kick off by going over the definition of critical thinking given in the syllabus and examining how the University of St. Thomas incorporates critical thinking into its mission statement.

You then move to the first sign you've posted and explain the content as if you were someone who only thought within that framework. So if I moved to the analytic philosophy sign I would only speak about critical thinking as the evaluation of argument and detection of logical fallacies. You then move to the second sign you've posted and give your understanding of the content as if you were solely concerned with that second perspective. So I would move to the scientific method sign and speak about critical thinking as the generation and testing of hypotheses and the application of the principle of falsifiability. Sometimes as I get to the different signs I'll put a different hat on—maybe a Minnesota Twins hat at one, a Green Bay Packers hat at another, an LA Lakers hat at a third, and so on. Students say that bringing in a simple spatial difference—speaking the language of a different theoretical paradigm when you are at a different station in the room—helps them realize that different perspectives can be taken on the same material.

A further variant on this exercise is to ask the class to generate questions about the topic after you've done your mini-review at each of the stations you've posted. You can then respond to the same question in several different ways by going to two or three of the stations and responding in the voice of someone answering just from that perspective. Finally, when you have done this a couple of times in class you can add a further complexity. This time, you divide the class into groups and ask different groups to go and stand at the different signs. You then pose a question or raise an issue about the material and you ask the groups to brainstorm for a couple of minutes on how they would answer the question, or respond to the issue, if they operated only within the framework represented by the sign they are standing by. The exercise ends with each group giving a summary of their responses.

Compiling an Assumptions Inventory

In this exercise you get into the habit of stopping a presentation you are making to compile, in front of the class, an Assumptions Inventory. This is, quite simply, an audit of the most important assumptions informing the material you've just presented. It can be adapted to almost any subject or topic, such as . . .

- Presenting your reasoning behind the way you've just presented a mathematical problem and demonstrated the solution

- Explaining how you've designed an experiment to measure velocity

- Describing how you discern the meaning of certain analogies used in a poem

- Summarizing the causal chain you've identified in a sequence of historical events

- Reviewing how a set of skills learned in a classroom can be applied to a real-life setting

- Justifying why you choose one theory over others as the best explanation for a particular phenomenon

The audit works as follows. At appropriate junctures in your presentation you pause to summarize the chief assumptions embedded in the presentation you've just given. You distinguish between explicit and implicit assumptions and then try to list the paradigmatic, prescriptive, or causal assumptions that have influenced your argument so far. You do your best to give examples of the most persuasive evidence for each of these assumptions and identify anything that's questionable about the assumption. This could be pointing out that some assumptions are less evidence-based than others, or that some have never been properly tested or challenged. You also explain which assumptions are more recent, which have never changed, and which you feel most, or least, confident about.

Modeling Point-Counterpoint

This activity is possible only if you are team teaching a class. Essentially, it requires two or more people to analyze an idea, or take apart a piece of content, from discernibly different perspectives in front of the class. I usually team teach two courses a year, and the point-counterpoint moments are often the ones that students pick out as the most engaging ones in class. This is where students see the faculty attempt to model what respectful disagreement and critical analysis of another's position look like. This is extremely helpful if you are asking students to do these things as part of their own small group discussions with each other.

Certain kinds of interactions are important to demonstrate when modeling Point-Counterpoint. Probably the most important is showing students how to pose questions that ask for evidence without attaching judgmental elements to them. Examples of these would be "Can you tell me more about . . . ?" "Why do you think that's the case?" "What's the most convincing piece of evidence for that view?" "How do you respond to Smith's research that challenges your position?" Other questions would seek clarification such as "If I understand you correctly you seem to be saying . . . " or "Can I just check that I've followed your argument correctly?"

Point-Counterpoint also allows you to show you try to incorporate, or build on, your co-teacher's comments, which, in turn, emphasizes for students the importance of careful listening. You can strive to answer questions addressed to you as fully and clearly as possible, and be ready to admit when you don't have an answer, or when you need some time to think through what you want to say. When you disagree with a coteacher's analysis, or you take a very different position on understanding a piece of content, you can say "I take a different view on this and here's why I think the way I do" or "My approach doesn't emphasize what you cover, here's my line of analysis." Often the greatest moments of delight for students noted on their Critical Incident Questionnaires are when two instructors publicly disagree on something. This immediately gets their attention and wakes them up.

Engaging in Structured Devil's Advocacy

This is a solo version of Point-Counterpoint. As part of your presentation you strive to spend some time presenting any arguments that counter your own assertions. A dramatic and theatrical approach is to state your opening position while you stand in one part of the room, and then to move to another part of the room, look back at where you were originally standing, and then direct a second set of comments back at that spot as if you were speaking to the person (yourself) who was just standing there. Here you deliberately state an alternative view, or you analyze the ideas you were just describing through a different research paradigm or a different theoretical framework. You are deliberately playing devil's advocate with the position you've just stated.

Structured Devil's Advocacy deliberately articulates a different perspective on what you've just said or opens up questions about it. You say things like "However, if look at this idea from another point of view you can see that . . . " or "A whole other interpretation is possible of this argument that calls many of its central assumptions into question." You can model critical analysis by presenting counter-arguments or rebuttals, in essence using the principle of falsifiability described in Chapter Two. When you do this you address your imaginary other self by name and say things like, "Stephen, what you're omitting to mention is . . .", or, "Of course Stephen, you could pursue a very different line of reasoning if you argue that . . . "

Using the Critical Incident Questionnaire (CIQ)

I began this chapter with a description of the Critical Incident Questionnaire (CIQ), so if you're unsure about what this instrument is and how it works just go back a couple of pages. Every time you report the results of the previous week's CIQ responses back to students you have the opportunity to model critical thinking for them. Each week as I report the form's responses back to the students, I make the point to them that in doing so I am applying critical thinking to my own actions as a teacher. This is because I am using students' perceptions to check the assumptions I am operating under as I set up and then teach the course. As I talk about their reactions to the last week's class I reflect publicly on the relative accuracy of the assumptions I was working under as I set up the activities I arranged for them. I discuss the assumptions informing the assignments I designed and those underlying the specific decisions I made in the midst of the class. I keep telling them that I am trying to demonstrate critical thinking in action— publicly checking my assumptions as a teacher by reviewing them through the different perceptions represented by the students in the class.

If no surprises are evident in the CIQ responses, and it is clear that most people felt the class had gone well, I say that the CIQ responses are still valuable because they allow me to do confirmatory critical thinking. Confirmatory critical thinking is what happens when we research an assumption that we've trusted intuitively, and discover that it is indeed a good one to follow. The CIQ can be confirmatory as well as challenging and often illustrates why our habitual assumptions are so well grounded. It's reassuring for students to know that critical thinking can be confirmatory, that sometimes it can lead to us committing even more strongly to assumptions we already hold. If they think that critical thinking only happens when they are forced to change everything they believed up to that point, then it is unlikely that many will wish to engage in it.

Ending Lectures and Discussions with Questions

Lecturers are often told that the golden rule of effective lecturing is to "tell 'em what you're going to tell 'em, tell 'em, then tell 'em what you've just told 'em." The problem with this rule is that it commodifies knowledge as a neatly bounded package of facts or concepts. Doing this is inimical to intellectual inquiry, particularly to the student's ability to make connections across subject areas and disciplines. Even more worryingly, ending with a summary of what's already been said establishes a sense of definitive closure, of the last word having been spoken on the subject.

I argue that good lecturers end their presentations by pointing out all the new questions that have been raised by the content of the lecture, and also by pointing out which of the questions posed at the start of the lecture have been left unanswered or been reframed in a more provocative or contentious way. This prepares students for the same practice in discussion where conversation sessions can be ended by asking students to volunteer the questions the discussion has raised for them rather than by giving a summary of "what we've learned today in our discussion." If possible, lecturers should spend the last ten minutes of a lecture asking students to write down the questions the lecture has raised for them, and then find a way to make some of these public. Students can be asked to speak their questions to the whole class, or they can be asked to share them with each other in small buzz groups of two or three. If they write them down, they can pass them to the lecturer, and have the lecturer read out a random selection. As hand held devices become de rigueur in classrooms, students can send their questions anonymously and electronically to a classroom whiteboard for review.

Even if none of these things are possible, your own behavior of finishing a lecture with a list of new questions the lecture raises for you, or ending with an acknowledgment of the omissions, ethical dilemmas, and contradictions that challenge what you've just articulated, is a powerful piece of modeling. You should be warned, though, that initially students will probably be very critical of this behavior. On CIQs they will record their frustration that the lecture didn't end only with a clear recap of the main points. They will see your behavior of ending with questions or raising problems as unnecessarily confusing, as pulling the rug out from under their feet. Over time, as you consistently explain how doing these things is your best attempt to model the spirit of critical inquiry you are trying to encourage in learners, students' frustration will often diminish.

Specific Experiences

One of the surest ways to strike terror into someone is to ask them to tell you what their assumptions are. This is an intimidating question for the most confident of us. First, we often don't know what our assumptions are and, second, it's often hard to define exactly what constitutes an assumption. So the response to being asked to disclose your assumptions is often to say the first thing that comes into your head, which is often a cliché or whatever you judge to be the thing you are supposed to say. For example, if anyone had asked me what my assumptions about parenting were when my kids were younger I probably would have said something like "be consistent," "let them know you love them," or "support them in whatever they want to do." The first and last of these assumptions are wrong, in my opinion. First, I was often inconsistent. I would change my "policy" on appropriate parenting behavior depending on the situation. Second, it is quite possible that I would sometimes judge that what my children wanted to do—eat only pizza perhaps—was wrong. Because my children are beacons of sweet reason I can't ever remember that happening—but it is quite possible that it could have.

We learn much more about what our assumptions *really* are when we're asked to explore highly specific experiences. For example, ask most teachers what assumptions they hold about what makes a good teacher, and what you will hear in response often mimics what their own mentors have told them, or what they have read in professional literature. They will also respond at a level of high generality. However, ask those same teachers to choose the day in the last month when they felt they did their best work, or the day when things went so badly they felt like quitting, and you will get a highly concrete answer. As you hear why they chose that day, and what it was about that day that was so wonderful or awful, you will receive reams of detail about the people involved, or about the dynamics of the incidents that provoked either delight or depression. These specifics are likely to tell you far more about what a person's assumptions actually are than if you asked them directly, "What are your assumptions?"

So when students describe the classroom activities that they find to be the most helpful in teaching them how to think critically, they usually reference scenarios, case studies, particular experiments, simulations, specific texts—anything where they deal with a very concrete situation. It is much easier for students to describe the assumptions they are operating under in reference to a specific activity or experience than to talk generally about the assumptions they hold about the best way to study engineering or what constitutes legitimate criticism in art history. So if you want your students to think critically you need to embed this process in very specific activities and ask a series of questions about how they completed those tasks. What inferential leaps do they make as they interpret the results of an experiment? Which evidence for confirming a hypothesis do they find the most convincing? What is unpersuasive or irrelevant about other evidence? Why does one theory seem to explain a particular sequence of events better than another? Any time you can focus a student's attention on why she made a particular choice out of the options available will be a much more fruitful entry into discussing critical thinking than talking about it in general terms.

Disorienting Dilemmas

A disorienting dilemma is a term usually associated with Jack Mezirow's groundbreaking work on transformative learning (Mezirow, 1991, 2000). It describes an unexpected situation that forces you to think differently about something you've taken for granted up to that point. Mezirow's work most frequently focuses on situations that come out of the blue and cause us to reappraise how we think about some part of life. For example, when you're fired after working diligently for years, you quickly reappraise your assumptions about institutional loyalty. When your partner suddenly leaves you, you rethink the assumptions you hold about how to nourish a healthy relationship. When someone close to you dies or you are told you have a life-threatening condition, your priorities are usually drastically reordered. Although disorienting dilemmas are often traumatic, they can also be pleasurable. For example, unexpectedly falling in love or becoming a parent for the first time usually causes you to rethink what is important in life.

Research on transformative learning (Mezirow and Taylor, 2009) documents how disorienting dilemmas are the most common triggers to a major reappraisal of our meaning schemes and meaning perspectives—in other words, to changing the usual ways we make sense of the local events in our lives, as well as the bigger issues. Exactly the same is true of critical thinking, at least if students' testimonies are to be believed. Time and again, students say that it takes facing something dramatically unnerving to compel them to think in different ways about it. But those unsettling classroom moments are the ones that they remember vividly and respond to strongly.

What a disorienting dilemma looks like will vary from discipline to discipline, subject to subject, topic to topic. What unites all of them is their unexpectedness. When a chemist sets up an experiment in which she assumes she knows in advance whether or not her hypothesis will be proven, and when the opposite occurs, this is a disorienting dilemma. When an English major is sure of the correct interpretation of a passage and reads an analysis that is totally different, this is the same thing. Any time a case study looks familiar to the student but the outcome of the case study is completely unexpected, this is a disorienting dilemma. A colleague of mine used to start a course by asking students to appraise a piece of work that had been generally well regarded in his field. After the students had shared their uniformly positive appraisals, he would publicly demolish the piece. That was certainly a way to shake students up early! Another colleague used to begin a unit on racism by lying down at the entrance of the classroom so students had to step over her to gain entry. For many students, the teacher admitting that he or she is wrong, or has made a mistake, is a disorienting dilemma. Seeing members of a teaching team disagree can be equally unsettling to students from cultures where teachers are revered as guardians of certitude.

The trick with designing a disorienting dilemma is that it has to be unsettling enough to shake students out of their comfort zone, but not so discomforting that those students will do their best to avoid dealing with it. One good way to introduce a disorienting dilemma is to begin by first demonstrating how you yourself dealt with something equally disorienting. As with many other things, the CIQ has been helpful for me in this regard. Sometimes I will feel good about how a class has gone only to read a CIQ response that criticizes me in a way that is both serious and wholly unanticipated. I will report this to the students and talk through how this disorienting feedback has affected me and what it's meant for how I conduct the class. Another thing I sometimes do is tell a teaching colleague before we teach a particular class that sometime during that class I want her to ask me the most unexpected and difficult question she can think of. It's good for the students to see me struggling to deal in the moment with a challenge from a colleague to my usual ways of thinking.

An Incremental Process

The final insight that comes from students about how they learn to think critically concerns the way this process unfolds over time. Basically, it seems that students across the disciplines respond best when a program or course designed to teach critical thinking begins with exercises that are nonthreatening and have little risk attached to them, primarily because the student's own reasoning and choices are not directly at play. Then, over time, the application of critical protocols moves closer and closer to a direct analysis of the student's own thinking and actions. Hence, at the end of the program or course the students are engaged in a direct critical analysis of their own ideas and forms of reasoning. But, in contrast to much of what I assumed to be the case for the first half of my teaching career, it is *not* a good idea to start a critical thinking sequence by focusing initially on the student's own reasoning and experiences. This is too intimidating, too close to home; there is too much at risk.

The opening phase of a critical thinking sequence should exhibit two initial features. First, there should be a clear and repeated attempt to describe in very specific terms what a critical thinking protocol looks like. This is what Chapter One in this book did with my initial outline of critical thinking as the hunting and checking of assumptions through viewing them from multiple perspectives. Students like as many examples as possible to be given of what this protocol looks like in action and how it can be applied to specific content. Second, students stress that an early and repeated modeling of teachers' own engagement in critical thinking is also useful. This initial phase is one characterized by considerable teacher scaffolding; that is, teachers providing models, protocols, and examples of the process that students can hang their own subsequent critical thinking activities on.

The second phase kicks off with students applying these critical protocols to problems that are specific to the discipline or subject. They are given examples of experiments, theorems, texts, arguments, case studies, or concepts in their fields and asked to apply critical analysis to them. What evidence did the designers of these experiments take most seriously? What assumptions were they making when they developed testable hypotheses about the nature of the phenomena they were investigating? How did theoreticians end up at their analyses? What kinds of reasoning (inductive, deductive, fallibilistic, analogical, etc.) did the author of a text use? How could assumption hunting be applied to a particular case?

Once students are in the rhythm of correctly applying critical protocols to content primarily authored by others (usually credible scholars in the field) then the process starts to move closer to the final phase in the sequence, the student's analysis of her own experience. Now, instead of turning a critical gaze on the reasoning processes used by experts in the subject the student is asked to turn it on herself. Perhaps she is asked to lay out her chain of reasoning behind a mathematical proof she has devised, the assumptions of reliability and validity she is applying to an experimental design, or the reasons that she feels one biblical interpretation is more accurate than another. But however it is done, the emphasis is now on the student examining her own reasoning process, instead of her laying bare the reasoning of scholars and experts in the field.

Summary

In this chapter I've worked to apply one of the intellectual traditions informing critical thinking explored in Chapter Two—the tradition of American pragmatism—to understand how to teach critical thinking. Just as pragmatism makes experience the center of its analysis, so I have argued that the key to teaching critical thinking is to understand how students experience the process. We've seen that it's learned best in groups that are structured to provide students with multiple perspectives on the content studied. We've seen that at the outset it's crucial for teachers to model their own engagement in critical thinking. We've learned that students find out much more about how to think critically when they apply that process in very specific activities. We've been informed about the importance of disorienting dilemmas in triggering critical thinking. And we now know that students learn the process best when it's sequenced incrementally to begin with learning basic protocols that are applied to work produced by others, and then over time to move closer and closer to a direct analysis of the student's own thinking and actions. In the next chapter we will look at the first part of this sequence and consider some introductory exercises and protocols in critical thinking.

4

Introducing Basic Protocols
of Critical Thinking

The last chapter concluded with the observation that students say they find it easiest to learn how to think critically when that process is sequenced incrementally. It works best when students begin by mastering basic critical thinking protocols, and then over time applying these protocols to their own reasoning and actions. In this chapter, I want to introduce some of these introductory protocols. But before doing that, let me say something on the thorny question of exactly when to introduce critical thinking activities in any educational program. As is true for most aspects of teaching, the decision when to push students out of their comfort zone so that they start to question their assumptions and view things differently, is highly contextual. There is no one-size-fits-all approach, and the most we can say with confidence is that a great deal of introductory teacher modeling is usually helpful.

Introducing Critical Thinking: Timing Is Everything

So exactly when should we make critical thinking a primary focus for students? There are two clear schools of thought on this, and both have validity, so let me review them briefly.

The first school holds that although in the best of all possible worlds it would be desirable for every act of learning to involve critical thinking, this is not how learning happens. Before you can think critically about something you need to have studied that "something" enough so that you have sufficient information and understanding to begin to make critical judgments about it. This information and understanding is what I was talking about in Chapter One when I introduced R. S. Peters' notion of the grammar of a subject. The grammar of a subject is its basic building blocks of content (the minimal information everyone needs to know about a subject) and its epistemology (the procedures and standards applied in the subject to judge whether knowledge is legitimate).

This first school of thought argues that before this grammar is learned it is unrealistic to expect students to be able to think critically about a topic. So most programs that have critical thinking as one of their goals begin with a fairly traditional process of information transmission, when students are assimilating basic content and learning how to judge what counts as legitimate knowledge in the area. This is why most introductory courses are of the survey type, where students are provided with a map of the subject that helps them understand the intellectual and skill terrain it covers. This first school of thought argues that critical thinking happens only after students learn how to read this map.

The second school of thought argues that it is always possible to incorporate critical thinking into courses introducing students to a new subject area. For example, proponents of teaching basic language who draw on the methodology of Paulo Freire (2005) point out that he developed a process whereby peasants could learn to read and write while concurrently becoming aware of power dynamics in their communities and becoming alert to their own oppression. Ira Shor's (1987) brilliant work on using students' everyday experiences to teach critical thinking falls into this vein, as when he helped students understand the workings of monopoly capitalism by analyzing the burgers they ate in the college cafeteria. In many freshman orientation courses there is a similar opportunity for students to do some basic critical thinking as they clarify a host of assumptions they hold about college life—how important it is to belong to a fraternity, what they think their teachers expect of them, how many hours of homework per week is realistic, and so on.

Even in more traditional, content-heavy disciplines, this second school argues that some element of critical thinking can be incorporated from the beginning. For example, when students learn the basics of a new language, one of the first things they learn are the rudiments of grammar such as declension or the presence of masculine and feminine nouns. It is easy to communicate that these are clearly human constructions, reflecting a culture's internal dynamics. When setting up an introductory science experiment, it is simple to teach how the methodology being used reflects assumptions the scientific community has about how to generate reliable knowledge. When teaching trainee nurses how to give an injection, the assumptions about why this is the correct way are usually clarified.

My position on integrating critical thinking into one's teaching is that it is always possible to some degree, even if only fleetingly. Just in the act of explaining why you've arranged the first class the way you have, why the first homework assignment is structured the way it is, or why the syllabus is organized in a particular way, you are letting students see that you are working from assumptions you've developed about the best way to teach the class. So for me the question is not whether or not critical thinking can be incorporated into the teaching of introductory courses, but rather the degree to which this is possible.

It seems to me that there are particular times in a course or classroom when critical thinking—clarifying and checking assumptions by viewing material from different perspectives—is particularly important. Some of these are . . .

- *When skills or knowledge have to be applied in the real world*—Students have to determine how to make abstract knowledge, or general skill sets, learned in a classroom fit a real-life situation. To do this the student has to be able to know which assumptions to follow, what cues to look for, and what evidence to take most seriously.

- *When independent judgment is needed*—Students are required to work through a complex theoretical problem, conceptual analysis, or mass of contradictory data and judge what is the most accurate interpretation or justifiable action. Given that this requirement parallels the work conditions that most graduates will enjoy, it is a survival necessity for college students to learn.

- *When alternative interpretations and perspectives are possible*—Here students are presented with data, texts, or situations in which it is important to learn about the multiple ways these things can be understood.

- *When actions and decisions need to be informed*—Here students are asked to explain the rationale for their actions so that they recreate the chain of reasoning that led them to a particular proof, a textual conclusion, or a decision to act in a certain way.

- *When rapid judgments are called for*—This is particularly the case in courses that seek to mimic the real conditions of the workplace, where students will be required to make quick judgments about how to react to situations in which they lack all the relevant data (such as engineering or human services professions).

- *When students are encouraged to see themselves as knowledge generators*—If a course objective is to get students to take responsibility for generating new knowledge or conducting new research in their discipline, they will have to articulate the assumptions they are working under as they set up experiments, interpret texts, or design practice interventions in their fields.

Building a Case for Critical Thinking

As students approach critical thinking for the first time in a new subject area, it is important that the ground be prepared properly by teachers' building the best case they can as to why critical thinking is important. One of the greatest errors that even experienced teachers make is to assume that because they are excited about a course and clearly see its relevance for students, those same students will share this excitement and sense of anticipation. As a general rule it is always important to try and build the best case you can, as early as you can, as to why students should take a particular course or learning activity seriously.

There are a number of ways you can build a case for critical thinking to students, and I will look at these in more detail in Chapter Seven, but for the moment it is important to mention the following approaches:

- *Using former resisters*—Invite students who have taken the course before, and who were themselves initially resistant to learning critical thinking, to visit the new class early in the term. They share with new students how they found the course content to be useful or relevant to them, why they turned from resisting critical thinking to seeing its importance, and whatever survival advice they have for new students on how to make it through the course. One or two words of endorsement from such students are worth far more than the most impassioned, rhetorical justifications you could come up with.

- *Real-life case studies*—If you have access to video vignettes, learning journals, YouTube excerpts, or even scenes from TV shows or movies that show critical thinking being applied in some situation this can help convince students of the importance of a learning endeavor.

- *Simulations*—If students go through a simulation early on in a course and it becomes clear in that simulation that the only successful way out of it requires them to question an assumption or to look at something differently, this can go a long way to convincing them that critical thinking is something they should be trying to develop.

- *Modeling*—It can't be overemphasized just how important it is for teachers to model their own engagement in critical thinking before they ask for a similar engagement from students. If students see you clarifying and checking your assumptions in front of them, or striving to understand or interpret material from as many different vantage points as possible, and if you explain how this is helpful to you as a practitioner of your discipline, this goes a long way to removing some of the suspicion or skepticism students will inevitably feel when you tell them you are going to ask them to think critically about the subject or topic.

- *Reward structure*—Another rookie mistake that even experienced teachers keep making is to tell students how important something is but then set up a reward structure that doesn't require students to excel in it. For example, many teachers say they want to use discussion to get students actively engaged in learning but then award students' grades solely on the basis of a midterm and final paper. So if students' demonstrating critical thinking is an important objective of the course there need to be multiple opportunities for this to be assessed. Unfortunately, as much as we would like students to be motivated by an intrinsic love of learning, higher education (like other sectors) has become so commodified that many students will only take seriously any activities that contribute to their grade.

So if you're grading for discussion participation, you need to let students know that the best discussion participation is when a student clarifies an assumption, comes up with a different way to check an assumption, discovers a new perspective on the material, and so on. In every assignment there needs to be built in some kind of critical audit in which students are asked to identify assumptions that have been challenged or confirmed during work for the assignment, or to document the new perspectives they gained on the material during their work for the assignment. I shall go into much more detail on this in Chapter Seven.

Voting on Teacher Assumption Inventories

A useful introductory protocol is to ask students to vote on the Assumption Inventory a teacher compiles. I described this instrument in the previous chapter during the discussion of modeling. Essentially, an Assumption Inventory is a moment when a teacher steps aside from the material and discloses the assumptions she is operating under in setting up an experiment a particular way, stressing some evidence over others, giving certain advice on how to apply classroom skills in a real-life setting, and so on. I urge teachers to do this in class from day one.

But there are a couple of nice extensions of this that involve students in applying an early protocol for critical thinking. One is to give students your inventory and then say that one of the assumptions you just identified as important to you was actually false, not justified by the data. You then ask students to choose which of your assumptions was the fake one. If you're in a large auditorium and students have clickers this can be done very easily. More cumbersome is to have a show of hands. If you want to take this particular extension further you can ask students to split into groups and join the other students in the class who voted for the same assumption you did. Each student group is then given three to four minutes to share with each other the reasons that they chose the particular false assumption they did. Students then gather as a whole class and each group gives its reasons for choosing their false assumption.

The other, and slightly more complex, extension of this activity is to give the students three or four assumptions—or three or four pieces of evidence that have genuinely influenced you—and then to ask them to choose the one assumption or one piece of evidence that they think you took most seriously. Here the students have to try and get inside your head, think back over the material you've just explained, and then make a judgment about the relative merit you accorded each assumption or chunk of evidence. As with the previous tweak of the Assumptions Inventory exercise, you can ask students to form into groups by the assumption or evidence chunk they chose, and then get them to brainstorm why they think you were most persuaded by it.

Using Clickers and Hand Held Devices

Clickers and other hand held devices (iPads, Androids, cell phones, Palm Pilots) are rapidly entering higher education classrooms as teaching tools, not just student communication devices. Instead of viewing these as distractions from the main business at hand— helping students learn content we deem valuable—we need to make a virtue of necessity and incorporate them directly into our teaching of that content. As technology evolves we can expect that students using some kind of hand held device will soon be as much a part of classroom activity as students using a pen to take notes was in the past. A hand held device allows students to provide information as fast as it takes them to press a key, and opens up multiple possibilities for incorporating elements of critical thinking early on in a course.

In his interviews with college teachers who used clickers, Bruff (2009) noted how these needed to be viewed as a stimulus to critical classroom discussion and not as an end in themselves. For example:

- A psychology professor who asked students to vote on the high, medium, or low construct validity of articles used the different clicker responses from students as a prompt to classroom discussion and then called for another round of votes

- A chemistry professor developed reason-focused questions that asked students to vote on why molecular reaction rates increased as the temperature of a reaction increased

- A pharmacy instructor asked students to choose from different treatment options and vote on the best insulin regimen to treat a patient newly diagnosed with type 1 diabetes

- An anthropology professor asked students to provide definitions of the term *civilization*, added one or two of his own, and then asked students to vote on the best definition (Bruff, 2009, pp. 89–93)

In each of these examples the point is not the vote but the discussion that follows after the vote that explores why students made the choice they did. The clicker vote is merely a way to engage students with content by asking them to make their best choice from multiple possible options. The critical analysis only emerges in the discussion of why they made the choice they did, the reasons they found certain evidence most compelling, or why they judged particular arguments to be more persuasive than others.

As hand held devices become as cheap as biros we can expect that these discussions will increasingly happen not just in speech, but on electronic classroom whiteboards. So, after students have voted on the kinds of questions described above, the teacher can project the results on a screen and ask the students to write their reasons for their choices directly onto their hand held device. These responses will then be projected for the whole class to see. This makes it much easier for an instructor to be critical of a response—to point out errors in reasoning, false inferences, unjustified assertions, and so on—without the student feeling personally humiliated. Since the responses projected on the whiteboard are anonymous, no one is publicly shamed or humiliated by being the focus of a teacher's critique.

Hand held devices are also helpful in drawing a map of the whole class's thinking. In the past, teachers have had to rely on classroom discussions, or on questions raised in lectures, to assess where students are in their ability to think critically about a topic. These approaches are inevitably skewed in favor of students who are confident enough to participate in discussion or to ask questions in an auditorium. This means waiting until students have submitted a class assignment to gain a sense of what different levels of understanding exist across a whole class. Now technology has provided a way for teachers to assess very quickly how the entire range of students thinks differently about something.

Conducting a Scenario Analysis

One of the most adaptable early protocols in critical thinking is the Scenario Analysis. Here you take a piece of material you are trying to teach and rewrite it as a description of an imagined event in which a fictional character is making a choice. Students are then asked to put themselves in the head of the character and try to identify the assumptions that character might be operating under. They give suggestions on how the character might check his assumptions, and then offer another way of looking at the scenario that the character clearly does not share. These scenarios are usually brief, from two paragraphs to a page. They are really bite size case studies and, because of their brevity, are easy to fit into any class period.

This exercise can be adapted to almost every subject and topic by writing the scenario as a situation in which a fictional character is making a judgment about the correctness of how a chunk of content should be understood or an intellectual skill organized. So, for example, you could write scenarios in which . . .

- A fictional chemist who is trying to understand the cause and effect relationship in a particular chemical reaction sets up an experiment to test what she feels is a plausible hypothesis. Students reading this scenario are then asked to identify the reasoning behind the chemist's choice of her particular hypothesis, and also encouraged to propose an alternative hypothesis that the fictional chemist could have chosen.

- A mathematician formulating a mathematical proof adapts a familiar mathematical protocol that the students are familiar with to construct an equation. Students reading this scenario are then asked to identify the reasoning behind the mathematician's adaptation of the protocol and also encouraged to propose an alternative of constructing an equation.

- A fictional psychologist studying a child with learning difficulties concludes the child is autistic. Students reading this scenario are asked to identify the assumptions the fictional psychologist was operating under when he made the diagnosis, and how he could have checked out those assumptions. Students then suggest alternative diagnoses that the fictional psychologist could have been made based on the information provided in the scenario.

- A fictional climatologist is researching greenhouse gas emissions and concludes from studying records of iceberg movement that global warming is a hoax (or a real threat). Students read the scenario and try to identify the piece of evidence the fictional climatologist took most seriously. They try to pose alternative assessments of the existence of global warming that the climatologist might have made had he focused on different information.

- A fictional triage nurse in an understaffed emergency room makes a decision about the relative seriousness of a patient's condition based on information he gathers from the patient. Students try to identify the information that they feel was most influential in the fictional nurse's diagnosis. They offer alternative plausible diagnoses that could have been made if the fictional nurse had focused on different information.

To illustrate what a Scenario Analysis exercise might look like let me give three examples of ones I've used in the past. The first is from a general workshop on critical thinking that I've offered for students across the disciplines. The second is from a "train the trainers" program. The third is a scenario I have used in leadership training, and is one that draws on a classroom incident that I mention a couple of times in this book. All three of them use the same basic format. A fictional character is faced with a situation in which she has to take action, and the students are asked the same three questions about the fictional character's actions . . .

1. What assumptions—explicit and implicit—do you think the character is operating under in this situation? List as many as you can.

2. Of the assumptions you've listed, which ones could the character check by simple research and inquiry? How could she do this?

3. Give an alternate interpretation of this scenario—a version of what's happening that is consistent with the events described but that you think the character would disagree with or has not noticed.

These three questions are focused on hunting and checking assumptions and on uncovering as many different alternative perspectives as students can propose. There is no question that asks participants to come up with advice for the fictional character. This is deliberate. I want the three questions to focus on research and inquiry, not on immediately providing solutions. The intent of Scenario Analysis is to show students that the quality of any advice offered is correlated with how well people are able to identify the assumptions they bring to their understanding of a problem. Action may be the point of critical thinking, but it will only be informed if it springs from a good understanding of a situation.

After each of the scenarios in Exhibits 4.1, 4.2, and 4.3, I provide examples of the kinds of responses students have given to them.

Exhibit 4.1. Scenario Analysis Exercise: Green Acres

John and Mary, a college educated couple with a young daughter, have decided to move out of Los Angeles to the San Fernando Valley. They will both continue to work at their jobs in the city but have decided that their daughter is being short changed in the quality of her life by being forced to grow up in L.A. Lately, John feels that the pressures of the city have been getting to all of them. He points out to Mary that there are more arguments between the two of them, that their daughter has begun wetting her bed, and that much of their precious leisure time at the weekends is spent on the expressway trying to get out of the city.

More particularly, John feels that bringing their daughter up in a dangerous and dirty city is not good parenting, and that sending her to a poorly funded public school will condemn her to an inferior education. To him, the suburban life style they see in the valley is more natural. There is more space, they can live in a house with a yard, their daughter can play in her neighborhood, and the lower housing costs mean they can afford to send her to a local private school.

John believes this move will improve their quality of life both environmentally and personally. Being away from the pressures of the city will help them build a stable, warm family life. Mary has agreed to his plan.

Instructions to Students

Please respond individually to the three questions below. Once you have completed your responses, find three or four other people and share your responses.

1. What assumptions—explicit and implicit—do you think John is operating under in this situation? Explicit assumptions are ones he is fully aware of. Implicit assumptions are ones that are influencing him but that he isn't so aware of. List as many of these two kinds of assumptions as you can.

2. Of the assumptions you've listed, which ones could he check by simple research and inquiry? How could he do this?

3. Give an alternate interpretation of this scenario—a version of what's happening that is consistent with the events described but that you think John would disagree with or has not noticed.

Typical Assumptions Students Propose

John's Assumptions

1. Living in the San Fernando Valley will improve their quality of life. (Explicit)

2. Commuting into the city will not be a problem. (Explicit)

3. Neighborhoods are safer in the valley. (Explicit)

4. Public schooling is inferior to private schooling. (Explicit)

5. Bedwetting is caused by the pressures of the city and so will cease in the valley. (Explicit)

6. Marital arguments are caused by the pressures of the city and so will cease in the valley. (Explicit)

7. Mary should support John's reasoning and his decision. (Implicit)

8. If John is happy the family will be happy. (Implicit)

9. The economic condition of the family will improve with the move. (Implicit)

10. John's analysis is correct and should be followed. (Implicit)

As each student group reports out their assumptions to the whole class, the instructor then adds an additional layer of complexity by asking students to try to distinguish which of these assumptions are paradigmatic, which are prescriptive, and which are causal. In the example above, (2) (5), (6), and (9) are causal, (7) and (10) are prescriptive, and (1), (3), and (4) are paradigmatic. Assumption (8) is particularly interesting as it could be labeled causal, prescriptive, and paradigmatic!

(Continued)

Ways of Checking the Assumptions That Students Often Propose

1. John should talk to Mary and his daughter about their life in L.A. He should ask them what brings them the greatest pleasure, and what most upsets them, about how they currently live. (I usually describe this as going to the source.)

2. Find a couple with a young daughter who have already made the change and interview them about its effect on their and their daughter's lives. (I usually call this consulting experiential pioneers.)

3. Sublet their L.A. apartment and rent a house in the valley for a year—view it as a trial run. (I usually call this pilot testing.)

4. Do an economic audit of the costs of the move—factoring in private school fees, gas etc. (I usually call this doing a cost-benefit analysis.)

5. Examine the family budget to see what savings could be made (again, doing a cost-benefit analysis.)

6. Research leisure opportunities in the city that could replace the need to drive out of the city on weekends. (I call this field research.)

7. Arrange to see a counselor to check out the state of the marriage—maybe the arguments are unrelated to city pressures. (I call this consulting experts.)

8. See a pediatrician/psychologist about the bedwetting—maybe it's unrelated to city pressures (again, consulting experts).

Alternative Interpretations Students Often Give

1. The real problem is the lack of communication between John and Mary. The arguments are caused by John's need to control family life, not by city pressures.

2. Moving to the valley will increase the pressure on all members. The commute will be horrendous and leave them even more tired and frustrated.

3. The pressures of private school education will add to the bedwetting problem. Moreover, their daughter will be educated in a school that does not look like the rest of Southern California.

4. The daughter's bedwetting is caused by something completely unrelated to the fact of living in the city and needs to be reviewed by a pediatrician.

Exhibit 4.2. Scenario Analysis Exercise: Giving Feedback

Eileen, an instructor in an interpersonal skills workshop, is troubled by the behavior of one of the workshop participants named Geoffrey. She feels that Geoffrey—a manager who is technically competent but seems unable to keep his staff team together for more than six months at a time—needs to see himself as his team members see him. Over the three meetings the course has had so far, Eileen notices that several behaviors are very predictable. Geoffrey invariably arrives late, with no apology, and usually leaves before the workshop session is finished. During the sessions he lounges in his chair with a bored expression on his face and rarely contributes to any of the discussions. He checks his laptop constantly for e-mail and often texts on his phone while Eileen is speaking. The only questions he asks are ones that Eileen feels call her authority into question, since they challenge her knowledge and pose different explanations than the ones Eileen has provided. To Eileen, these behaviors all add up to an arrogance and hostility that will be severely dysfunctional for Geoffrey as he moves about the organization.

Eileen decides to write a formal memo to Geoffrey pointing out the effect his nonparticipation is having on the group. She wants to put on record her misgivings about his pattern of behavior. In the

(Continued)

memo she picks out the specific behaviors of Geoffrey's that bother her (reading e-mail, texting, looking bored, not bothering to contribute, never asking good questions, arriving late and leaving early) and points out their negative effect. She asks him to work on reducing these behaviors over the next two meetings and points out that if he can eliminate these tendencies his power and prestige in the organization will grow.

1. What assumptions—explicit and implicit—do you think Eileen is operating under in this situation? List as many as you can.

2. Of the assumptions you've listed, which ones could Eileen check by simple research and inquiry? How could she do this?

3. Give an alternate interpretation of this scenario—a version of what's happening that is consistent with the events described but that you think Eileen would disagree with.

Typical Assumptions Students Propose

1. Geoffrey's behavior is a deliberate and studied attempt to show disrespect to Eileen.

2. The short time Geoffrey's teams stay together is because of his lack of communication skills.

3. Others in the group are bothered by Geoffrey's actions.

4. Geoffrey's actions will harm his organizational career.

5. Eileen has created ample opportunities for people to contribute and Geoffrey has chosen not to avail himself of them.

6. The relevance of the workshop is clear to participants.

7. Eileen has accurately diagnosed the meaning of Geoffrey's behavior.

8. A written memo is a good way to give feedback on nonverbal behavior.

9. Geoffrey arrives late because he is disinterested in the workshop.

10. Geoffrey leaves early to show the workshop is of little use to him.

11. Geoffrey's questions are asked only to call Eileen's authority into question.

12. When Geoffrey texts he is not communicating about the workshop.

13. No other participants share Geoffrey's apparent concerns.

14. Geoffrey's laptop use has nothing to do with the workshop content.

Ways of Checking These Assumptions That Students Often Propose

1. Ask group members (using an anonymous and private form of data collection) how they feel the group is going and what problems they see emerging.

2. Talk to Geoffrey about how Eileen feels about his behavior and ask him how he feels about the class.

3. Ask Geoffrey's supervisors why his teams stay in place for such a short time.

4. Ask Geoffrey's ex-team members why they left and how they felt about their time in his team.

5. Study the characteristics of the most successful members of the organization.

Alternative Interpretations Students Often Give

1. Geoffrey's behavior is caused by shyness. His apparent disinterest masks severe introversion. When he arrives late and leaves early he says nothing about it so as not to draw attention to himself. He rarely contributes to discussion because of his shyness. What Eileen assumes is an expression of boredom is an unwillingness to make eye contact because of his social awkwardness.

(Continued)

2. Eileen has created a cold climate in the group that makes participation difficult.

3. The members of the group have been forced to show up. They
have complained to Geoffrey and he has volunteered to show
Eileen how stupid the whole course is.

4. Geoffrey is so good at his job that the company uses his team as
a training ground. People are moved out after three months so
that new people can benefit from his expertise.

5. Geoffrey's behavior represents a learning style that is heavily
focused on introspective processing of information. His use of
texting and his laptop are his way of creating connections between
the subject matter of the workshop and his own experiences.

6. Geoffrey's questions represent either confusion about the course
content or curiosity about it. They are asked awkwardly because
of his shyness and introversion.

_____

_____

Exhibit 4.3. Scenario Analysis Exercise: The Anti-Racist Ground Rule

David is a White college teacher working on a campus that is 90%
White European Americans. In recent months the campus has experienced a number of racially motivated hate crimes. Crosses have
been burned, swastikas daubed on the Jewish frat house, and racist
epithets sprayed on the side of the building housing the minority
students' center. As a response to these events the university has
initiated a program of anti-racist workshops involving students who
have been identified as influential campus leaders. The hope is that
after participating in these workshops, these leaders will spearhead
an attempt to condemn and prevent these racist acts.

The college has asked for faculty to volunteer to lead some of these workshops. Although he has no experience working in this area, David wants to do something to help, so he signs up. From the few discussions he's led in the past concerning the dynamics of race and racism, David knows things can get contentious very quickly. He's seen discussions that have been designed to decrease racism actually incite it and lead to minority students dropping out of class.

To make sure that the anti-racist workshops don't fall into the same pattern of actually making the situation worse, David decides he will institute a ground rule to guide conversation in the workshop he will be running. His ground rule is that if a person of color discloses an experience in which he or she has been the target of racist speech or actions, the White students should not try to convince the student that he or she misperceived the situation, and saw racism where it really didn't exist. One of the topics the workshop is supposed to address is racial micro-aggressions—the subtle and small gestures, remarks, and actions that Whites exhibit that people of color perceive as racist but that Whites don't recognize as such. David wants to make sure that White students don't dismiss examples of racism they are confronted with, and that they don't try to maintain that such events are all in the heads of students of color. He believes that the ground rule that White students should not try to talk students of color out of their belief that they have experienced racism will help keep the group's focus on racial micro-aggressions.

1. What assumptions—explicit and implicit—do you think David is operating under in this situation? List as many as you can.

2. Of the assumptions you've listed, which ones could David check by simple research and inquiry? How could he do this?

3. Give an alternate interpretation of this scenario—a version of what's happening that is consistent with the events described but that you think David would disagree with.

(Continued)

Typical Assumptions Students Propose

1. Workshops are a good response to hate crimes.

2. The students chosen to participate in the workshops are people whose voices carry weight with other students in the broader campus community.

3. Students will change behavior if their racism is pointed out to them.

4. The ground rule will protect students of color from further racism.

5. Students of all races will observe the ground rule.

6. Students of color will appreciate the ground rule.

7. White students are unaware of their racist actions.

8. David is nonracist.

9. David has the authority to insist the ground rule is observed.

10. The ground rule will decrease racist thoughts and feelings in White students.

11. Talking about racism can be done calmly.

12. White faculty members are the people best qualified to lead the workshops.

Ways of Checking These Assumptions That Students Often Propose

1. Study how other campuses have responded to hate crimes and the effectiveness of any anti-racism workshops they have instituted.

2. Ask students of color how they feel about the proposed ground rule.

3. Ask students across campus to nominate the most influential student leaders.

4. Ask faculty who have experience in these kinds of workshops their opinion of the ground rule.

5. Review anti-racist workshops run at other campuses and find out what exercises and approaches worked best.

6. Ask community leaders in the area how they have responded to racism in businesses and government agencies.

7. Institute some form of anonymous ongoing evaluation to see if the ground rule is having the effect intended for it.

8. Ask faculty colleagues of color their opinion of the ground rule.

Alternative Interpretations Students Often Give

1. The ground rule will lead to White students feeling they have been labeled as racist before they have had the chance to contribute to a discussion. It will increase their feelings of resentment and harden their resolve not to take the workshop seriously.

2. The students of color will perceive the ground rule to be condescending and patronizing, because it implies they are unable to stand up for themselves when pointing out examples of racial micro-aggressions.

3. The ground rule itself is a racial micro-aggression because it springs from an unarticulated assumption that Whites are the "saviors" of people of color.

4. The ground rule is primarily designed to make David feel better about himself and to increase his own feeling of self-importance. It is designed to allow him to congratulate himself on his own anti-racist righteousness.

5. The workshops will be perceived as a public relations exercise by students of color, who will view them as exercises in image manipulation designed to make sure enrolment doesn't suffer.

Four points need to be made about the Scenario Analysis technique just demonstrated.

The first is that it is a social learning exercise, one in which students work in groups to focus on uncovering and checking assumptions by viewing them through different perspectives. Although the exercise begins with the student individually completing the three questions about the scenario, it is in the group sharing that the real learning occurs. Students come to realize they need others to help them see things they've missed, a major reason, in the preceding chapter, that students' preference for learning critical thinking through social learning was emphasized. The exercise works best when different students identify assumptions that come as a surprise to their peers, and when they propose widely varying explanations of what could be happening in the scenario.

The second point is that this exercise also builds on an insight students offer (summarized in Chapter Three) of how they best learn critical thinking; in this case through a concentration on specific experiences. Each of the scenarios focuses on a concrete situation, and students find it much easier to hunt assumptions when there is a specific experience to explore. Scenarios can be written in more complex ways by adding multiple characters who all have to make choices, and giving more nuanced information that complicates their options. For example, in the second "Giving Feedback" scenario, the situation described is productively complicated if the two main characters exhibit different racial identities; if Eileen is African American and Jeff is European American, students will suggest different assumptions. Or perhaps a wrinkle can be added with a sentence or two that describes how one of the characters has come out as a Gay or Lesbian person. But you should hold off the temptation of adding multiple characters or complicating variables until students feel comfortable applying the protocol to single character scenarios.

Third, it's important to stress is that there is no right or correct answer to any of the questions. Telling students this at the outset takes a lot of the pressure off their shoulders. Now they don't need to worry about whether their understanding of the scenario is the proper or "correct" one. In fact I usually tell students that the more assumptions and interpretations they generate, and the more ways they propose for the fictional characters to check those out, the better. The intent of the exercise is to provide an introductory engagement in the critical protocol of unearthing and checking assumptions by viewing them through different perspectives. Because it is not the students' own reasoning at stake, and because all the attention is on the fictional character's assumptions and interpretations, students are mentally freer to participate than if we began with an example from their own lives.

Fourth, the scenario is deliberately designed as one in which the student is not required to apply critical thinking to her own assumptions. By focusing on a fictional character the pressure is off students because there is very little at stake. They are not being asked to imagine themselves in the scenario and say what they would do in a similar circumstance. Were that the case the perceived risks and threats of this approach would be much higher. But even if the scenario happens to be close to one the student has experienced, there is no pressure on the student to disclose that fact. All they are being asked to do is be a mental detective regarding the thinking of a fictional individual.

What is the instructor's role in a Scenario Analysis? Well, the instructor usually writes the vignette and runs the exercise, essentially coordinating the different responses that groups come up with in their discussions. In the later phases of this exercise instructors do offer judgments and clarification. When students are reporting out the different assumptions they've identified, they often need help in distinguishing between implicit and explicit, and between paradigmatic, prescriptive, and causal assumptions.

When they are suggesting different ways the actors in the scenarios could check out the accuracy of their assumptions, these have to be within the range of possibility. When proposing alternative interpretations of the scenario it is the teacher's job to find out why the students came to their alternative interpretation and to ask them to provide information from the scenario that justifies their interpretation.

In fact this third part of the exercise—offering alternative interpretations—is usually the one that students find it hardest to complete. What often happens is that they offer alternative recommendations for action, telling the character how they should behave differently, rather than giving an alternative interpretation of what's happening that fits the brief facts given. I usually have to stress that the one thing students doing Scenario Analysis should *not* do is offer any advice to the fictional characters as to how they should resolve their situation differently. This is very deliberate on my part. Unless I specify very clearly that no advice should be given, the students will spend the bulk of their time discussing what John, Eileen, and Geoffrey should do. Removing that possibility from the exercise means (theoretically, at least!) that students will focus all their attention on assumptions and interpretations.

In passing, I might add that the same dynamic is true of teachers. Get a group of teachers together over coffee or a beer and as soon as one of them brings up a problem they're facing and asks for help, the first thing the other group members will do is start telling the teacher in trouble what to do. What is skipped over is the critical scrutiny of how the teacher has framed the problem, whether or not it's the real problem to focus on, what assumptions the teacher brings to understanding and resolving the problem, and the different approaches that could be taken to addressing it. This is why in my book *Becoming a Critically Reflective Teacher* (Brookfield, 1995) most of the exercises I suggest for teachers' critical conversation groups focus not on brainstorming solutions to problems but rather on understanding what assumptions teachers hold about their problems, and what different understandings of these problems can be generated.

Summary

This is the first of the chapters that has primarily focused on techniques, in this case introductory exercises with the aim to familiarize students with the basic protocol of critical thinking in a way that is as playful and nonthreatening as possible. I have focused particularly on the Scenario Analysis exercise because that's the one I've had greatest success with across the disciplines. It can be adapted to any subject area simply by writing it in the form of a scenario in which a fictional character (practitioner, scholar, researcher, or student) is deciding how to create knowledge in that discipline, or trying to judge which knowledge can be trusted as valid and reliable. To students the focus of each scenario seems far away from their own reasoning patterns; after all, they're concentrating on the inferences and interpretations a fictional individual is making in each scenario. Of course in the debriefing of the exercise students learn a great deal about their own assumptions, and they realize what perspectives and interpretations they've missed when they hear other students submitting theirs.

The next chapter continues this practical focus. I move to the second phase in the incremental process of learning to think critically, which, for want of a better term, I've labeled intermediate. Here I explain how the process of critical thinking is brought somewhat closer to an analysis of the student's own reasoning but is still removed enough to be reasonably comfortable.

5

Developing Critical Complexity
Intermediate and Advanced Protocols

In workshops I often liken the process of critical thinking to physical exercise. Let's assume you've been selected to represent the U.S. soccer team in the World Cup Final—the ultimate honor for any American soccer player and the most testing ordeal you'll ever experience. (The World Cup Final makes the Super Bowl look like a neighborhood kick around in the park.) To prepare for this moment would take years of preparation, during which there would be training camps, warm up exhibition matches, games to qualify for the tournament, group-round games in the first stage of the tournament itself, the knockout round of the tournament, and, finally the whole enchilada—the World Cup Final itself.

Playing in the World Cup Final is to me the soccer equivalent of applying critical thinking directly to your own assumptions and experiences. It's the most testing intellectual ordeal you'll ever face and takes a great deal of training and preparation. To continue the metaphor, suppose you did no training before the World Cup Final, no roadwork, no ball training, no strength or cardiovascular work-outs, you just sat on your sofa watching videos of past finals. Chances are that as soon as the whistle was blown to start the match you would run after the ball and immediately hear two snaps as your hamstrings went. You'd go down in a heap and be writhing in agony on the patch in front of millions of viewers.

The same thing is likely to happen if students begin a critical thinking process with the most demanding task of all—applying critical thinking directly to their own ideas and experiences. This is the intellectual equivalent of playing a World Cup Final with no physical warm ups or preparatory training. In both situations you need to arrive at this peak experience only after a substantial period of training in which you learn protocols that, with practice, become second nature. If the activities discussed in Chapter Four are the introductory protocols (in soccer terms, the initial training camps and warm up exhibition matches) students learn, then the current chapter deals with intermediate and advanced phases of critical thinking. The intermediate exercises I describe bring the critical thinking focus closer to the person's experience but are still experienced as being at one stage removed. In soccer terms, this is the two-year period when you play your regional qualifying matches to see if your team is good enough to go the World Cup Final tournament. The advanced exercises that I describe in the chapter after this will focus directly on the student's own assumptions, perspectives, reasoning process, and experience—in soccer terms, the World Cup Final itself.

Intermediate Protocol 1: Crisis Decision Simulation

I begin this section with an exercise that is far removed from the student's own life. This is because it is easier to contemplate different ways of interpreting something if the object of attention is not close to home. It's so much easier to fantasize about what you would do if you won the lottery than to think through how to spend the limited income you earn when your wants and needs far outstrip your resources. So the opening activity—Crisis Decision Simulation—is one that is clearly one no student has ever had to face.

The Crisis Decision Simulation is an exercise that students conduct in groups. The instructor designs a simulation in which students are asked to imagine they are faced with having to take action, or make a choice, in a situation where no one clearly appropriate option is available. They are also put under the constraints of time. Students have no more than a few minutes to decide as a group how they are going to respond to this crisis. Crisis Decision Simulation is a slightly more elaborate version of the Heinz Dilemma often taught in courses on developmental psychology. In this dilemma Heinz is caring for his wife, who will die if she does not receive a particular drug. The cost of the drug far exceeds Heinz's resources, so he breaks into the pharmacy and steals the drug. Students are asked to give their opinion on the morality of Heinz's breaking the law to save his wife.

As with the Heinz Dilemma, there is no right answer to a Crisis Decision Simulation. The point is for groups to be asked to make a choice under duress, and then, during debriefing, for them to uncover the reasoning processes that led them to that particular choice. What evidence did they take most seriously in the simulation? Whose arguments during the group discussion held sway, and why was this? What were the inferential leaps people made as they came to a decision? How many different options were generated for group members to choose from? Exhibit 5.1 is an example of a Crisis Decision Simulation I use in my workshops.

The Crisis Decision Simulation is clearly a highly artificial exercise using an overly dramatic example. So students don't really feel they are making a choice that resembles anything that they will have to do in real life. Declaring up front that there is no correct answer removes the need for students to try and guess which one they "should" choose. In the Nuclear Bubble example every person requesting admittance to the dome has legitimate reasons for being chosen. So on the newsprint postings the students focus on assumptions, on evidence, and on different viewpoints expressed, rather than being preoccupied with whether or not the correct choice has been made.

Exhibit 5.1. The Nuclear Bubble: A Crisis Decision Simulation

There has just been a nuclear attack on your country. Because you had forewarning of this attack, you took the precaution of constructing a geodesic dome made of radiation-repelling, transparent plastic. You stocked it with enough oxygen, food, water, and medical supplies to sustain ten people while the radiation levels receded outside the dome. Your intention is that this ten will then go out and start civilization again.

One day the ten of you look out of the dome to see a group of survivors stumbling across the scarred landscape toward the dome. As it happens, you have enough supplies to allow one more person into the dome. The survivors begin banging on the dome, pleading to be let in. You switch on the radiation-filtering intercom you've installed and tell the survivors that one can be admitted and that they should take turns telling your group why they should be let in.

The first survivor says he is a *family farmer* and has been self-sufficiently growing his own food all his life. He should be admitted because of his agricultural expertise. After all, he argues, unless the basic demands of life are met and enough food is produced, the group will die from hunger.

The second survivor says she is a *radiation sickness specialist* and that since none of the group have lived through a nuclear attack before no one knows how their bodies will respond to the lingering levels of radiation that are bound to be left outside. She makes the point that it doesn't matter if everyone is a superb farmer—if they are too sick to move they will all die.

The third survivor says she is a *teacher*. She argues that the point of living is not mere survival but the generation and preservation of the culture that creates meaning and provides richness to existence. She says humans are adaptable enough to pay attention to survival needs such as finding food, but that it takes specialist training (which she has) to be able to create an educational system that nourishes the soul and makes life worth surviving for.

The fourth survivor is a *pregnant woman*. She says she has the gift of life within her and pleads for the group to save her unborn child.

The final survivor is a *hand-to-hand combat trainer and weapons specialist*. He argues that it is highly unlikely that this is the only geodesic dome built to survive the attack and that once the group leaves the dome to venture out into the world they will face other groups fighting for the few scarce resources left to support life. If the group does not know how to defend itself they will inevitably be killed, or left to die, by groups who are tougher and better trained in fighting and who will hog the necessary survival resources for themselves.

Instructions to Group Members

Find four other people to form a group of five. You have ten minutes to decide which of the survivors you will admit. There is no right answer and all answers are plausible.

Once your group has made its choice spend another ten minutes answering the following questions and putting your responses on sheets of newsprint.

1. How did the group decide its choice? Did members talk this through till they reached consensus? Did they take a vote? Was the choice split or did a majority support the choice? Which assumptions informed your choice of your decision-making method?

2. What was the strongest argument made that convinced group members to choose one of the five?

3. What assumptions was this argument based on? What was the best evidence supplied to support this argument?

4. What were the main viewpoints expressed that challenged your group's final choice?

5. If you had more time available, how could you check out whether or not your choice was a good one?

Intermediate Protocol 2: Critical Debate

Another highly theatrical intermediate critical thinking protocol is the Critical Debate exercise. Here, the teacher chooses a
contentious issue within the field of study on which opinion is
divided among scholars or practitioners, and then she frames this
issue as a debate motion. The motion is announced to students
and they are asked to divide into two teams. The first team will
prepare arguments to support the motion, and the second team
will prepare arguments to oppose it. People volunteer by a show
of hands to work on one of the two teams.

Once the class has divided itself into two teams then the
teacher plays a trick that she can only play once! She tells
the students that she is switching their votes so that they will
actually be on the team opposite to the one they volunteered
for. Hence, all those who volunteered for the team to draft arguments to support the motion will now be on the team that drafts
arguments to oppose the motion. Similarly, all those who have
volunteered to draft arguments for the motion will now make up
the team opposing it.

Each team is given 10–15 minutes to come up with the best
arguments they can and then another five minutes to decide
who will present these arguments in the debate. Each team then
has five minutes to present their arguments. After these initial
presentations the teams reconvene for another five minutes to
caucus and draft rebuttal arguments. The person who presents
the rebuttals should not be the person who presented the initial
arguments. The rebuttal arguments are presented and the exercise concludes with a free vote on the motion. Here people are
told they can follow their own thinking and vote whichever way
they want.

After the vote the experience of participating in the debate is
discussed with the whole class. Students are asked how it felt to
argue against positions they were committed to. They are asked

to share any new ways of thinking about the issue that were opened up for them, and any new understandings of the issue that emerged for them.

The final phase in the Critical Debate exercise takes the form of a homework assignment on the activity. Students are asked to write a brief follow-up Reflective Audit on the debate in which they document . . .

1. Assumptions they held about the issue that were clarified or confirmed by the debate

2. Assumptions they held about the issue that surprised them or that emerged during the debate

3. How they could check out these new assumptions

4. Any new perspectives on the issue that suggested themselves during the debate

5. How their existing assumptions were challenged or changed by the debate.

Intermediate Protocol 3: Exemplars and Flaws

This exercise comes a little closer to home because, unlike the Critical Debate exercise, students are actually making a choice that represents their real opinion. But the choice seems somewhat impersonal because it is a choice of another person whom the students admire or criticize, or of an abstract piece of work such as a mathematical proof or historical explanation that the students feel is accurate or flawed. Like Critical Debate the exercise can be adapted to any discipline or subject area, though the essential idea stays the same.

Exemplars and Flaws begins with the student focusing on a topic and choosing either someone who has contributed useful knowledge to that topic or some concept that moves understanding of the topic of the area forward in some way. This is the

"Exemplars" part of the exercise. She makes her choice individually, uninfluenced by peers.

Some examples of the instructions for this part of the exercise might be . . .

- Of the mathematical proofs we've covered this year, which is the most elegant?

- Of the explanations for the historical event we've just researched, which is the most convincing?

- Of the laws of physics we've studied so far this term, which has the greatest predictive power?

- Of the poems we've reviewed up to now, which demonstrates the most insight into the nature of love?

- Of the psychological theories offered for schizophrenia, which do you think is the most plausible and complete?

- Which of the readings assigned in class for this week was the most interesting or well written?

- Of the business leaders we've seen in action so far, who would you most want leading your organization?

- Of the colleagues you've worked with in your field practicum, whom do you most admire and what is it about this person that is so admirable?

After students have made their choices individually they are put into trios and asked to share their responses with each other. Each student takes a turn to name her choice and explain why she made the choice she did. When she has finished her explanation the other two students then tell her about the assumptions they think she holds about the subject. They let her know, from their perspective, what kind of arguments and evidence she seems most drawn to, what perspectives seem to be most interesting to her, which parts of the exemplar she chose she feels most strongly about, and the epistemological assumptions she holds about what kind of knowledge she feels is most reliable. Once the first student has heard her colleagues give her feedback about her choice of an exemplar, then the second student in the trio has the spotlight and the process is repeated, and so on to the third.

The "Aberrations" part of Exemplars and Flaws reiterates the process outlined above, except that this time the student focuses on something she finds wanting in the topic. Examples of this might be . . .

- Of the logic theorems we've covered this year, which has the weakest links?

- Of the explanations for the movement of population we've just researched, which is the least convincing?

- Of the accounting procedures we've studied so far this term, which is the most cumbersome or prone to error?

- Of the films we've viewed up to now, which is the most confusingly edited?

- Of the sociological classifications offered of different social classes, which do you find most confusing?

- Which of the readings assigned in class for this week was the least convincing or worst written?

- Of the theologians we've studied, who do you feel would do the greatest harm if he or she were in charge of your congregation?

- Of the authors you've studied throughout your program, whom do you think is least qualified to guide students' learning?

As with the Crisis Decision Simulation it is important to let students know there is not a right or correct answer for this exercise. The point is to set up a group learning activity in which peers help the student become aware of her own reasoning processes, the sorts of evidence she is drawn to, how she decides what constitutes legitimate knowledge, and so on. The most helpful part of this exercise is its focus on a particular text, concept, or individual that students are forced to choose. The specificity of this choice is what students say they like since the choice of a particular exemplar or aberration can tell a lot about the general assumptions a student holds about a topic.

Intermediate Protocol 4: Quotes to Affirm and Challenge

This is a close companion to the Exemplars and Flaws exercise just described, except that this focuses only on written work students have just reviewed. I have used this exercise when I have been trying to focus a classroom discussion on a particular text. One of my frustrations as a discussion leader (and also as a student) is when students have been asked to read a piece to prepare for the class but the ensuing discussion stays at a level of generality. Quotes to Affirm and Challenge was designed to prevent this happening and to keep attention on particular passages or pages in a reading. But I have also tweaked it to be a critical thinking exercise that helps students become aware of the assumptions that inform their visceral responses to different parts of a text.

The exercise begins with an assigned text that students read before class. Their task is to choose one quote they wish to affirm in the text and one that they wish to challenge. They can choose a quote to affirm for any reason. Maybe they agree with what the quote says, maybe they like the way it's expressed, maybe the quote gave them new information or a new perspective, maybe it provided an example that made a lot of other material much clearer, perhaps it states the most important point in the text—there is no right reason for choosing a quote. The choice of a quote to challenge follows the same logic. There is no right reason for choosing a selection. Maybe the quote is so confusing the student has no idea what it means, maybe it seems biased, maybe it expresses something the student disagrees with, maybe it makes inferential leaps that aren't justified in the student's opinion, maybe it seems immoral, and so on.

Students come to class having chosen their two quotes. They form into small groups of about five and each member takes a turn to propose a quote they wish to affirm and the reasons for doing this. When everyone in the small group has proposed a quote to affirm, the group then chooses *one* of the five quotes submitted to report back to the larger class. The "quote to challenge" portion of this exercise follows the same procedure, with the caveat that the quote to challenge that the group decides on cannot come from the same person who brought the quote to affirm to the group.

The two quotes chosen by each small group are then written on a sheet of newsprint and each group posts its quotes at a different place in the room so that the whole class can see each pair of quotes that each group has chosen. Posted next to the quotes are the reasons that each group chose the two quotes it did.

We then move to the whole-class portion of Quotes to Affirm and Challenge. Students read the quotes posted around the room that others have affirmed or challenged and the reasons for their selections. I then ask them to pick out a pair of quotes chosen by a *different* group that interests them and that they wish to talk more about. Students then move to the posting containing these new quotes. At the station they've chosen they meet other students who were also drawn to these particular quotes. These students read the reasons for choosing these quotes posted by the original group and add to this list anything new that they think of, as well as commenting on the reasons already listed.

A few minutes later I ask the original small groups to reconvene and go back to their original posting and read what comments have been added to this. I give them time to discuss the new comments and introduce the homework for the next week. This is a brief Reflective Audit (my term for one-page homework papers that build on an exercise the students have done in class) in which each student has to answer three questions . . .

Exhibit 5.2. Quotes to Affirm and Challenge: Reflective Audit

1. What were the two quotes you brought to class and why did you originally pick them? If you had to do this exercise again on the same text, would you still choose these quotes? If "yes," what was it in other students' comments that convinced you that your original choice was a good one? If "no," what was it in other students' comments that convinced you to alter your original choice?

2. What was the pair of quotes proposed by another group that you chose to discuss and why did you choose them? As you talked to other students who chose the same posting you did, what new information or perspectives did you learn about the topic? If nothing new to you was discussed, what parts of your thinking were confirmed?

3. What does your participation in this exercise tell you about your own patterns of thinking on this topic? What arguments, or what kinds of evidence, are you drawn to, and what are you confused by? What do you assume constitutes good research or scholarship in this topic, and what constitutes poor research or scholarship?

One of the reasons I like the Quotes to Affirm and Challenge exercise so much is because students are "suckered" into thinking it is an easy homework assignment. After all, they only have to pick out two quotes—how hard can that be? Students think they're getting away easy, since they can choose two quotes quickly before they enter the room, or even as they're waiting for the class to start. This exercise also gets good responses from students because at no point is there any whole-class, large group discussion—the event many students fear the most. The student does all the work either on her own or in small group conversation. I feel that the design of the exercise—its structure—is the teacher here, a good example of what Finkel means by teaching with your mouth shut (Finkel, 2000).

But although this looks initially like an easy assignment it becomes increasingly complex and challenging. Students are really being asked to engage in metacognition, in thinking about their thinking, one of the hardest parts of critical self-reflection. But they are helped by the fact that this exercise, like so many productive ones in critical thinking, is a social learning exercise for much of the time. When the groups first get together and have to choose the quotes they want to post to the whole class, students have to share the reasons for their postings and write these on the newsprint. When students move to new postings and meet other students drawn to those same postings, they again have to clarify what drew them to those stations—but this is done with other students. And when they get back to their original postings they have to read other students' comments on the quotes their group chose and discuss what this means with their original group members.

The hardest part of the exercise is the Reflective Audit that has to be completed. This is an individually completed assignment (though it could be done as a group assignment if necessary) in which students are asked to review their patterns of reasoning and the assumptions they hold about what constitutes legitimate, and poor, scholarship on the topic. If students have not taken the exercise seriously up to that point, and just picked random quotes out of the air two minutes before the class meets, this is when they are found wanting and when they lose points from their overall class grade.

But I repeat, this kind of metacognition is hard to exercise, and the first times students try to do it the results usually fall far short of where eventually I want the students to be. Just how difficult it is was brought home to me early in my career when I was reviewing applications from candidates who wished to enroll as doctoral students in adult education at Columbia University, Teachers College. We used to ask applicants for the doctorate to choose a contentious issue in the field, state their position on it, list the assumptions that informed their position, and then state the counter arguments to it. After three or four years not one applicant had managed to do this! Consequently, we changed the admission assignment and instead gave applicants two extracts written by well-known authors in the field who were at opposite ends of the ideological spectrum (Malcolm Knowles and Paulo Freire). Applicants were asked to identify the differences between them and state the different assumptions each was working under. Most applicants had great difficulty doing this.

So if applicants for a doctoral degree at Columbia are unable to identify their own assumptions, let alone the assumptions of leading figures in the field, then how much more difficult will it be for a freshman, or even a senior in an honors program, to do the same. This only underscores the importance of a great deal of initial teacher modeling of critical thinking, and of a sequenced approach to teaching it. Before students can be asked to do the basic meta-cognition involved in the Reflective Audit for the Quotes to Affirm and Challenge exercise, they will have had to have a lot of practice doing the sort of basic, introductory protocols outlined in the previous chapter.

Advanced Protocols

The final phase of critical thinking—the point at which it's most fully realized—is when students think critically about their own decisions, choices, and reasoning. At this stage students have nothing to hide behind. They are being asked to identify and research assumptions that have informed their actions and structured their thinking, some of which they believe in implicitly, and some of which have defined who they are up to that point in their lives. This is the intellectual equivalent of inviting a demolition expert to place charges at the foundation of your own house so it can collapse and allow you to rebuild a sounder structure from the ground up. It is an intimidating and for most people, a highly threatening prospect. It should be no surprise then that students struggle greatly with this final phase and that they are very resistant to engaging with it.

What makes this final phase more palatable, however, is that it happens only after initial teacher modeling and after the student has participated in several basic and intermediate protocols. It is also focused on specific choices and decisions the student has made, and so is very concrete and recognizable. Advanced protocols thus have the advantage of familiarity because they adapt the same features used in the basic and intermediate variants. First, they are social learning exercises in which students rely on peers to help them identify and then research assumptions that have been influential in guiding their thinking and choices. Second, they focus on specific actions, choices, or decisions, not on trying to discern general assumptions the student holds about a whole discipline or subject. Third, they are informed by the teacher's modeling her own engagement in them. It is more important than ever with advanced protocols that students see teachers struggling to apply the same protocols to their own reasoning and actions.

I hope by now you see how the insights summarized in Chapter Three regarding what students say helps them learn to think critically (watching a lot of teacher modeling, going through an incremental sequence that gradually brings the focus closer and closer to the student's own thinking, focusing on specific experiences, making sure it happens through group work with peers) inform the protocols described in the current and preceding chapters. The next activity—the Critical Conversation Protocol— follows all these insights. So although it's a long way removed from the introductory Scenario Analysis protocol described in Chapter Four, its format is essentially the same. Both Scenario Analysis and Critical Conversation are social learning activities that focus on specific choices, actions, or experiences. Both also implement the basic critical thinking process explained in Chapter One in which students try to identify assumptions, consider how these could be checked, and explore different perspectives on the topic.

Critical Conversation Protocol

The Critical Conversation Protocol is an activity that should be placed toward the end of a critical thinking program. Its level of complexity is such that students need to be prepared properly for the experience, and instructors need to make sure they model what the process looks like before inviting students' engagement. A critical conversation is a focused conversation in which someone is helped

1. To come to an awareness of the assumptions she is operating under.
2. To investigate whether these assumptions are well grounded.
3. To look at her reasoning and actions from different viewpoints.
4. To think about the implications of the conversation for her future actions and thinking.

In a process of structured critical conversation I suggest that people think of playing one of three possible roles—storyteller, detective, or umpire.

The *storyteller* is the person who is willing to make herself the focus of critical conversation by first describing some part of her thinking, practice, or experience.

The *detectives* are those in the group who help her come to a more fully informed understanding of the assumptions and actions that frame her thinking, practice, or experience.

The *umpire* is the group member who has agreed to monitor the conversation with a view to pointing out when people are talking to each other in a judgmental way. She also keeps the group focused on the discrete stages in the exercise.

All participants in the group play all three of these roles at different times. The protocol is so rich and complex that it happens several times, but each time the roles switch so participants have the chance to be the storyteller at least once, the umpire at least once, and the detectives several times. The idea is that if this is done multiple times, the behaviors associated with each role gradually become habitual.

The exercise has five discrete stages and the person chosen to be the umpire has the responsibility to make sure the stages are followed in sequence. The umpire is mostly a nonspeaking role. She interjects only if the group is going off track or if she judges that someone is breaking the ground rules for the exercise. Exhibit 5.3 shows how the activity proceeds.

Although this is a heavily structured and artificial exercise, the intent is for these dispositions to become so internalized that the ground rules and structure outlined above eventually become unnecessary. And, although I've presented this as a neatly sequenced exercise with five discrete stages, the reality is that of course it isn't! As the conversation proceeds past the designated question period, the detectives think up new questions that they

Exhibit 5.3. The Critical Conversation Protocol

1. The Storyteller Tells the Tale (10 minutes)

The conversation opens with the person who is the storyteller describing as concretely and specifically as possible an incident from her learning that for some reason was a problem. In the natural sciences this could be an experiment that, to the storyteller, went disastrously and puzzlingly wrong. In the humanities it could be an aesthetic engagement with art, philosophy, or literature, in which the student was the only person to experience a work of art or set of ideas in a particular way that set her off from the mainstream. In social sciences it could be a theoretical paradigm that the student was unable to understand or one that, once understood, seemed to have no application to the content it was supposed to explain. In the applied human sciences it could be a nurse or a teacher who was faced with a serious dilemma that seemed to have no clear resolution.

The learning incident is one that is recalled because it was particularly frustrating. Most probably it is an incident that leaves the teller somewhat puzzled by its layers and complexities. The storyteller describes the incident in her own words and without any questions or interruptions. Her colleagues, who are in the role of detectives, attend to her remarks very carefully. They are listeners with a purpose.

The detectives are trying to identify the explicit and implicit assumptions the storyteller holds about what are supposedly correct ways of understanding the problem she discloses. Some of these will be general assumptions about the procedures used to judge whether or not knowledge can be trusted in the discipline. Some will be about how a good scholar should behave, or what a correct intellectual protocol or research methodology looks like. Some will be more specific to the particular topic, assignment, or action described. These will have to do with the choices the storyteller made and the actions she took. The detectives are listening particularly for assumptions the storyteller holds about what counts as legitimate knowledge. They listen also for assumptions that are hegemonic; that is, ones that seem admirable and useful to the storyteller but that actually work against her best interests.

The detectives are also asked to imagine themselves inside the heads of the other researchers or learners in the story (if there are any) and to try to see the events through their eyes. If this is an incident involving only the learner, and no teachers or other students were involved, the detectives try to think of different intellectual orientations in the field that might help deal with the confusion the storyteller is recounting. If possible, the detectives make mental or written notes about plausible alternative interpretations of the story that fit the facts as they hear them but that would come as a surprise to the storyteller.

2. The Detectives Ask Questions About the Event (10 minutes)

After the storyteller has finished speaking, the detectives are allowed to break their silence to ask her any questions they have about the events she has just described. The detectives are searching for any information that will help them uncover the assumptions they think the storyteller holds. They are also looking for details not provided in the first telling of the story that will help them relive the events described through the eyes of the storyteller or through the eyes of the other participants involved, if there are any. This will help them understand these events from the different participants' perspectives.

The ground rules they must observe concern how they ask questions of the storyteller. They can only ask questions that request information (Can you say more about . . . ? Can you explain again why you decided to . . . ?), not questions that pass judgment (Are you seriously telling me that you . . . ? Why on earth would

(Continued)

you . . . ?). Their questions are asked only for the purpose of clarifying the details of what happened. They must refrain from giving their opinions or suggestions, no matter how helpful they feel these might be. Detectives also should ask only one question at a time. They must avoid asking multiple questions masquerading as a single request for information. They should not give advice on how the storyteller should have acted.

As the storyteller hears the detectives' questions she tries to answer them as fully and honestly as possible. She also has the opportunity to ask the detectives why they asked the particular questions they put to her. The umpire points out to the detectives any examples of judgmental questions that they ask, particularly those in which they imply that they have seen a better way to respond to the situation. An example of such a question would be one beginning, "Didn't you think to . . . ?"

The umpire brings the detectives' attention to the ways in which their tone of voice and body language, as well as their words, risk driving the storyteller into a defensive bunker. Essentially the umpire serves as the storyteller's ally, watching out for situations in which the storyteller might start to feel under attack.

3. The Detectives Report the Assumptions They Hear in the Storyteller's Descriptions (10 minutes)

When the incident has been fully described and all the detectives' questions have been answered, the conversation moves to the assumption-reporting phase. Here the detectives tell the storyteller, on the basis of her story and her response to their questions, what assumptions they think she holds.

This is done as nonjudgmentally as possible, as a reporting back exercise. The detectives seek only to state clearly what they think the storyteller's assumptions are, not to judge whether they are right or wrong. They are asked to state these assumptions tentatively, descriptively, and nonjudgmentally, using phrases such as "It seems as if . . . ," "I wonder if one assumption you might be holding is that . . . ," or "Is it possible that you assumed that . . . ?" They state only one assumption at a time and do not give any advice about the way the learner *should* have understood or responded to the incident described. The umpire intervenes to point out to detectives when she thinks they are reporting assumptions with a judgmental overlay.

4. The Detectives Give Alternative Interpretations of the Events Described (10 minutes)

The detectives now give alternative versions of the events that have been described, based on their attempts to relive the story through the eyes of the other participants involved or to understand the learning event through alternative intellectual paradigms. These alternative interpretations must be plausible in that they are consistent with the facts as the storyteller describes them. When appropriate, detectives should point out how power or hegemony plays itself out in the different interpretations they are giving.

The detectives are to give these interpretations as descriptions, not judgments. They are describing how others involved in the events might have viewed them, not saying whether or not these perceptions are accurate. They are speculating how the learning event might look when viewed from a different intellectual framework, not saying that this is the one the storyteller should have used. They should not give any advice here.

As the storyteller hears these alternative interpretations she is asked to let the detectives have the floor so that they can state their case as fully as possible. After they have described how the situation might look through the eyes of other participants or from a different intellectual vantage point, the storyteller is then allowed to give any additional information that would cast doubt on these interpretations. She is also allowed to ask the detectives to elaborate on any confusing aspects of why they are making the interpretations they are. At no time is she expected to agree with any interpretations the detectives offer.

(Continued)

5. Participants Do an Experiential Audit (10 minutes)

Finally, the ground rules cease to be in effect any longer and the detectives can give whatever advice they wish. The storytellers and detectives state what they have learned from the conversation, what new insights they have realized, what assumptions they have missed or need to explore further, what different understandings they have as a result of the conversation, and what their reflection means for their future actions. The umpire gives an overall summary of the ability of participants to be respectful listeners and talkers and also gives her perspective on the story.

---

want to ask that will help them tell the storyteller what her assumptions are and offer her new perspectives. So the assumption giving and the alternative perspective reporting periods are always peppered with questions.

In my experience using this with thousands of different participants the most frequent job the umpire has to do is step in when people give advice in the guise of asking questions, reporting assumptions, or providing alternative perspectives. We are so culturally conditioned to move straight from being told the problem to providing the solution, that the intermediate stages of critical analysis are completely forgotten. Yet problem solving can be done uncritically, as when no one asks whether the problem we're spending time solving is the real problem at issue or in whose interests is it that the current problem be solved. Critical problem solving tries to unearth the assumptions that frame why someone sees something as a problem, it tries to unearth the assumptions informing how people take action to solve the problem, and it constantly explores different perspectives that have not previously been considered.

Although I began using this exercise with students, I have since broadened it to all sorts of different situations. I have used it at retreats to help a group of practitioners come up with new ways of responding to wearyingly familiar problems. I have used it in faculty conversation circles in schools, colleges, and seminaries. It has been used in nursing education training and in executive development workshops for global corporations. I have also used it as a way to shake up meetings. It seems to be infinitely adaptable and is really very simple to use, providing the ground rules are clearly understood and enforced.

One caveat needs issuing however. I would never use this without first doing a teaching demonstration of how the process works, in which I play the roles of facilitator, umpire, and storyteller. When I do this I carry three different baseball caps with me. I wear red when I'm the umpire, because I need to put a red light on to stop detectives from being judgmental, bombarding the storyteller with questions, and offering advice. I wear a green one when I'm playing the role of storyteller, because I've received the green light to tell my story. And I wear an orange one when I'm in my role as facilitator, to signify pausing to take questions about how the exercise should proceed, explaining next steps in the activity, laying out initial ground rules, and so on. Critical Incident Questionnaire (CIQ) responses from students have consistently reported that the teaching demonstration is invaluable in helping students understand the intricacies of the process and alerting them what to watch out for. It also, of course, is consistent with what students tell us about the importance of teachers modeling for them what critical thinking looks like.

Summary

In this chapter I have tried to describe a typical incremental sequence of intermediate to advanced exercises that teach students how to think critically. Each of the protocols discussed share some basic similarities. They are all social learning activities in which students serve as reflective mirrors helping their peers see things differently. They all focus on specific tasks, concepts, experiences, individuals, or practices, rather than on general, discipline-wide frameworks. And they are all sequenced to move closer and closer to the student's direct analysis of her own thinking and experiences.

In the next chapter I turn my attention to one the most frequent bugbears students complain about—being told to write a critical review of a text with no idea what the teacher means by the term *critical*.

6

Reading and Writing Critically

Up to now we have focused mostly on classroom activities in which students' engagement in critical thinking happens through speech. This is not surprising given that students say the best environments for them to learn to think critically are those involving peers helping them discover assumptions and viewpoints they otherwise would miss. But most assessment of students' ability to think critically happens through tests and essays, in other words through the written word. The ultimate example of this is the doctoral dissertation in which students write a book length study of a topic through which critical thinking is interwoven.

Speaking critically and writing critically are two very different processes. In speaking we have nonverbal and gestural tools available to us that we can use to underscore different elements in our argument. When you critique someone else's ideas and they are standing in front of you, your comments are more likely to have subtlety, to be shaded by a concern not to make the person turn away in disgust, anger, or embarrassment. Make the same critical points in writing and the primary stylistic concern is usually to be clear. But the same clarity valued so much in writing is often experienced by the receiver of criticism as an overly aggressive bluntness, far more threatening and objectionable than if the same points were made in a face-to-face exchange.

As more and more courses are taught in a hybrid or wholly online fashion, the ability to write critically is even more crucial than it was in the days of wholly face-to-face classes. But although students are often told that analyses of literature should be conducted critically, there is remarkably little specific assistance given on how to do this. As an example, I taught for ten years in a university program in which fostering critical thinking was a cardinal value, and I asked students to demonstrate this in every paper they were required to write. Yet not once did I give any guidance on how to do this, other than to tell them to look for assumptions that authors were operating under. When students finally confronted me with the fact that I had never actually explained what I meant by a critical analysis of literature, I was forced to be much more specific in my directions. So if this chapter is of any help to you it is because of those students' complaints.

Writing critically and speaking critically are the same, however, when it comes to the basic model of critical thinking outlined in Chapter One. Irrespective of the medium through which students show they are thinking critically, the same processes are emphasized—looking for assumptions, coming up with different ways to check those assumptions, and reviewing ideas and actions from multiple points of view. So any critical analysis of a text needs to contain, at a minimum, the following features:

- An effort to lay bare the assumptions the author is operating under, particularly assumptions the author has about what constitutes legitimate knowledge and which methods produce such knowledge.

- An appraisal of the reliability and validity of the author's conclusions or theoretical explanations.

- An assessment of the clarity of the writing—the degree to which its meaning is fully communicated, illustrated with ample examples, and guides the reader through the text.

- An overall evaluation of the relative merits of the text—both as a stand-alone piece of work, and in comparison to other scholarship in the area.

Misunderstandings of Critical Reading

One of the barriers students face in writing critically is their misunderstanding of exactly what this process entails. For example, if a student thinks a critical analysis of a major theorist in the field, a canonical text, or a widely accepted theorem involves showing how the theorist, author, or proof is wrong, this is an incredibly intimidating prospect. It would take an extremely confident, or extremely foolish, student to produce a demolition of a piece of work that was widely referenced, published in several languages, and generally regarded as authoritative. So one of the first things teachers have to do is wrestle learners away from the mistaken notion that criticism is inherently negative, which brings us to our first misunderstanding.

That It's Negative

For many of us the word *critical* carries negative connotations. Being critical is equated with cynical pessimism, with taking great pleasure in knocking down what other people have created; in short, with attacking and destroying what we portray as the naive and shortsighted efforts of others. It is important to say from the outset, then, that critical reading is a process of appraisal, involving the recognition of *positive* as well as *negative* elements. In fact, using the words *positive* and *negative* is mistaken because it only serves to reinforce a false dichotomy that we have to reach a verdict that something is good or bad. What critical reading and writing are all about is assessing the accuracy and validity of a piece of work. This means that we will usually find aspects of research, philosophy, or theory that we dislike, disagree with, and find incomplete or overly narrow. But we will also find aspects that seem to us well described, recognizable, and informative. Few pieces of writing we read in a doctoral program will be so unequivocally wonderful or awful that we can adopt a film critic approach to its appraisal, giving it an intellectual thumbs up or thumbs down. If we are reading critically we will almost certainly find that our appraisals are multilayered, even contradictory (as in when the same passages both excite and disturb). But central to all critical reading is the acknowledgment of what we find to be well grounded, accurate, and meritorious in a piece of scholarly writing, as well as what we find wanting.

That It Always Leads to Relativism

Critical reading and writing makes us aware that knowledge is always culturally and disciplinarily constructed—always the product of particular people thinking in particular ways at particular times in particular places. A common response to this discovery on the part of readers is to lapse into a relativistic state of defeatism. They conclude that because nothing seems to have universal certainty (even what passes for the laws of physics change according to time and place), no ideas have any greater legitimacy than any others. This conclusion can induce a kind of intellectual lethargy, a disconnection from the world of ideas.

In fact, critical reading can increase our sense of connectedness to a text by increasing our ability to give an informed rationale as to why we hold the convictions and beliefs we do. When we give a piece of literature a careful critical appraisal we have a sense of its strengths and weaknesses. The intellectual convictions we derive from this appraisal are informed by this same even-handed sense of what is strongest and weakest about our convictions and about why, on balance, we hold these even as we recognize their shortcomings. The point at which the best critical readers operate is the point of informed commitment so valued by the pragmatic tradition summarized in Chapter Two. Informed commitment means being able to give a rationale and to cite evidence for our ideas while always being open to reexamining and rethinking these in the light of further experience.

That It's Only for the Philosophically Astute

Because so much academic writing on critical thinking is grounded in the paradigm of analytic philosophy and concentrates on argument analysis, it is easy to conclude that critical thinking is not for the philosophically challenged. But critical reading (one form of critical thinking in action) is not restricted to those who pursue majors in logic. I prefer to think of it as a survival skill within the competence of all, irrespective of their formally defined educational level. In fact, as extensive research into how people reason in everyday situations shows (Sternberg, Forsyth, Hedlund, Horvath, Wagner, and others, 2000), the ability to clarify assumptions, analyze evidence quickly, assess the importance of contending contextual variables, and come to informed decisions is evident in many nonacademic contexts of adult life. Indeed, critical thinking informs how many of us negotiate and survive what we see as transforming episodes in our adult lives (Taylor and Cranton, forthcoming).

That It's the Preserve of Politically Correct Left-Wingers

Because one stream of writing on critical thinking, critical analysis, and critical reflection emanates from adherents of the Frankfurt School of Critical Social Theory—a body of work interpreting and revising Marx for the contemporary era (Brookfield, 2004)—there is a tendency to equate any activity with a name that includes *critical* with left-of-center political views. Students sometimes complain that for some teachers critical reading has a predetermined ideological outcome of turning the student into anything from a liberal to a neo-Marxist. In adult education programs where I have taught, this feeling sometimes expresses itself in the charge that my choice of texts shows I am anti-business. Given that critical theory's main critique is of the logic of capitalism, this complaint from students is hardly surprising.

However, it is important to remember that one of the most frequent responses to reading texts critically is for students to become much more skeptical of ascribed authority and much more likely to question ideas that were previously taken for granted. Since we live in a culture in which capitalist ideas are invested with such taken-for-granted authority that they constitute the dominant ideology, one possible consequence of critical thinking and reading is the student's questioning of the moral basis and universality of this ideology. Critical theorists are quick to point out, however, that, critical reading in a totalitarian communist society would call into question the taken-for-granted authority of those dominant left-wing ideologies.

The point about critical reading, properly encouraged, is that critical questions are asked of all ideologies, disciplines, and theories. So a critical social science turns a skeptical eye on all claims to universal validity. For a teacher to mandate in advance—either explicitly or implicitly—that only one ideological interpretation or outcome is permitted in a discussion or assignment is to contradict a fundamental tenet of critical thinking. That tenet holds that all involved—including teachers—must always be open to reexamining the assumptions informing their ideological commitments. For teachers this imperative is particularly important, since one of the best ways in which they can teach critical thinking is for them to model the process in their own actions. I hope, personally, that a critical reading of texts results in students becoming more skeptical of conservative ideologies, and more aware of the inhumanity of monopoly capitalism. And I feel a duty to make my bias known. But I also must continually lay out my own assumptions, and the evidence for these, and invite students to point out omissions in my position and to suggest alternative interpretations that can be made of the evidence I cite. For me to decree that "proper" or "real" critical thinking occurs only when students end up mimicking my political views would be the pedagogic equivalent of papal infallibility. I would kill at the outset any chance for genuine, searching inquiry.

That It's Wholly Cognitive

Critical reading, like critical thinking, is often thought of as a purely intellectual process in which rationality is valued above all else. The concept of rationality figures so strongly in work of critical theoreticians such as Habermas that it's not surprising to find it prominent in discussions of critical thinking and reading. However, critical reading as it is outlined here recognizes that thought and reasoning is infused with emotional currents and responses. Indeed, the feeling of connectedness to an idea, theory, or area of study that is so necessary to intellectual work is itself emotional. Even our appreciation of the intellectual elegance of a concept or set of theoretical propositions involves emotional elements.

So in critical reading we pay attention to our emotions, as well as our intellect. In particular, we investigate our emotional responses to the material we encounter. We can try to understand why it is that we become enthused or appalled, perplexed or engaged, by a piece of literature. As we read work that challenges some of our most deeply held assumptions, we are likely to experience strong feelings of anger and resentment against the writer or her ideas, feelings that are grounded in the sense of threat that this work holds for us. It is important that we know this in advance of our reading and try to understand that our emotional reactions are the inevitable accompaniment of undertaking any kind of intellectual inquiry that is really challenging.

Components of a Critical Review of a Text

In this section I want to outline what for me are the component elements of a critical review of a text. Not all of these will be in every analysis a student submits. For example, if it is a groundbreaking text in a new area it is harder to trace the text's intellectual antecedents, or to compare it to other works in the area (since none will have been published yet). But as a general rule, a written critical analysis of a text should locate the text in an area of scholarship, it should demonstrate an understanding of what the author is intending, it should identify assumptions, omissions, and alternate perspectives, and it should take a position on the relative merits of the text in terms of its accuracy, comprehensiveness, validity, and clarity.

Understanding the Text in Terms the Author Sets

Before beginning any written critical appraisal, the text must be understood in the terms the author sets for it. A critical analysis is rendered completely invalid if it doesn't understand the author's basic arguments. In terms of basic intellectual courtesy and honesty, anyone writing a critical analysis of a text needs to show that they understand what the author is trying to do and how she has set about accomplishing her task. As someone who has published extensively, I know from personal experience how frustrating it is to read a critique of my work that is based on a partial reading of it and that critiques me for omissions that are actually located in a separate part of the text.

It is also invalid to critique a text for not doing something the author has explicitly acknowledged she is not trying to do. Critical commentary should begin by focusing on the project the author has set for her work. It is, of course, legitimate to disagree with this project, to claim it is wrongly directed, poorly conceived, too limited or wide in scope, and so on. But the writer of any critique must begin by showing she has a thorough understanding of what the author is trying to do, and a good working knowledge of how she is trying to do it. This can be done in several ways:

A student can provide emblematic excerpts, quotes, and author examples that capture accurately what the text represents. There is nothing that demonstrates a student's understanding of key ideas better than if she can find a clear example of a complex proposition the author is advancing, whether this be one in the text or one that she provides. The foundation of a good critical review of a piece of literature is the student's showing that she understands the arguments and information presented from the author's viewpoint, and that she can explicate the text's intended meanings.

Students can show they are aware of the full range of the author's scholarship and the place that the text under analysis occupies in that body of work. If the work is an extension of earlier work, that needs to be acknowledged, as does any significant new directions that are taken in the text. Perhaps the text revises or even disavows earlier work, or maybe it marks a complete break with what went before. All this should be in a critical review. If the text represents a watershed that precedes subsequent work of importance, its place in the trajectory of the author's intellectual development should be recognized.

Students should be able to identify the chief assumptions that inform an author's work, particularly the assumptions the author makes about what comprises legitimate knowledge. Depending on the discipline students could try to identify (1) paradigmatic assumptions the author holds—those that shape the author's whole outlook on an area, (2) prescriptive assumptions—the epistemological assumptions the author makes about what should be considered appropriate methods for establishing truth, or (c) causal assumptions—those the author proposes to explain particular dynamics, proofs, and relationships covered in the work.

When it seems appropriate, students could also review the chief published critiques of the work that already exist, together with any acknowledgments they need to make regarding their debt to those existing critiques or their departure from them.

Students can show how the work analyzed fits in a broad map of scholarship in the field. If the field is organized by its different research methodologies, by its different philosophical orientations, or by its focus on specific content, the location of the work in these categorizations can be identified.

The intellectual antecedents of the particular work can be acknowledged. This could be a case of identifying the previous work conducted by others that the author is building on, the methodological or philosophical schools the author takes most seriously, or the way the work builds cumulatively on earlier stages in the author's own intellectual project.

Conducting a Critical Analysis of the Text

Once the student has shown a clear understanding of what the author intends a text to accomplish, and once she has understood the author's arguments and conclusions from the "inside" (that is, in the author's own terms), the business of critique can begin. This is when the detailed taking apart of a work begins. Here, students can apply the critical protocol outlined in Chapter One to ask the following questions:

- What are the assumptions—paradigmatic, prescriptive, and causal—an author operates under? To what degree is each of these assumptions accurate and valid?

- What potentially fruitful explanations or interpretations of the material explored are neglected or omitted?

- Of those explanations and interpretations offered, which are most accurate and valid, and why is this the case?

- What inconsistencies or contradictions does the text reveal? Are there times when a contention offered in one part of the text is contradicted by a statement or argument elsewhere?

- Which are the strongest of arguments that are advanced, and why is this so?

- Which elements of different arguments does the author adduce the most convincing evidence to support?

- When claims and contentions are made, and to what degree are these grounded in documented empirical evidence?

- When, if ever, does an author's personal preferences masquerade as objective conclusions?

- To what degree are the author's conclusions predetermined by the methodological or philosophical paradigm in which she works? If they are, does the author acknowledge this influence?

- How far do the major conclusions or interpretations in a study clearly follow from earlier arguments and explanations? What is the discernible developmental flow to a text?

- When generalizations are advanced about broad categories that are studied, to what extent are the particular illustrations intended to support these generalizations reliable and valid?

- How open are authors about their biases? What significant unacknowledged biases does a piece of work contain?

- How well do authors communicate their meaning? Which parts of their arguments are the easiest to follow and why is this? Which parts of their arguments are confusing?

- When new concepts, terms, or proofs are offered, how well does the author illustrate these with clarifying, helpful examples?

Taking a Position

Finally, what distinguishes a critical review of a text from a descriptive summary or précis is the student taking a position on the relative merits of that text. For many students this is the hardest part of writing critically. It may seem outrageous to students to contemplate critiquing the work of scholars who are well established in the field they are studying. Many students offer initial appraisals that are strong on affirmation and weak on omissions, unsupported conclusions, or unwarranted inferences. This is hardly surprising. When students are in the early stages of encountering a subject, it is often unrealistic and unfair to expect them to judge how well a particular piece stacks up against a whole body of work conducted by multiple scholars. So the capacity to take a position on the merits of a piece of work depends on the student's familiarity with the broad discipline. As with other aspects of thinking critically, the learner needs a grasp of the "grammar" of the subject (as outlined in Chapter One) before being able to make appraisals of particular contributions to that subject.

As always, directions to students on how to write a critical appraisal of a text should emphasize always that it is an *appraisal*, not a demolition, and that an appraisal involves assessing what the text does well as much as what it neglects. Typical questions that a student can address in a critical appraisal are

- How contemporary is the piece of work being analyzed? Is it up to date in utilizing new research and the most recent methodologies or paradigms?

- How well does the work explain or describe the topic it addresses? Can you assess its explanatory power or descriptive exactness compared to other, similar texts on this topic?

- How does the work compare to other, similar work conducted on the topic? Is the emphasis mostly on reiterating what is already known? Does the work add new information or insight? Are explanations or theorems offered with more or less comprehensibility than in other, similar work?

- How sound is the argument offered in the text? To what degree do conclusions follow from evidence? Are the author's inferences clearly documented and justified?

- What degree of self-criticality is evident in the text? If appropriate, how does the author include criticisms of her work or strive to identify areas of possible weakness in her arguments or methodology?

- To what degree does the author clarify the intellectual precedents to her work? Does she acknowledge relevant prior work in the area? Is the text explicitly situated in a stream of similar research? If not, does the author indicate what is unique about the text compared to other work in the subject area?

- In terms of other work in the subject, how appropriate, accurate, and helpful are the examples, metaphors, and analogies used to illustrate concepts and explanations?

- What is the explanatory range of the text compared to other works in the area? Does it encompass all possible examples of the phenomena studied? If not, are the limits to its explanations acknowledged?

- To what degree does the work invite refutation, extension, or refinement? Does it indicate fruitful directions for future research and scholarship?

- When specialist language is used in the text, how well does the author justify its adoption?

How to Teach Critical Writing

Critical writing follows three of the same general processes of critical thinking outlined in the discussion in Chapter Three of what students say are the best methods for learning to think critically. It needs to be sequenced incrementally, beginning with small-scale tasks and as much scaffolding as possible—such as ample provision of good examples of critical writing. It needs to be learned socially, with peer critique an inherent part of the process. And faculty must engage in the process in front of students by modeling it, explicitly and repeatedly. Let's take a look at each of these in turn.

Incremental Sequencing

As already indicated, probably the most intimidating thing for many students is to be told to write a critical analysis of a text. But this is made much more palatable when they are eased into this by exposure to the different tasks involved. Students repeatedly affirm that being provided with multiple examples of what a well— and badly—written critical analysis looks like is enormously helpful. This is particularly the case if the examples provided are from work completed by students in previous courses. Of course, the trick is to give examples that are specific enough to be helpful but that do not offer an easily transposed template that a student can copy uncritically.

When I post examples of earlier students' good and bad attempts to write critically I typically develop a color-coded or formatting guide to what I wish students to notice.

Color-Coded Critical Feedback

Red—for sentences where the student identifies different assumptions an author has made.

Green—for sentences where the student identifies contradictions, inconsistencies, or omissions in a text.

Blue—for sentences where the student provides an example of where inferences follow, or do not follow, from evidence in the text.

Yellow—for sentences where the student appropriately identifies aspects of a text that are either particularly clear or particularly confusing.

Underlined—for sentences where the student demonstrates how a text is situated within a subject area or how it defies easy categorization.

Italics—for sentences where the student clearly shows he has captured an author's intended meaning, perhaps through a particularly appropriate example the student provides.

Boldface—for sentences where the student clearly takes a position on judging the relative merits of a piece compared to other work in the area.

Sequencing critical writing means starting small, with students analyzing a paragraph or page, rather than critiquing a whole chapter. One useful exercise in this regard is Quotes to Affirm and Challenge, described in the previous chapter. Another is the Hatful of Quotes exercise.

Giving Specific Feedback

One of the most important events in a sequence of learning to write critically is when teachers provide regular and specific commentary on students' writing. Of course the drawback to this is that faculty are so busy working with ever larger classes that stressful overload becomes the norm. Asking them to provide individualized feedback on students' writing is then experienced as cruel and unusual punishment. But getting in the habit of asking a few simple questions can help students improve their ability to do close and critical readings of material. In particular, students need to be made aware of their tendency to make broad but unsupported generalizations about a piece of writing. Many supposedly critical reviews of texts contain sweeping conclusions that students have picked up from reading secondary interpretations, or

---

Exhibit 6.1. Hatful of Quotes

Prior to a discussion of a text the leader types out sentences or passages from the text onto separate slips of paper. In class she puts these into a hat and asks students to draw one of these slips out of a hat. Students are given a few minutes to think about their quote and then asked to read it out and comment on it. The order of contribution is up to the students. Those who feel more fearful about speaking go last and take more time to think about what they want to say. Because the same five or six quotes are used, students who go later will have heard their quote read out and commented on by those who spoke earlier. So even if they have little to say about their own interpretation of the quote, they can affirm, build on, or contradict a comment a peer has already made on that quote. This exercise is a good way to create a safe opportunity for everyone to speak. Those who are diffident get to say something, thus building confidence for subsequent contributions.

Adapted for the purposes of teaching critical reading and writing the teacher chooses particular quotes that

- Have assumptions (causal at first, then prescriptive, and finally paradigmatic) embedded in them
- Contain inferences (valid and invalid) from data that are expressed clearly or confusingly
- Display a good or poor use of appropriate illustrative examples
- Contain inconsistencies or contradictions

As students move through a course or program the material they explore increases in length, breadth, and complexity. Students move from paragraphs to pages, from chapters to books, from pieces that focus on one idea to those that introduce multiple variables and perspectives, and from theoretical schools to whole genres.

---

from peers, with no citations or indications exactly where in the text evidence can be found that support these generalized verdicts. Once students see faculty repeatedly raising the following questions they soon get into the habit of writing in a way that forestalls them:

- Can you provide a specific quote or sentence in the text that illustrates your meaning?

- Where in the text does the author argue this point?

- What other interpretations could be made of this data that the author doesn't consider?

- You seem to have identified an assumption here—is it causal, prescriptive, or paradigmatic?

- Why do you think the author argues this point so strongly?

- Your comment here seems to contradict what you wrote in the previous paragraph—can you say more about why you think these two comments are not inconsistent?

- Your sentences don't seem to connect to each other here—can you provide a link between them?

- I can't follow your meaning here—can you rewrite your sentence to make your meaning clearer?

Finally, one discipline that benefits students is that of being asked at the end of each assignment to raise at least two questions regarding the material they've studied. What these questions are is not in any way specified in advance. But if a student hands in a paper that doesn't contain these questions then the paper is returned as incomplete. The questions can be as simple as ones about the meaning of a particular sentence, or as complex as, say, ones about future directions for research or the misapplication of an analytical framework.

Writing as Peer Learning

If critical thinking is experienced as a social learning process in which peers bring your assumptions to your attention and point out interpretations and perspectives you've missed, then the same holds true for critical writing. I suggest that if at all possible critical writing be a two-stage process in which students first give each other feedback on early drafts before submitting final drafts to faculty for their evaluation. One obvious difficulty with this approach is that students are often reluctant to give each other any kind of negative feedback and consequently emphasize the positive aspects of their appraisal far more than the negative or neutral aspects. So if students are to be asked to give each other critical feedback on early writing drafts then two conditions need to be in place. First, faculty needs to model what this process looks like (something I address at the end of this chapter), and, second, students need highly specific protocols and templates to help structure the process. The following is one suggested peer critique protocol.

The specific instructions in a critical writing protocol will alter depending on the kind of student it is intended for. But the general point remains valid. If you are going to ask students to conduct a critical review of each other's writing, then the more specific the directions, the better. In addition, a good protocol should have a roughly equal balance between directions that ask for positive and negative appraisal.

Faculty Modeling

One of the most helpful things that faculty can do when they teach critical reading and writing is to demonstrate for students how they apply this to their own work. This is much more easily arranged

Exhibit 6.2. Peer Critique Writing Protocol

Your task is to give specific feedback to your learning partner on the extent to which the partner's writing exhibits a critical approach. In your partner's draft, please identify the following . . .

1. The three sentences where you think you best understand what your partner is trying to convey

2. The three sentences where your partner's meaning was least clear to you

3. The sentence where an example most accurately illustrated the meaning of a conclusion

4. The sentence where an example least accurately illustrated the meaning of a conclusion

5. The sentence or paragraph where your partner made clear an assumption she held about the material studied

6. The sentence or paragraph where your partner neglected to clarify an assumption she held about the material studied

7. The paragraph or passage where your partner provided what she felt was an accurate interpretation of the material

8. The paragraph or passage where your partner missed a possible alternative interpretation of the material

9. The paragraph or passage where your partner made her most accurate inference from the data

10. The paragraph or passage where your partner made her most questionable inference from the data

11. The paragraph or passage that contained the clearest transitions between sentences as your partner built an argument

12. The paragraph or passage that contained the most confusing transitions between sentences as your partner built an argument

when a course is team taught, since different team members can follow protocols such as the one outlined in the preceding section and apply them to each other's work in front of students. When I have done this in team-taught courses there is always a flurry of comments on the Critical Incident Questionnaires (CIQ) to the effect that students find these the most helpful and engaging moments of the class session. This is particularly the case for the parts of the protocol where one faculty members tells another about the least clear transition in their work, the most questionable inference, the most inappropriate example, the assumptions that were missed, and so on.

But most of us teach for most of our time solo, so we have to find ways of modeling the protocol as a form of self-appraisal. As a well-published author, I am fortunate in that I can choose a published article or chapter of mine and review it as if it were written by a third party. In fact, when I do this the first time with a group of students I usually remove my name from the materials I give them, so they don't know that I'm the author. After my own appraisal of the work I then invite students to add their own comments—a process which is much more freely engaged in when students don't know that I'm the author they're critiquing.

The advent of online technology has made this process of modeling critical writing much easier to accommodate. We can post examples of our own work together with our own critical appraisal of our piece. Exhibit 6.3 shows one example I use— an early draft of the first page of my book *Becoming a Critically Reflective Teacher* (Brookfield, 1995).

Summary

This chapter has focused on the ways critical thinking is evident in students' writing. I have argued that many of the themes outlined in Chapter Three regarding what students say helps them learn to think critically are paralleled in how they learn to write

Exhibit 6.3. Example: Faculty Modeling of Critical Reading

We teach to change the world. The hope that undergirds our efforts to help students learn is that doing this will help them act toward each other, and to their environment, with compassion, understanding, and fairness. But our attempts to increase the amount of love and justice in the world are never simple, never ambiguous. What we think are democratic, respectful ways of treating people can be experienced by them as oppressive and constraining. One of the hardest things teachers learn is that the sincerity of their intentions does not guarantee the purity of their practice. The cultural, psychological, and political complexities of learning, and the ways in which power complicates all human relationships (including those between students and teachers), mean that teaching can never be innocent.

Teaching innocently means thinking that we're always understanding exactly what it is that we're doing and what effect we're having. Teaching innocently means assuming that the meanings and significance we place in our actions are the ones that students take from them. At best, teaching this way is naive. At worst, it induces pessimism, guilt, and lethargy. Since we rarely have full awareness of what we're doing, and since we frequently misread how others perceive our actions, an uncritical stance toward our practice sets us up for a lifetime of frustration. Nothing seems to work out as it should. Our inability to control what looks like chaos becomes, to our eyes, evidence of our incompetence.

Breaking this vicious circle of innocence and blame is one reason why the habit of critical reflection is crucial for teachers' survival. Without a critically reflective stance toward what we do we tend to accept the blame for problems that are not of our own making. We think that all resistance to learning displayed by students is caused by our own insensitivity or un-preparedness. We read poor evaluations of our teaching (often written by only a small

(Continued)

minority of our students) and immediately conclude that we are hopeless failures. We become depressed when ways of behaving toward students and colleagues that we think are democratic and respectful are interpreted as aloof or manipulative. A critically reflective stance toward our teaching helps us avoid these traps of demoralization and self-laceration. It might not win us easy promotion or bring us lots of friends. But it does increase enormously the chances that we will survive in the classroom with enough energy and sense of purpose to have some real effect on those we teach.

1. The three sentences where you think you best understand what the author is trying to convey

   Teaching innocently means thinking that we're always understanding exactly what it is that we're doing and what effect we're having.

   What we think are democratic, respectful ways of treating people can be experienced by them as oppressive and constraining.

   Nothing seems to work out as it should.

2. The three sentences where the author's meaning was least clear

   The hope that undergirds our efforts to help students learn is that doing this will help them act toward each other, and to their environment, with compassion, understanding, and fairness.

   But our attempts to increase the amount of love and justice in the world are never simple, never ambiguous.

   The cultural, psychological, and political complexities of learning, and the ways in which power complicates all human relationships (including those between students and teachers), mean that teaching can never be innocent.

3. The sentence where an example most accurately illustrated the meaning of a conclusion

   We read poor evaluations of our teaching (often written by only a small minority of our students) and immediately conclude that we are hopeless failures.

4. The sentence where an example least accurately illustrated the meaning of a conclusion

We become depressed when ways of behaving toward students and colleagues that we think are democratic and respectful are interpreted as aloof or manipulative.

5. The sentence or paragraph where the author made clear an assumption he or she held about the topic

Teaching innocently means assuming that the meanings and significance we place in our actions are the ones that students take from them.

6. The sentence or paragraph where the author neglected to clarify an assumption he or she held about the topic

But it does increase enormously the chances that we will survive in the classroom with enough energy and sense of purpose to have some real effect on those we teach.

(This is a causal assumption that is stated as an empirical fact.)

7. The paragraph or passage where the author provided an accurate interpretation of the material

At best, teaching this way is naive. At worst, it induces pessimism, guilt and lethargy.

8. The paragraph or passage where the author missed a possible alternative interpretation of the material

We teach to change the world. The hope that undergirds our efforts to help students learn is that doing this will help them act toward each other, and to their environment, with compassion, understanding, and fairness.

(Many teachers have nothing like this agenda; they are there simply to make sure students learn the material.)

9. The paragraph or passage where the author made the most accurate inference from the data

We think that all resistance to learning displayed by students is caused by our own insensitivity or un-preparedness.

(Continued)

10. The paragraph or passage where the author made the most questionable inference from the data

A critically reflective stance toward our teaching helps us avoid these traps of demoralization and self-laceration.

(This is stated as an obvious cause and effect link, when in fact it represents the author's bias.)

11. The paragraph or passage that contained the clearest transitions between sentences as the author built an argument.

Teaching innocently means thinking that we're always understanding exactly what it is that we're doing and what effect we're having. Teaching innocently means assuming that the meanings and significance we place in our actions are the ones that students take from them. At best, teaching this way is naive. At worst, it induces pessimism, guilt, and lethargy. Since we rarely have full awareness of what we're doing, and since we frequently misread how others perceive our actions, an uncritical stance toward our practice sets us up for a lifetime of frustration. Nothing seems to work out as it should. Our inability to control what looks like chaos becomes, to our eyes, evidence of our incompetence.

12. The paragraph or passage that contained the most confusing transitions between sentences as the author built an argument.

We teach to change the world. The hope that undergirds our efforts to help students learn is that doing this will help them act toward each other, and to their environment, with compassion, understanding and fairness. But our attempts to increase the amount of love and justice in the world are never simple, never ambiguous. What we think are democratic, respectful ways of treating people can be experienced by them as oppressive and constraining. One of the hardest things teachers learn is that the sincerity of their intentions does not guarantee the purity of their practice. The cultural, psychological, and political complexities of learning, and the ways in which power complicates all human relationships (including those between students and teachers), mean that teaching can never be innocent.

(This paragraph contains six distinct themes—that teachers want to change the world, that this involves fostering compassion, understanding, and fairness, that teaching is never simple, that when teachers believe they're working democratically they are actually working to constrain students, that sincerity does not guarantee purity (whatever that means), and that teaching's complexities mean it is never innocent. These are trotted out one after the other with minimal links or transitions. In addition, the paragraph makes many sweeping generalizations, none of which are supported by evidence. It also creates inferences—such as working democratically can be constraining—that are stated but not explained. Finally, the paragraph is full of prescriptive assumptions about what teachers should do, none of which are explicitly acknowledged.)

---

critically. Reading, writing, and thinking critically cannot really be separated, and in writing critically one is forced to think more clearly about where one stands and to choose which arguments are felt to be the most convincing. All three processes benefit from being sequenced incrementally, from being learned in groups, and from being demonstrated and modeled by teachers. In the next chapter I delve further into how to design course assignments that foster critical writing, and I explore how to integrate critical thinking into course design.

7

Integrating Critical Thinking Across the Curriculum

Of all the objectives highlighted in the mission statements of various institutions of higher education in North America, two stand out. One has to do with what might broadly be called civic engagement; that is, with helping students become responsible citizens concerned to defend democracy. The other is to foster critical thinking. In my own home University of St. Thomas the two are linked, and critical thinking is identified as one of the elements of morally responsible leadership that advances the common good. Given that critical thinking is lauded so widely in colleges and universities, one might reasonably conclude that faculty across schools, programs, and departments all share a common commitment to initiating students into this process.

There is a problem with this assumption, however, one that was discussed in Chapter Two. Although teaching students to think more critically is commonly espoused, the way this is conceived and practiced varies considerably from department to department, program to program. A natural science program that regards critical thinking as equivalent to becoming skilled at hypothesis formulation and testing is very different from a social science program that regards critical thinking as the ability to identify ideological manipulation. Any institution that wishes to foster critical thinking across the disciplines thus needs to ensure that students and faculty have a shared understanding of the process.

Chapter One outlined the basis for such an understanding in arguing that four generic intellectual operations were common to all forms of critical thinking: (1) identifying the assumptions that frame our thinking and determine our actions, (2) checking out the degree to which these assumptions are accurate and valid, (3) looking at our ideas and actions from several different perspectives, and (4) on the basis of all this, taking informed actions. It also proposed a basic typology of different kinds of assumptions that critical thinking unearths and scrutinizes—paradigmatic, prescriptive, and causal. In the current chapter I want to take this general understanding of critical thinking and explore how it could inform curricula across a whole institution.

My assumption is that if a common understanding of critical thinking is explicitly embedded in the different disciplines that comprise a college or university's offerings, students will benefit. A shared language among faculty will consistently underscore for students the centrality of critical thinking to all intellectual work. It will also allow faculty to talk to each other across disciplinary differences. If students see and hear faculty sharing a common critical language they will better understand that fostering this kind of thinking is the point of higher education. And the confusion from hearing the same term—*critical thinking*—being employed in very different ways will be considerably reduced.

Beginning Systemically

Before thinking about how critical thinking can be integrated into different schools and programs, we need to consider how the importance of critical thinking can be underscored on a system-wide basis. A good first place to start is with the institution's mission statement. Obviously, this should include an explicit commitment to developing critical thinking as the core intellectual project of the university. Since an institution's mission statement is then reproduced in school, program, and department materials, there needs to be an agreed on, common definition of critical thinking that can be quoted in all program descriptions and course materials. One such definition might be the following:

Defining Critical Thinking

Critical thinking describes the process by which students become aware of two sets of assumptions. First, students investigate the assumptions held by scholars in a field of study regarding the way legitimate knowledge is created and advanced in that field. Second, students investigate their own assumptions and the way these frame their own thinking and actions. Thinking critically requires us to check the assumptions that we, and others, hold, by assessing the accuracy and validity of the evidence for these assumptions and by looking at ideas and actions from multiple perspectives. A person who thinks critically is much better placed to take informed actions; actions that are well grounded in evidence and that are more likely to achieve the results intended.

If a common definition such as the preceding can be agreed on, this can then be reproduced in all program publicity materials, course descriptions, and syllabuses. How each department or program would decide that the generic processes outlined above were met would vary. With regard to the first set of assumptions— those that scholars in a discipline hold about how legitimate knowledge is created and advanced—departments would differ in what they required. A course in biochemistry would expect students to understand why certain protocols were commonly adopted in experimental design. A course in photography would encourage students to explore how aesthetic standards developed in the field. A clinical practicum in nursing would want students to know the standards for nursing education established by the National League of Nursing. A course in sociology would ask students to consider why certain theoretical frameworks for explaining the functioning of social systems evolved as they did.

In each program, course, or syllabus statement, the lexicon would therefore be that of the common definition outlined above, but its manifestation—how it was recognized and assessed in terms of specific student learning operations and practices—would look very different. Needless to say, a critical thinking approach would insist that students not only be aware of the genesis and development of these disciplinary standards and frameworks, but also that they would be able to critique them. This would entail students taking a position on those that had greatest legitimacy and expressing why they believed that to be the case. It would also involve students identifying whose interests were served by the existence of a particular protocol and whose interests were harmed.

With regard to the second set of assumptions—those students hold about their own thinking and actions—the language in different disciplines could be quite similar. After all, whether a student is a physicist, theologian, pharmacist, or psychologist is really irrelevant, since students in all those areas will hold assumptions about the specific topics and subject matter they study. And their actions, whether they be intellectual actions (such as favoring a particular proof, theoretical framework, or experimental protocol), field-based, applied actions (such as adopting a particular diagnosis method, clinical protocol, or interview format), or socio-political actions (such as joining a Socialist league or college Republican organization, working to repeal pollution control legislation or organizing demonstrations at meetings of the World Trade Organization), all follow from their assumptions.

An Example: Critical Thinking in Food and Consumer Science

As a specific example of how a general definition can be developed for students, the following is a definition I developed for the College of Food and Consumer Sciences at Iowa State University in 2003.

What Is Critical Thinking?

Life is a series of decisions, some small, some much larger. Whom we date or choose as friends, the work or career we pursue, which political candidates we support, what we choose to eat, where we live, what consumer goods we buy, whom we marry and how we raise children—all these decisions are based on assumptions. We assume our friends will be trustworthy and won't talk about us behind our backs. We assume our career choices will be personally fulfilling or financially remunerative. We assume politicians we vote for have our, or the community's, best interests at heart. We assume that the foods we choose to eat are healthy for us, and so on.

These assumptions are sometimes correct. At other times, however, the assumptions we base our decisions on have never been examined. Sometimes we hold these assumptions because people we respect (friends, parents, teachers, religious leaders) have told us they are right. At other times we have picked these assumptions up as we travel through life but can't say exactly where they've come from. To make good decisions in life we need to be sure that these assumptions are accurate and valid—that they fit the situations and decisions we are facing.

Critical thinking describes the process we use to uncover and check our assumptions. First we need to find out what our assumptions are. We may know some of these already (these we call explicit assumptions) but others we are unaware of (implicit assumptions). To uncover these implicit assumptions it is often helpful to involve other people (friends, family, work colleagues) who help us see ourselves, and our actions, from unfamiliar perspectives. Sometimes reading books, watching videos, or having new experiences such as traveling to other cultures, going to college, or being an intern help us become aware of our assumptions. Once we know what our assumptions are we enter the second phase of critical thinking, that of research. We try to check out our assumptions to make sure they are accurate and valid. To do this we also need to consult a wide range of sources—talking to people with experience in the situations in which we find ourselves, reading relevant literature, searching trusted Web sites, consulting experts, and so on. The third and final phase of critical thinking puts the first two stages into practice by applying our analysis to our decisions. Decisions based on critical thinking are more likely to be ones we feel confident about and to have the effects we want them to have.

So, in summary, critical thinking involves three interrelated phases:

1. Discovering the assumptions that guide our decisions, actions, and choices

2. Checking the accuracy of these assumptions by exploring as many different perspectives, viewpoints, and sources as possible

3. Making informed decisions that are based on these researched assumptions

(Informed decisions are based on evidence we can trust, can be explained to others, and have a good chance of achieving the effects we want.)

A College or University-Wide Freshman Seminar on Critical Thinking

A few years ago *American Educator*, the journal of the American Federation of Teachers, asked on the cover page in bold capitals "Can Critical Thinking Be Taught?" and answered "Not in the Way You Think." Inside, the lead article argued a familiar perspective; namely, that "it makes no sense to teach critical thinking devoid of factual content" (Willingham, 2007, p. 10). Summarized briefly, Willingham argued that before people can think critically—that is, before they can take multiple perspectives on an issue or body of knowledge, solve problems, draw inferences, assess accurate evidence, and so on—they need to have a full appreciation of what Chapter Two described as the internal grammar of a subject area. To recap, the grammar of a subject comprises its internal rules for truth, its central concepts, and the criteria it employs to judge excellence in the area. Furthermore, argues Willingham, critical thinking is inextricably intertwined with domain knowledge and is highly contextual. Hence, a student may learn to think very critically in one area but be unable to think this way in another that seems similar. The illustration Willingham provides is of students who are taught to see the conduct of the American revolutionary war of independence from the British and American sides, but who find it almost impossible to view World War II from the German, Italian, or Japanese perspective. The article concludes that teaching critical thinking skills independently of a subject matter context is nonsense, a conclusion that calls into question the thousands of discrete critical thinking courses taught in North America.

I believe that the first of Willingham's conclusions is accurate and that critical thinking can only be learned and practiced from within domain knowledge, but that the second is premature. I think that critical thinking courses *are* appropriate and that they do not need to be taught within the context of academic subjects or disciplines. Rather, critical thinking can be taught within the context of the student's own life. The curriculum for such courses comprises the events students have experienced as they enter college and face the challenges and difficulties of young adulthood.

Part of the student experience is realizing the limitations of "life rules" learned in adolescence that are supposed to guide you successfully through your college years. Another is being free of parental constraints for the first time and needing to take responsibility for your decisions and choices. Dealing with loneliness, feeling that everyone is making friends except you, deciding which courses to take, how much time to devote to study, where to study, how to negotiate living with a room mate you've never met, when and how much to drink—all these situations require students to make choices based on assumptions they hold about the best course of action. So the texts for such introductory critical thinking courses are students' own experiences as they enter the college years: the assumptions, and ways of assessing the accuracy of these, that students develop to explain the situations they face, solve their problems, and guide their actions.

Most freshman year students have to take some kind of orientation course equipping them to adapt to college life, learn about expectations for academic work, and gain practice in the study skills students will need to succeed. Time management, working well in groups, textbook reading, note taking, preparing for tests, college writing, plagiarism, and critical thinking are often covered. In addition to study skills, such a course typically covers accessing the array of campus resources, money management, communication skills, living with diversity, maintaining a healthy lifestyle, and balancing social and academic life.

I suggest that where critical thinking is a central part of the college or university's mission statement, a mandatory *Freshman Seminar on Critical Thinking* be established. This would introduce students to the basic protocol outline in Chapter One. Critical thinking would be understood as a process by which we try to identify the assumptions framing our reasoning, decision making, and choices, mostly by trying to open ourselves up to perspectives we have not considered before. This course could actually weave into it much of the content covered by Freshman Year Orientations. The course could begin with students being asked to consider a number of realistic Scenario Analysis exercises (along the lines of the method outlined in Chapter Three) in which the central character in the scenario is trying to make money decisions, respond to plagiarism he has observed, balance the demands of work with taking necessary relaxation, prepare for a tough exam, deal with racism or sexism he is witnessing or experiencing, or negotiate a relationship with an important faculty member that is not going well.

Each Scenario Analysis would introduce the basic three questions we ask in critical thinking: What assumptions are people acting under? How could they check out the accuracy and validity of these? And what are different ways of understanding the situation? As students completed scenarios individually and then in groups they would be asked to report out any causal, prescriptive, or paradigmatic assumptions they had uncovered, and to share the different interpretations of the scenario they had generated. The seminar would then split into disciplinary based groups so students could work with others who are also studying natural sciences, human services, business, arts and humanities, social sciences— whatever the college's disciplinary divisions might be. In these disciplinary-based groups activities such as Crisis-Decision Simulation, Exemplars and Flaws, Critical Debate, or any other of the intermediary exercises outlined in Chapter Five would then be introduced. This course would be invaluable in explaining the primacy of critical thinking to students (and their parents) new to the institution, and could also position its importance to alumni and future donors.

Building a Case for Critical Thinking

Once an institutionwide definition of critical thinking has been adopted and embedded in program and departmental materials, the next step is to consider how a case for critical thinking could be built that clearly demonstrates its utility for students and faculty. Too often the importance of critical thinking is declared as self-evident, with no effort to explain just why it's so important.

In Chapter Four I touched on the mistake of doing this, and briefly summarized some ways of building a case to students. I also tried to do this in Chapter One, by showing how important critical thinking had been in helping me get to grips with clinical depression. I revisit this theme in more detail below, and I present a six-step process for building a case for critical thinking to students who are either unfamiliar with the process or skeptical of its relevance to their lives.

Step 1: Research the Students' Culture

This seems such an obvious beginning step in all teaching situations, yet so often it's neglected. But the more we know about those we teach, the better placed we are to respond to any resistance they display. If we know something about the different values, expectations, experiences, and preferred learning styles of our students, we can adjust our teaching approaches, assignments, and forms of assessment accordingly. The more information we have about these things the more likely we are to choose materials, and use approaches, that our students find congenial. Knowing these things also helps us make a better, more contextually informed case for the learning we are asking them to undertake.

Finding out about student culture is made much easier with the advent of social media, where students' interests, enthusiasms, and dislikes are on public display. Even as my advancing age distances me further and further from my own students, I can use such publicly available media to find out about their favorite music, TV shows, sporting passions, even student slang. One instructor I met asks her students to nominate their favorite TV shows and then promises to watch the top-nominated show for the duration of the semester. Her intent is to trawl the show for examples that illustrate the ideas she is teaching. Not every course or subject lends itself to this approach, but as more and more courses integrate technology into face-to-face classes, it is now quite normal for a student gallery to be posted on WebCT, Blackboard, or whatever E-learning platform the institution adopts. Consequently, before the first class meeting it's quite possible for instructors to gain a limited sense of who their students are, and their previous history as learners at the institution.

There is, of course, a whole stream of theorizing on culturally relevant, culturally contextual, culturally sensitive, or culturally responsive teaching (Ginsberg and Wlodkowski, 2009; Gay, 2010; Herrera, 2010; McKinley, 2010). Central aims of such teaching are to build on skills and dispositions that students bring from their home cultures, and to help students take action to address social and political inequality. Culturally responsive teachers are urged to find out as much as possible about their students' communities by attending community events, students' baseball games, cultural festivals—anything that gives teachers material they can use to make connections between their students' experiences and the material they are trying to teach. In higher education Ira Shor and his colleagues (Shor, 1987; Shor and Pari, 1999; Pari and Shor, 2000; Souto-Manning, Ayers, and Shor, 2010) have done some brilliant work building on Paulo Freire's insights about the need to situate the development of critical consciousness in learners' own language and experiences.

Of course, as teachers' lives get busier and busier, and the importance of standardized rankings such as those contained in the *U.S. News and World Report* become more and more powerful, teachers can legitimately claim that spending their weekends researching students' communities leaves them no lives for themselves. Without proper attention to our souls, and time spent renewing them, teachers working in increasingly diverse and ever larger classrooms, where students' culture of entitlement is sometimes very strong, is a sure recipe for burnout. But wherever teachers can fit researching their students' culture into the corners of their lives, the pay-off can be immense. Anytime a teacher can argue that a student needs to learn to think critically in order to negotiate a specific situation in the student's life, the case for critical thinking is strengthened.

Step 2: Involve Former Resisters

In trying to convince new students of the importance of critical thinking we are always working against the fact that our own expressions of its importance will be met with some skepticism. Students will say "of course you're going to tell us it's important that we think critically—after all, you earn your living from teaching it!" But the voices of former students who were resistant to learning critical thinking, but who subsequently came to appreciate its value for them, will have far greater credibility than ours. Organizing a first-class alumni panel made up of three or four resistant students who were in the course in previous years can be very effective in puncturing early resistance. A few words from these former resisters will have a much greater effect than any appeals you can make.

Step 3: Take Students to Real-Life Sites Where Critical Thinking Is Evident

In skills-based courses that prepare students for real-life work, taking students on a field trip to a site where critical thinking is clearly being deployed in the cause of doing good work can be a wonderful way to build a case for its utility. In the human services professions (such as teaching, social work, nursing, criminal justice), the world of business, or in vocational schools teaching technical trades (information technology, media arts, the hospitality industry, and so on) the applicability of learning to real life is valued highly. Instructors are often adjuncts, hired primarily for their vocational experience. Real-life examples pepper these classrooms and guest speakers are often brought in to show how classroom learning connects to the world of work. In addition, field trips, sometimes, even internships, are arranged to help students make connections between their developing skills and future careers.

Of course, a visit to a real-life site where critical thinking is being employed will have little meaning unless workers at that site have been taught how to make their own critical thinking public, and how to demonstrate its role in their work. Critical thinking is useless in pedagogic terms if it remains implicit, something the worker does without making its presence clear to visiting students. So any field trip needs to be prepared for thoroughly, by teaching the workers or practitioners involved how to communicate to observers their own practice of critical thinking. For example, in medical residency training, doctors taking rounds can speak out loud the assumptions informing their diagnoses and treatments, they can check these out against their own experiences, the experiences of colleagues, and the reactions of patients, and they can ask both students and colleagues to suggest alternative possible explanations for the patient's condition and how it might lead to different treatment options.

Step 4: Use Real-Life Simulations

In Chapter Five we already discussed one particular application of a simulation, the Crisis-Decision Simulation. If you remember that simulation, it involved a highly dramatized situation of a group of students in a radiation-free geodesic dome deciding which of a number of survivors of a nuclear holocaust they were to let into their dome. (As I wrote this chapter the 2011 Tsunami that hit Japan and crippled the Fukushima Daiichi nuclear power plant made the simulation eerily relevant). That is not the kind of simulation I'm thinking of here.

A simulation designed to illustrate the importance of critical thinking will be one grounded in the realities of students' lives. With adult students it could be one where students have to imagine a situation in which they are trying to balance multiple obligations, responsibilities, and loyalties (to family, work, friends, church, community). With more traditional aged students it could also focus on dilemmas students often face on campus. Typical ones might be

- Seeing friends engage in binge drinking or use racist stereotypes, and wondering when, if, or how to intervene

- Deciding what the price of loyalty to a friend is when that friendship is blocking you from participating in student life

- How to respond to plagiarism when it either (1) draws directly on your own work or (2) does not disadvantage you in any way

- How to respond to a racial micro-aggression when you are a racial minority of one or two in a mostly White institution

- When choosing a major, how to decide whether to study something that fascinates you but holds poor job prospects or something that is less interesting but is more likely to lead to employment on graduation

Such simulations begin with the teacher asking students to generate—individually, on their own—as many possible responses to the situation as they can come up with. Students are then placed in groups and told to share their responses with each other, along with the reasons they made them. At a very basic level this teaches students how people interpret the same situation very differently. Students are then told to try to identify the assumptions that lie behind their different solutions, and to decide which had been checked and which were unchecked. They are also asked to study the evidence they gave to justify the responses they made to specific problems, and to identify when this evidence draws from beyond their own personal experience.

When students see how many of the assumptions that informed their solutions are completely unresearched, and how often they draw only on their own personal experience, they are brought face to face with the risks of acting uncritically. When the simulation adds information that would have been uncovered through a simple checking of assumptions, students realize how many decisions in their lives have perhaps been made uncritically, and how dangerous this can be. The simulations outlined above will typically foreground power dynamics and the influence of socialization, dominant ideology, and culture.

Step 5: Model Your Own Critical Thinking

The missing link in much college teaching is the regular attempt by teachers to model the learning behaviors and dispositions they have requested of students. Far too often students are told that a certain task or learning activity is good for them but have never seen the teacher engaged in the very activity that is being urged on them. For example, one of the mistakes I have made many times in my career is to walk into a classroom on the first day of a new course, announce to students that I believe in discussion and group work, and tell them why the experience of working collaboratively will be good for them. Then I assign topics to students and put them into small discussion groups. The trouble with this scenario is that it omits a crucial element. I have neglected to model in front of the students an engagement in the very activity—participating in discussions with peers—I am prescribing for them.

As teachers we have to earn the right to ask students to engage seriously in learning only if we first model our own serious commitment to it. This is as true for critical thinking as it is for any other learning endeavor. If we want students to believe us when we say critical thinking is good for them, we have to show them how it's good for us too. In Chapter Three I have already touched on what students say about the importance of seeing teachers model critical thinking. In addition, Chapter Ten focuses solely on this theme. So I refer you to those sections of the book for more analysis of this issue.

Step 6: Make Sure the Reward Structure Is Consistent

Nothing torpedoes teachers' good intentions quite so effectively as urging students to participate in activities that the teacher values but that the students have decided are not rewarded by whatever evaluation system is in place. It is this realization that totally changed my thinking on grading students for participation in discussion. For many years I relied heavily on discussion as a way of teaching but graded students on the quality of their papers. Not surprisingly, student take-up in discussion was extremely spotty—a few naturally garrulous extroverts (or egomaniacs) tended to be responsible for 90% of the conversation. Once I fully realized just how much student behavior was determined by the response to the questions "Will this be on the test?" I developed a Grading Participation Rubric that specified in advance a number of concrete behaviors that I was looking for as evidence of good participation. Examples of these are

- Ask a question or make a comment that shows you are interested in what another person says.

- Ask a question or make a comment that encourages another person to elaborate on something they have already said.

- Bring in a resource (a reading, Web link, video) not covered in the syllabus but that adds new information/ perspectives to our learning.

- Make a comment that underscores the link between two people's contributions and make this link explicit in your comment.

- Post a comment on the course chat room that summarizes our conversations so far and/or suggests new directions and questions to be explored in the future.

- Make a comment (online if this is appropriate) indicating that you found another person's ideas interesting or useful. Be specific as to why this was the case.

- Contribute something that builds on, or springs from, what someone else has said. Be explicit about the way you are building on the other person's thoughts—this can be done online.

- Make a summary observation that takes into account several people's contributions and that touches on a recurring theme in the discussion (online if you like).

- Ask a cause-and-effect question—for example, "Can you explain why you think it's true that if these things are in place such and such a thing will occur?"

- Find a way to express appreciation for the enlightenment you have gained from the discussion. Try to be specific about what it was that helped you understand something better. Again this can be done online if this suits you better.

The same logic informing how to grade for discussion participation holds true for how to grade for critical thinking. Students need to understand how the reward system for the course works, and how engaging in critical thinking is the practice that is most important.

Here are some ways this can happen:

In discussion groups—Students can be assessed by the extent to which they clarify their own, and others', assumptions, by the number of different interpretations or explanations of a phenomenon they generate or by the way they identify causal, paradigmatic, or prescriptive assumptions.

In lectures—Students can receive evaluation on their evolving critical thinking with the use of clickers or poll questions. Lecturers can pose a problem or outline an explanation for something, and then ask a question about the assumptions informing the solution to the problem or the assumptions framing the explanation. Students regularly vote on which assumptions offered in a poll are the most correct and then the whole spread of results can be shown to the class. The lecturer can then lead a whole class discussion—or ask students to form into small groups and hold their own discussions—on why certain assumptions were chosen more frequently than others.

This is a wonderful way for lecturers to build in elements of critical thinking, even with groups of many hundreds. Alternatively, the lecturer can pose a problem and then ask students to discuss possible solutions in buzz groups, ending with them writing these electronically on Whiteboard. Since Whiteboard submissions are anonymous, lecturers can point out errors in thinking without humiliating individual students.

In small group work—Directions can be given to small groups that clarify critical thinking as the purpose. One direction is to ask students to consider a problem and generate as many possible responses to the problem as they can. In reporting out their small group work, students attach an assumptions inventory to their responses that identifies causal, prescriptive, and paradigmatic assumptions that lie behind the solutions they post. A very effective instruction is to tell small groups that their task is to generate questions about a topic. So instead of having to come up with an answer, groups post all the questions concerning a problem that have come up at their table.

But the most effective way to build a focus on critical thinking throughout a course is to make sure that the language of critical thinking is deliberately embedded into every course unit and course assignment.

Integrating Critical Thinking into Specific Course Assignments

In this section I deal with what happens when the rubber really hits the road; that is, when instructors start to embed a specific request for critical thinking in all their assignments and students start to realize this will be one of the things expected of them across their college years. There are limits to how complex this can be at the beginning of a program—that depends primarily on the knowledge of the subject the student brings to the course. It's often hard for students to think critically about something that they are encountering for the first time. For students who are novices, nonmajors, or who are encountering material for the first time, it is harder to involve them in identifying and checking their own assumptions about a subject. But even introductory courses can include assignments that get students into the habit of looking for assumptions.

Introducing Critical Thinking in the Syllabus

At the start of the semester there should be a clear statement of critical thinking contained in the syllabus that communicates to students just what they will be expected to do throughout the course. We have reviewed the elements that need to be in these statements in different places in this book, mostly arguing that critical thinking involves (1) identifying the assumptions that frame our thinking and determine our actions, (2) checking out the degree to which these assumptions are accurate and valid, (3) looking at our ideas and actions from several different perspectives, and (4) on the basis of all this, taking informed actions. Along with this definition should be an example drawn from the content that the course is covering that shows the reader what critical thinking looks like when it's applied to some aspect of the course's content.

Creating Connections to Critical Thinking

Every course unit should explain its scope and objectives wherever possible by referencing critical thinking. Even if the module is one where there is a heavy diet of information transmission from the teacher to the student, it is still possible to point out that this content-heavy immersion is necessary if the student is to think critically about this material at a later point in her studies. Of course, if the course is one where critical thinking is being directly taught and applied, then each module needs to begin by stating explicitly that this is the case.

As students begin work on the module, two elements need to be evident early on. First, the instructor should provide a parallel example of how critical thinking can be applied to material that is not the unit studied, but that is not too far away from it either. This will help situate critical thinking in the unit being studied, without providing a template that students can copy and simply drop into their work. Second, the teacher should give at least one example of how she's applied critical thinking to similar material in the past. This will underscore its relevance to the unit of study and also model the teacher's own commitment to the process.

Creating Critical Thinking Assignments

When the specific assignment focus is on the student's practice of critical thinking, the assignment instructions should ask students some of the following questions . . .

- Which causal, prescriptive, or paradigmatic assumptions are evident in a piece of text, a proof or theorem, an explanation of a phenomenon, or in the generation of a new concept or hypotheses?

- What are the causal, prescriptive, or paradigmatic assumptions you bring to your analysis of a topic?

- What are the sources of evidence or authority that you take most seriously, and what are the reasons for this?

- Of the different resources used for the completion of the assignment—online searching, reading textbooks, studying other students' notes, listening to information delivered in lectures, information contained in the course packet, conversations with peers, and so forth— which yielded the most helpful information in working through the assignment, and why do you think this was the case?

- What are the real-world applications of the knowledge or skill you've just learned? How can this knowledge or skill help you deal with specific situations and problems you face outside the classroom?

- What is the Deliberate Error contained in the unit? (This is where the teacher deliberately inserts an error into each unit, exercise, or module.) Why do think this was the error? What was it about the error that brought it to your attention?

Embedding Critical Thinking Audits into Specific Assignments

In Chapter Three I mentioned how helpful it is for students when they see us providing regular critical thinking audits in lectures and seminars. A Critical Thinking Audit is a brief pause in which the teacher—or in this case, the student—provides a brief snapshot of where she is in her thinking as she is working through an exercise, module, or even a whole course. Here are examples of six different types of audits:

Audit A

Which of the assumptions covered so far are primarily causal?

Which of the assumptions covered so far are primarily prescriptive?

Which of the assumptions covered so far are primarily paradigmatic?

Audit B

Who is benefitting from this work?

Who is being harmed by this work?

How is power being exercised in this area?

Audit C

Where is further study needed?

Which evidence is most open to question?

Which assumptions could not be checked adequately?

Audit D

What assumptions have been confirmed?

What assumptions have been challenged?

What new assumptions have been discovered?

Audit E

What evidence was most accessible?

What evidence was most accurate?

How did the learning "fit" the real world?

Audit F

Whose voices are missing from this work?

What different explanations or interpretations are possible for this work?

What ethical questions are raised for you about the work?

You can write Critical Thinking Audits as (1) unit audits dealing with one particular chunk of knowledge, (2) as midcourse audits allowing you to see where students are in their understanding of the material halfway through a semester, or (3) as course completion audits where students look back at the territory they've just covered. What these audits look like will obviously vary from course to course, subject to subject, but they always focus on the same core competencies: are students looking for assumptions and are they making judgments about the validity and accuracy of the evidence for these assumptions?

Maximizing the Capstone Experience

Many departments, schools, colleges, and universities plan their four-year program with the idea that a *Capstone Experience* will be the final intellectual effort, the piece of work that accomplishes two things: it allows the student to see how far they've come since their Freshman Days, and it offers them the chance to do intellectual work at the highest possible level after four years of intensive study. To me, making the Capstone Experience or the Capstone Project a piece of work focused explicitly on applying critical thinking is a no-brainer. The Capstone Project could ask students to look at an area they were familiar with through a whole new intellectual paradigm. Or students could make a deliberate attempt to ferret out all the unacknowledged assumptions that had influenced them over their four years. They could write an intellectual biography of how they changed their thinking on a subject and what kinds of causal, prescriptive, or paradigmatic assumptions were challenged and confirmed along the way. However it's done, making critical thinking the central element of a capstone would close the circle nicely.

Summary

In this chapter I have tried to show how critical thinking as a learning process can be integrated across the whole college experience, beginning with a Freshman Seminar and ending with a Capstone Experience. Given that so many colleges and universities proclaim their fealty to this kind of thinking, it would not take much to ensure this commitment was embedded into every phase of a student's academic studies. This will not always be easy, primarily because of the different intellectual traditions informing critical thinking I outlined in Chapter Two. But people from different disciplinary backgrounds share a desire to ferret out assumptions, a willingness to generate multiple explanations for topics, and a focus on assessing the accuracy and validity of evidence. These make a college's comprehensive commitment to critical thinking across the disciplines completely feasible.

In the next chapter we turn our attention to how this kind of learning can be situated in a group discussion. What does a critical discussion look like? How can students' participation in such a discussion be assessed? What discussion processes foster critical thinking? And what might be the kinds of questions raised in critical discussion?

8

Making Discussions Critical

In Chapter Three I reported that students say that they learn critical thinking best when it happens in groups. It seems that it is much easier to discover assumptions and contemplate alternative perspectives when this is done with a group of peers who are all grappling with the same material. If critical thinking is understood as a social learning process, then it is not surprising to find that many teachers use group work, and particularly discussion, to teach it. After all, don't discussion group members call each other to account, ask for evidence, and generate multiple viewpoints on an issue?

There's no doubt that in some discussions this does happen. But just having people talking in a group bears no necessary correlation to critical thinking. In fact, you could argue that the converse happens; that the existence of groupthink quickly steers a group down the path of one wrong-headed analysis. Given the number of conversation groups I've been involved in, where the lack of any critical standards for judging the merits of particular contributions meant that lies, half-truths, stereotypes, and unwarranted generalizations went unchallenged, it is clear that just having a discussion doesn't mean critical thinking is happening.

The problem of uncontrolled, uncritical, discussion groups was written about eloquently (some would say objectionably) almost half a century ago by Herbert Marcuse (1965). Marcuse argued that a misunderstanding of democracy had led to discussion leaders overemphasizing the fact that everyone's voice had value. In the intent to honor and respect each learner's voice, discussion leaders had to act as if each person's contribution carried equal weight to everyone else's. All a student needed to say was "this is my experience" and it was very difficult for a teacher to probe this without appearing intrusive and somehow dismissing the person's life experiences. A discussion leader's concern to dignify each student's personhood could easily result in a refusal to point out the ideologically skewed nature of particular contributions, let alone saying someone is wrong.

In Marcuse's view, the ideology of democratic tolerance in discussion groups meant that "the stupid opinion is treated with the same respect as the intelligent one, the misinformed may talk as long as the informed, and propaganda rides along with falsehood. This pure tolerance of sense and nonsense is justified by the democratic argument that nobody, neither group nor individual, is in possession of the truth and capable of defining what is right and wrong, good and bad" (1965, p. 94). So even if a student is spewing racist stereotypes the instructor would feel reluctant to challenge that directly, instead saying something mealy-mouthed like there are always multiple viewpoints on any issue.

I well remember a session I ran where a student of color disclosed an example of racism and a White student tried to talk the student of color out of it, saying it was unintentional, not meant to be exclusionary. My insistence that we institute a ground rule that says that White students accept as true and valid any experiences of racism recounted by students of color (an application of the Methodological Belief technique that Stephen Preskill and I discuss in our book *Discussion as a Way of Teaching*, 2005) was met by the White student telling me that the classroom was now not a safe space anymore, so I could forget about any further contributions from this person.

What Does a Critical Discussion Look Like?

There are different ways to answer this question, some focusing on the content discussed, some on the processes being followed. Where the focus is on the critical analysis of content, the minimum conditions for critical discussion are as follows:

- A prime focus is on members identifying assumptions—their own, their peers', the teacher's, and the text's. Some of these will be implicit, some explicit. Some will be causal, some prescriptive, and some paradigmatic. Some will focus on power dynamics, some on hegemony.

- Once assumptions have been identified the discussion will then focus on the degree to which these assumptions are accurate and valid.

- The discussion will also attempt to fix the contextual validity of an assumption—situations in which it is more, or less, appropriate.

- Whenever a statement is made that generalizes beyond one person's experience, the group members focus on uncovering the evidence for that generalization.

- The group keeps a record of the links in an inferential chain that leads to a conclusion that several in the group agree with.

- Group members seek constantly to generate as many different perspectives as possible on the issue at hand, with no one being shut down prematurely.

- Members will constantly be on the alert for groupthink and will be suspicious of any early consensus that emerges.

Where the focus for critical discussion is on the conversational processes to be followed—the ways that people should try to structure their talk—the intent is to have formats that allow the widest array of voices heard, provide regular opportunities for all to contribute, and build in reflective pauses and interludes necessary for good critical thought. Hence, criteria for judging whether or not discussion is conducive to critical thinking might be the following:

- Structures are in place to ensure that everyone in the group is regularly given the floor to make a contribution, whether or not they're trying to get into the conversation.

- Time limits or some other method is instituted to prevent any one person, or group of people, dominating the conversation.

- No one feels the need to respond immediately to another person's contribution. So the group is comfortable with periods of reflective silence that are recognized as integral to critical thought.

- Group members constantly try to seek out similarities and differences between different contributions and to point out connections.

- Power constantly moves around the group. No one person or clique ever moves automatically center stage to take control of the conversation.

- Every time a new idea or concept is added to the conversation, the group strives to supply examples that illustrate its relevance.

- Group members regard active listening to each other as the most important part of good communication.

Discussion Exercises to Foster Critical Thinking

In this section I provide a selection of exercises that foster the kinds of behaviors outlined above. Some of these focus more on the critical analysis of content, others on creating space for the greatest diversity of voices to be heard. Ideally, of course, process and content are both addressed to some degree in each of these exercises.

Circle of Voices

This is one of my most favorite discussion protocols, and one I use a great deal at the beginning of a group's time together. It has two basic purposes. The first is to give everyone a chance to contribute on a topic before any premature consensus emerges. The second is to teach the importance of active listening so that a discussion can develop organically, constantly looping back to, building on, and extending earlier contributions.

Participants form into groups of five and a question for discussion is announced. Groups are allowed up to three minutes silent time to organize their thoughts and responses to the question. During this time they think about what they want to say on the topic once the circle of voices begins. This silent preparatory time is crucial to this and to so many other discussions intended to provoke critical thinking. Yet the dominant classroom practice of discussion is to announce a question and then ask for immediate responses. If people are to do something as complex as try to uncover assumptions and generate new perspectives they need regular periods of quiet processing, or contemplative, time.

After this silent period the discussion opens with the first round of conversation. Each person has the floor for up to a minute to say whatever it is they wish to say regarding their response to the question posed. During the time each person is speaking no one else is allowed to interrupt. This first round is really a series of uninterrupted mini-monologues, which seems a strange thing to do as part of a discussion. But it is crucial for the second part of the exercise.

After everyone has had the chance—uninterruptedly—to say their piece, then the discussion opens out into a more free flowing format. As this happens a second ground rule comes into effect. Participants are only allowed to talk about another person's ideas that have already been shared in the opening series of mini-monologues. People cannot jump into the conversation by expanding on their own ideas; they can only talk about their reactions to what someone else has said. The only exception to this ground rule is if someone else asks a student directly to expand on her ideas.

An important benefit of using the circle of voices at the start of a discussion is that it prevents the development early on of a pecking order of contributors. Introverted, shy members, those whose experience has taught them to mistrust academe, or those who view discussion as another thinly veiled opportunity for teachers to oppress or offend, will often stay silent at the beginning of a course. The longer this silence endures, the harder it is for these individuals to speak out. By way of contrast, in the circle of voices everyone's voice is heard at least once at the start of the session.

Circular Response

The Circular Response exercise was developed in the 1930s by the adult educator Eduard Lindeman to help community groups prioritize their concerns and settle on a manageable agenda. Like the Circle of Voices its intent is to democratize discussion participation, promote continuity, and give people some experience of the effort required in respectful listening. In this process participants sit in a circle so that everyone can see each other. The optimal size for this exercise is 8–12 participants.

Like Circle of Voices, the process has two rounds of conversation. The first round begins with each person in turn taking up to a minute to talk about an issue or question that the group has agreed to discuss. As with *Circle of Voices*, when someone is speaking in this first round there are no interruptions allowed. Once the first person has spoken, the person to the speaker's left speaks for up to a minute. However, the second speaker is not free to say anything she wants. She must incorporate into her remarks some reference to the preceding speaker's comments and then use this as a springboard for her own contribution. This doesn't have to be an agreement—it can be an expression of dissent from the previous opinion. The important thing is that the first speaker's comments are the prompt for whatever the second speaker says. This process moves around the circle with every speaker responding to the previous speaker's comments. The process ends where it started— with the opening speaker. Only this time the opening speaker is responding to the comments of the person who spoke before her. When this first round of conversation is over then the group moves into open conversation with no more ground rules. Questions can be asked about opening contributions, clarifications sought or offered, new ideas introduced.

Whenever I have used this exercise I invariably observe that in the first round of conversation heads lean in as each person sees how their contribution to the discussion is responded to. This is really an online threaded discussion happening synchronously in a face-to-face classroom. Unlike an online classroom, however, you don't need to wait for hours or days to see what someone will do with your comment. Circular Response is not an introductory discussion exercise in my opinion. There is often high anxiety around the prospect of having to speak in a way that responds immediately to another's contribution. To help ease this anxiety I always say that speakers can take a few moments to think about their response; they don't have to spring straight into speech after the previous speaker has stopped talking. I also make it clear that it is fine to say that you can't think of a response to the previous speaker's comments; but if you do this then you need to say why you're having difficulty making a connection. Is it because you have no experience that fits the previous speaker's? Are you unfamiliar with the language or terminology used? Do you find some of the argument hard to follow?

Chalk Talk

This exercise was introduced to me by Steven Rippe, a student in an Organizational Development class I taught at the University of St. Thomas. He, in turn, learned it from Hilton Smith (Smith, 2009) of The Foxfire Fund. Chalk Talk is a silent and visual way to engage in discussion without speaking. It takes as long as it takes and it's over when it's over. I've used it mostly in 10-minute bursts as a reflective prep for spoken conversation. It can also be a good way to unearth the concerns of a wide range of organizational members before building agendas for change. Here's how it works:

1. The leader writes a question in a circle in the center of the board—for example, "What are the assumptions behind Brookfield's model of critical thinking?" She places several sticks of chalk by the board.

2. She then explains this is a silent activity and that when people are ready they should write a response to the question on the board. They are also free to write responses to what others have written, pose questions about comments already posted, answer questions posted, draw lines between responses on different parts of the board that seem to connect, or between startlingly different responses to the same question, and so on.

3. Whenever they feel ready people get up and write something in response to the original question or to subsequent comments that are posted. Sometimes there are long silences or pauses between postings.

4. The facilitator also participates by drawing lines connecting comments that seem similar or contrasting, writing questions about a comment, by adding her own thoughts, and so on.

5. When a suitably long silence ensues the facilitator asks if people are done. If the activity is over then the class moves into speech about the postings on the board.

I like Chalk Talk for several reasons. One is that it has never badly misfired! Another is that it always produces contributions from far more people than would have been offered had I thrown the question out to the whole class and asked for comments. Often well over half the group post something in a 10-minute *Chalk Talk* session, compared to the 10% of students who would have dominated a whole-class discussion. It also honors silence and allows introverts to order their thoughts before posting. Of course, those same introverts may feel inhibited about writing something while everyone is watching. But since in *Chalk Talk* there are usually several people up at the board writing simultaneously, this is not too much of a drawback.

Spot the Error

Here the teacher tells students that at some point in the discussion she will deliberately make a contribution that she knows to be false. This could be something she says that is a factual error or something that displays a conceptual misunderstanding. It could be agreeing with a false argument made by a participant, a comment where something is asserted as fact with no basis in evidence, an attribution to the text that is unjustified, even something as simple as giving the wrong author's name to a particular book. Toward the end of the class students are given 30 seconds to write (anonymously!) what they think the mistake was on a piece of paper. These are then passed to the front, shuffled, and handed to the teacher. The teacher reads a selection of these out and discloses what the error was. She also has the chance to comment on other errors students thought they detected. As technology becomes cheaper students will soon be able to post their suggestions anonymously on a classroom electronic whiteboard where everyone can see their comments.

Structured Silence

Earlier in the chapter I argued that periods of quiet contemplation were an integral part of any group process focused on uncovering and checking assumptions, or considering alternative perspectives. One of the ways to make this silence a regular part of the classroom rhythm is to plan for periods of Structured Silence.

Every 15 to 20 minutes stop the discussion and call for a period of intentional silence of maybe two to three minutes. This is a reflective pause when discussion participants are asked to think quietly about *one* of the following questions (you choose which one depending on where the discussion has gone at that session):

- What was the most important point made in the last 15 minutes?

- What was the most puzzling or confusing point made in the last 15 minutes?

- What question do we most need to address in the next period of our discussion?

- What new perspective or interpretation was suggested for you in the last 15 minutes?

- What assumptions that you hold about this topic were confirmed for you in the last 15 minutes? Why was this?

- What assumptions that you hold about this topic were challenged for you in the last 15 minutes? Why was this?

Students make notes in response to the question on 3 × 5 cards you provide. When they've finished the cards are handed to the front, shuffled, and you (or students you choose randomly) read out several of the cards. This helps structure the next 15-minute chunk of discussion, and also gives you a sense of what meanings students are creating about the current discussion. Again, the increasing access to technology will mean this will soon be available in many classrooms via a class electronic whiteboard on which students can post anonymously.

Inferential Ladder

When the speech of a discussion can be slowed down group members can start to identify the Inferential Ladder they are building and climbing. An Inferential Ladder is the term commonly used to describe the steps of reasoning that lead to action. As generally articulated in North America, the first step—the first rung on the ladder—is our perceptions of the world, everything we see happening around us that hits our five senses. The second step is the selection and highlighting of certain bits of all this random and overwhelming sensuous information. We choose to focus on particular pieces of the world "out there" because we can't process it all, and we give meaning to the information we select. On the basis of the information selected as important, we construct assumptions. These assumptions then help us form conclusions and develop strong beliefs. The final rung of the ladder we construct is the action we take based on these beliefs.

Although the term is often attributed in the United States to the work of Chris Argyris (Argyris, 2010), and to Peter Senge's adaptation of it (Senge, 2006), I was aware of it as an undergraduate in England in the 1960s, probably because of the post–World War II work of the English archeologist Christopher Hawkes (Evans 1998). I understood it then to be more as the construction of a series of assumptions, each one building on the other, that ends in an action. It is like constructing a ladder in which the first rung—the foundational or paradigmatic assumption if you like— determines the building of the second rung (perhaps a prescriptive assumption), which, in turn, determines the building of the third rung (maybe a causal assumption). The causal assumption seems to be determining the action, but it is really traceable back to the paradigmatic assumption, the first rung on the ladder. If any of the rungs in the ladder are faulty, sooner or later it will break, the whole chain of reasoning will collapse, and the action based on it will fail.

In class I draw a ladder on the board, or on newsprint, comprising four rungs. As described above, the bottom rung is labeled *paradigmatic*, the second labeled *prescriptive*, the third labeled *causal*, and the top labeled *action*. At the start of the discussion I tell students that if any of them hears a paradigmatic, prescriptive or causal assumption either expressed explicitly or embedded implicitly within the conversation, that they should get up and write it next to the rung of the ladder concerned. The discussion doesn't stop when this happens, and students are constantly getting up and down to add their particular contribution. At first students find this a little weird (after all you don't usually get up in the middle of a discussion to write something on the board) but after a few times it become familiar and routine. As hand held devices and electronic whiteboards become common, students will be able to do this while sitting down.

Let me give an example in Table 8.1. Suppose I'm at a conference and I'm running a session in which readers of this very book (or Kindle) you now hold in your hand have met to discuss with me the topic "What's the best way to teach students to think critically?" As we talk I can imagine people getting up and down to write any number of responses in the boxes below. I've tried to generate some that might emerge and entered them by the relevant rung of the ladder.

Now this is a pretty sophisticated example of an Inferential Ladder but I use it because all readers of this book will be able

Table 8.1 The Best Way to Teach Students to Think Critically

Top Rung: **Action**	The teacher attempts to model every critical thinking activity before she asks students to do this
	Teacher evaluations and performance appraisals focus on how well teachers develop critical thinking in students
	Discussion and group learning formats are the preferred method for teaching critical thinking
	Student assessment approaches focus on the demonstration of critical thinking skills
	Curricula and programs are carefully structured to introduce critical thinking to students over a period of time and through increasingly complex exercises
	Courses are team taught so faculty can model critical dialogue
Third Rung: **Causal**	Students learn critical thinking by seeing teachers model it in front of them
	Critical thinking needs to be sequenced, beginning with exercises that are far away from a student's experience, but that move gradually closer and closer to it
	Social, group, and discussion learning formats work best for critical thinking because students serve as critical mirrors for each other
	Social, group, and discussion learning formats work best for teaching critical thinking because students bring different interpretations and perspectives to the table

(Continued)

Table 8.1 (Continued)

Second Rung: Prescriptive	The best teachers model criticality
	The best courses develop critical thinking
	The best students are those who are adept at critical thinking
	A good program should put critical thinking as its top learning objective
	Decisions informed by critical thinking are better than those taken instinctively
	Assessing critical thinking should be a teacher's, or program's, top priority
Bottom Rung: Paradigmatic	Critical thinking can be taught
	Critical thinking is essentially the same process across disciplines
	Critical thinking is the most important intellectual capacity students can develop
	Everyone can learn to think critically
	Thinking critically is an excellent preparation for life

immediately to understand how the ladder works (there's a causal assumption right there!).

At a suitable point toward the end of the discussion the leader calls a halt to the conversation and the focus turns to the ladder that's on the board. Students and teacher try to trace connections between the assumptions on different rungs. Particular attention is paid to the bottom rung and the question is raised, What's the evidence for each paradigmatic assumption? At this point, students start to see the power of paradigmatic assumptions—of how so much flows from them, and of how often they are unsupported by any evidence, other than the evidence of authority. In other words, they are true because someone deemed authoritative (an "expert" on critical thinking like me, for example!) has declared them to be true.

The Appreciative Pause

Thinking critically in discussion—with all the performance anxiety students feel about speaking extemporaneously, thinking on their feet, having to sound smart, and so on—is emotionally exhausting as well as intellectually demanding. This is why the last activity I mention—The Appreciative Pause—is so necessary.

One of the least practiced behaviors in discussion is to show appreciation for how someone has contributed to our learning. The Appreciative Pause is a technique that focuses deliberately on this behavior. In discussions where critical thinking is the focus, it is particularly important that there be regular opportunities for students to show each other how peer feedback has helped them identify and check assumptions, and generate multiple perspectives. After all, if critical thinking is a social learning process in which peers are the most necessary ingredients, and if we can't become aware of our own assumptions without the help of peers, then it makes sense to keep your peers committed to the process by letting them know how their contributions have helped your learning.

The Appreciative Pause works as follows. At least once in every discussion the instructor calls for a pause of a minute or so. During this time the only comments allowed are from participants who acknowledge how something that someone else said in the discussion (*not* the instructor) has contributed to their learning. Appreciations are often given for

- A question that was asked that suggested a whole new line of thinking

- A comment that clarified something that until then was confusing

- A comment that opened up a whole new line of thinking

- A comment that helped identify an assumption

- A comment that provided helpful evidence

- A comment that identified a gap in reasoning that needed to be addressed

- A new idea that is intriguing and had not been considered before

- A comment showing the connection between two other ideas or contributions when that connection hadn't been clear

- An example that was provided that helped increase understanding of a difficult concept

This can easily be done online by establishing an Appreciation Board, where students only post comments outlining how their peers have helped them grapple with critical thinking. Comments would accumulate over time to give a permanent record of the things peers have done that have been particularly appreciated. This can be reproduced for future courses to let new students see the importance of peer support and critique, and it can also prompt some new exercises that teachers can experiment in using.

The Post-It Appreciation

A variant on this I have experimented with is the Post-It Appreciation. This is done when participants work in synchronous, face-to-face groups to come up with responses to a problem or question. After a suitable time each group posts a record of its discussion, or a list of its suggestions. Post-It pads are distributed around the room next to each posting. Students are told to wander around the room and when they see a suggestion a group has made that they appreciate in some way, they write their appreciation of it on a Post-It note and place the note right by the comment on the newsprint they've found helpful. Perhaps they think the suggestion fits well with a problem they're confronting, or maybe it raises some important new information or provides a different, but helpful, perspective on the issue.

After a few minutes clusters of Post-Its become discernible at different points on the postings. This gives an immediate visual record of which elements of the postings generated the most comments. Group members read out the Post-It notes to the whole group and these themes are then discussed further with the whole group.

Critical Questioning Approaches

As we have seen throughout this book so far, asking questions is at the heart of critical thinking. In fact, the basic protocol introduced in Chapter One can easily be stated as four questions applied across disciplines and situations:

- What assumptions do we hold about the topic or situation under examination (particularly regarding what counts as legitimate knowledge)?

- How can we check these assumptions out for accuracy and validity?

- What alternative perspectives, explanations, or interpretations can we bring to bear on this topic or situation?

- What action should we take informed by our critical analysis?

These questions, or some variant of them, are embedded in many of the exercises and approaches outlined in the previous chapter. But one obvious place for practicing critical questioning that we have not addressed up to now is in classroom discussions. The kinds of questions we ask frame in a very significant way the answers we get. Closed questions of a Yes/No, Right/Wrong nature produce closed responses. Open questions yield a wide array of contributions. Open questions don't need to be deliberately vague or ethereal. When David Hagstrom, author of *From Outrageous to Inspired* (2004), and then principal at Denali Elementary School in Fairbanks, Alaska, spontaneously asked two parents and two teachers, "What do you want for your children at this school?" he didn't really expect the responses to lead to a complete reconceptualizing of the school's mission. As Hagstrom himself recounts, asking this one question opened the floodgates and provoked many additional questions. The parents replied simply that they wanted their children to be explorers and discoverers in school in the same ways that they were explorers and discoverers outside of school. When Hagstrom asked his second question, "How do we make this happen?" there was no turning back.

Learning to ask critical questions is not an interrogatory project but a way of inviting people to wonder. Wondering, of course, can then lead to all kinds of alternative possibilities being envisioned. A seemingly simple question like the one Hagstrom asked helps us identify what really matters to us as well as helping us clarify directions we wish to take. Why are we doing things this way? What might it look like to do things differently? What have we always wanted for this intellectual, educational, or political community? How could we make that happen? What are we trying to achieve? These are the first order questions that frame how we work. Who are we? What do we want to be remembered for? What do we stand for? What are our commitments? What are we becoming? These questions help us gauge how closely our actions and values are aligned.

Asking the questions above can be an unsettling, even rebellious act. It disturbs both those being asked (particularly if they're comfortable with the way things are) and those in power (who would rather people did not ask such questions). The edgy, daring side of questioning can also be an antidote to routine, to convention, to automatically pursuing more of the same. Questioning is also a practice that embodies respect. It demonstrates that we care enough about what others are thinking by trying to find this out through our questions. Indeed, one of the indicators of a good discussion is the extent to which participants themselves learn to practice the art of critical questioning.

Early on in any course or program where classroom discussion is intended to be a crucible for critical thinking students need to learn that there are a few simple categories of questions to bear in mind. Although the potential range of questions that can be asked in a discussion is limitless, three types of critically oriented questions are fairly common: questions to identify assumptions, questions about evidence for assumptions, and questions that generate multiple perspectives.

Opening Questions to Identify Assumptions

Since assumption hunting is at the core of critical thinking, students need to get into the habit of asking questions that identify assumptions. Usually asking a direct "What assumptions are you operating under here?" sort of question doesn't get you very far. It is vague, yet intimidating, at the same time. Vagueness and intimidation is a hard double-whammy to pull off, but a question like that will do it! Such a question is entirely legitimate, of course, but here (as with so many things in teaching, and in life) timing is all. When students have warmed up by dealing with less overt questions about their assumptions they are better equipped to answer such a direct approach.

When asking opening questions designed to identify assumptions it is best to ask students to focus on possible assumptions that the researchers, scholars, or practitioners they are studying are making, rather than focusing initially on assumptions the students themselves hold. As Chapter Three pointed out, critical thinking is learned incrementally, and students warm up for the rigor of identifying their own assumptions by first getting in the habit of focusing on those of others.

So what questions might we substitute when we're trying to start the process of getting students to be aware of their assumption? Some examples are

- Is one of the assumptions the author is operating under that . . . ? (Here providing one concrete assumption gives the student something to hold on to, to react to; it has a reassuring specificity.)

- When I've faced similar problems I've sometimes assumed that. . . . Does that assumption seem to fit here? (Again, this question gives the student something specific to respond to, rather than being confronted with an intimidating vagueness.)

- What cause and effect relationships do you see in this part of the study? (This focuses the student on causal assumptions, which are the easiest for students to grasp initially.)

- It seems that three possible assumptions behind this research/experiment might be. . . . Which of them seems most likely to you? (Like a multi-choice test, the request to choose between alternatives suggested has a concreteness to it that is reassuring. The critical assessment comes in the follow-up discussion about why students chose assumption [a], [b], or [c].)

- What's the most accurate assumption you find in this work? (One of the blocks to critical thinking is that students believe it always involves seizing on an error, or mistake. This question lets them know critical thinking is a process of appraisal, and that often it involves affirming what's accurate and well grounded about a piece of work.)

- What do you think is the most explicit assumption the author/researcher is making here? (Often starting with the idea of explicit assumptions—ones the author is open about and makes public—is helpful for students. They realize that they don't always have to uncover something that's hidden.)

- What word, phrase, or concept the author uses do you think indicates an assumption she holds? (Sometimes focusing on finding just a word or short phrase is a good entry into discovering assumptions.)

Opening Questions About Evidence

The obvious follow-up to questions that focus on identifying assumptions is to ask questions designed to uncover the evidence informing the assumptions already identified. Students need to learn early on that identifying assumptions is just the start of critical thinking, and that checking their accuracy and validity is when critical analysis really takes off. Again, the framing of these questions needs to communicate that checking is not just the application of the principle of falsifiability discussed in Chapter Two, not just focusing on what's wrong, omitted, misconceived, or biased. Critical questions also ask what's well grounded, what accurate inferences are being made, what has been well explained, and so on.

Some examples of questions that focus students on uncovering and assessing evidence are

- Pick a conclusion the author/researcher seems to have made. What's the most convincing piece of evidence provided to support this conclusion? (This gets students in the habit of starting with the conclusions section and then tracing back the flow of reasoning or research provided.)

- If you have to pick one piece of evidence in this study that you find most persuasive or convincing, what would that be? (Asking for just one piece of evidence sometimes focuses the discussion for students in a helpful way.)

- If you have to pick one piece of evidence in this study that you find least persuasive or convincing, what would that be? (This is the obvious counterpart to the question just posed above.)

- Of the arguments made or conclusions drawn, which one is most clearly grounded in evidence the author provides? (Again, this focuses on choosing just one piece of a text, rather than going straight to a more challenging meta-analysis.)

- If you were trying to convince a skeptic of the validity of this research, what evidence would you select from the study? (This provides practice for the student at making hypothetical leaps, trying to understand the material as the author understands and presents it.)

Opening Questions to Generate Multiple Perspectives

Open-ended questions, especially those beginning with why and how, are more likely to provoke students' thinking and problem-solving abilities and make the fullest use of discussion's potential for expanding intellectual and emotional horizons. Of course, using open questions obliges the facilitator to keep the discussion genuinely unrestricted. It is neither fair nor appropriate to ask an open-ended question and then to expect participants to furnish a predetermined or preferred response.

In critical thinking terms the purpose of open-ended questions is to help generate as many different understandings, interpretations, or explanations as possible. Of the three categories of critical questions discussed, these are the ones that have the least predictable results in a discussion. Their openness can unleash a storm of creativity or stop people solidly in their tracks. Consequently, they should be the last of the categories of questioning to introduce into the discussion. To respond well to an open-ended question students need to feel comfortable enough with their understanding of the material that they are not thrown by a question that deliberately puts them off center.

- Lets look at this topic/problem and start with a different premise, such as. . . . What would the topic/problem look like if this is the starting point for our analysis? (Here the teacher jump-starts the process by suggesting a switch in how the topic is framed and then invites students to take this new framing wherever it seems to go.)

- Instead of looking at this from the author's viewpoint, how do you think author X or Y would approach this? (Again, offering a concrete beginning point, such as how a different theorist or researcher would treat the problem, gives students experience of looking at things differently, yet keeps them reassuringly tied to a specific viewpoint.)

- Try to imagine you've never read any previous work on this topic. Where would your instinct tell you to start? (A much more difficult question to answer.)

- Let's try to think of the most unlikely or off-the-wall ways of understanding this, the weirder the better! What would they be? (Here you're giving permission for a variation of brainstorming. Students sometimes respond well to the invitation to weirdness, particularly if you begin by making a strange initial suggestion yourself!)

- Whose perspective is missing in this work and what would it look like if it was included? (Here you ask students directly to think about research perspectives

they have studied and speculate what difference
including them would make.)

- What would happen if different data were included in
this research? (A variant of the question above.)

- What radically different examples could you give of
this concept? How would these different examples take
our analysis in a different direction? (Sometimes the
specificity of asking for an illustrative example helps
get students into a more creative vein of thought.)

- Is there an idea or factor that you think has been
deliberately excluded here? Why do you think that's
happened? (This familiarizes students with the idea
that intellectual work always represents someone's
point of view or agenda, and that academic publishing
has gatekeepers who keep a discipline's regime of truth,
discussed in Chapter Two, intact.)

- What are some different options available that X could
have explored in solving this problem? (Here you just
throw out a free-for-all invitation to think of multiple
options the author could have considered.)

- What questions or issues have been raised for us today?
(This teaches students that critical discussion always
generates new lines of analysis. It can also be a good
set-up for the next class session.)

- What remains unresolved or contentious about this
issue? (A variant on the question above.)

Direct Questions Addressed to Students

Once students are used to discussing the sorts of questions posed
in the three categories above, where the focus is on someone else's
assumptions, work, or reasoning, then the ground is laid for ques-

tions that address the student's own thinking. Now teachers are better placed to ask students potentially intimidating questions such as

- What's the assumption you're making that you're least confident about?

- What's the assumption you're making that you're most confident about?

- What's a causal/prescriptive/paradigmatic assumption you're making here?

- What's a good example of what you are talking about?

- What do you mean by that?

- Can you explain the term you just used?

- It seems that X is an explicit assumption you have. What do you think might be some implicit assumptions you hold?

- Can you tell us why you think your conclusion is accurate?

- How do you know that?

- What data is that claim based on?

- What does the author say that supports your argument?

- Where did you find that view expressed in the text?

- What evidence would you give to someone who doubted your interpretation?

- What's the piece of evidence you've got for your view that you feel most confident about?

- Can you put that another way?

- Why do you think that's true?

- Can you give a different illustration of your point?

- What do you think you're leaving out?

- What do you think X would say about your analysis?

- What do you think you might have missed?

- What's the most different way of presenting your argument you can come up with?

- What's the most off-the-wall illustration of your point you can imagine?

- Whose work or views might you have ignored?

Summary

In this chapter we've built on the insight offered by students in Chapter Three that critical thinking is best experienced as a social learning process in which peers are indispensible. Since discussion is probably the most social of all teaching approaches, it seems particularly suited to developing students' critical thinking skills. However, we have seen that critical discussion is not the same as having students talk to each other in a directionless way. Certain exercises and forms of questioning are much more fruitful in prompting critical thinking, than others. The focus needs to be kept on identifying assumptions, assessing evidence, determining ladders of inference, generating multiple perspectives, and the conditions underlying informed action. And discussion sessions need to be sequenced so that they begin with critical analyses and responses to work produced by others in the field, and then gradually come round to focus directly on students' own reasoning.

9

Misunderstandings, Challenges, and Risks

We are now at the penultimate chapter of the book, a time that seems ripe for reviewing some of the most frequent misunderstandings, challenges, and risks of critical thinking. This could have been done earlier, of course, but I wanted to lay out in the first eight chapters a basic protocol for critical thinking, an analysis of the different ways it's understood, and a review of how it's learned. I also wanted to take readers through a series of introductory and complex exercises for teaching it, and then through an understanding of how it's practiced in writing and in discussion. Now that an approach to teaching critical thinking has been fully explored, let's turn to some of the chief misunderstandings people have about what this process involves and how it's implemented.

Misunderstandings of Critical Thinking

Whenever I'm on a newly formed task force on critical thinking, or I'm trying to explain the idea to students for the first time, a number of misunderstandings of critical thinking typically emerge. First, people often have a knee-jerk reaction against it because they assume being critical is the same as tearing something down, belittling or demeaning someone, or finding fault. Second, there is the objection that thinking critically about everything (and it's usually framed that way, as a generic process exercised across different areas of life) leads to the paralysis of analysis. If we can always find fault or view something differently, so this argument goes, we never actually get round to doing anything concrete! Third, and to the other extreme, a lot of the work on criticality seems to follow a narrative of fundamental change. This narrative begins with the person thinking and acting uncritically, then having some sort of epiphany that leads her to change in very fundamental ways. People think that entering onto critical thinking will therefore always involve dramatic transformation. Fourth, problem solving and critical thinking are often collapsed as if they were one and the same process. This may sometimes be true, but problem solving is not always the same as critical thinking, and we need to know when problem solving is being done uncritically. Finally, there is sometimes the sense that critical thinking is a finite process that always ends with a clear outcome or resolution. Again, there are times this is the case. But more often than not, a critical analysis will raise more, and more complex, questions than the ones originally posed.

Critical Thinking Is Negative

As I alluded to in the discussion of critical reading in Chapter Six the term *critical* has a popular connotation of finding fault in a negative way. So, when someone asks, "Why do we always have to be so critical?" they are not posing a rhetorical question with an obvious answer ("because it helps us take more informed actions that are grounded in experience and assumptions that have been properly analyzed"). No, they are usually bemoaning what is seen as the nit-picking approach to life, in which someone is never satisfied and always has to find fault with everything. One of the hardest attitudinal shifts to get students to make is from misperceiving criticality as always finding fault, to understanding it as a process of appraisal, in which we recognize those of our actions that are well grounded, and those of our assumptions that are correct, just as much as we discover those actions that are taken only because of force of habit, or those assumptions that don't fit a situation.

When introducing the process of critical thinking it is often far better to start with elements of positive appraisal, so students can understand that this is an integral part of the process. As a teacher you can introduce autobiographical examples of times when the assumptions you held about students, or about how to teach critical thinking, were proved to be accurate. An early Scenario Analysis can focus on students proposing the most accurate assumptions held by the character in the scenario. When reporting out the Critical Incident Questionnaire (CIQ) it is crucial that the teacher spend plenty of time describing those assumptions she made that were borne out by students' experiences. So if a small group discussion has gone well, and it's clear this is because the teacher assumed that students would appreciate her giving clear ground rules that prevented anyone from dominating, this should be revealed. For many teachers, myself included, doing this smacks of self-aggrandizement. But if we want students to understand that positive appraisal is always in the critical mix, we need to begin by modeling this.

The other thing we need to do (and I've described in Chapter Seven how I've tried to do this) is to make sure that across all our classroom and assignment instructions, we always ask students to focus on what was confirmed, as much as by what was challenged, in their engagement with critical thinking. So along with asking which assumptions were confirmed, we ask students to tell us the sources of evidence or authority that students take most seriously, and what their reasons for this are. We also can ask which of the different resources students used in an assignment—online searching, reading textbooks, studying other students' notes, listening to information delivered in lectures, information contained in the course packet, conversations with peers—yielded the most helpful information in working through the assignment, and why they thought this was the case.

Critical Thinking Freezes Us from Taking Action

It is easy to see why this objection arises. In a culture in which people of action (it's no coincidence that we talk of action heroes) are often prized over people of thought, it's not surprising that reflective analysis or questioning is sometimes viewed as a suspicious waste of time. If you're the kind of person who keeps raising questions at meetings, and who always wants to look at the assumptions behind decisions, then you risk gaining a reputation as someone who diverts people from the real business at hand—getting things done. For someone who has no positional power and authority, one of the hardest organizational dynamics to negotiate is to raise questions about the assumptions informing key decisions in a way that appears helpful and productive rather than obstructive or nitpicking.

The paralysis of analysis phrase is a cliché because it's true. Because there is always something that we've missed in a situation, always a perspective we haven't considered or an assumption we haven't checked, there is sometimes a real temptation to put off doing anything until we've conducted another round of analysis or gathered additional information. I imagine most readers have lived through situations where forming a task force to review a problem is actually a substitute for doing something about it. You can put off dealing with a seemingly intractable problem for a long time by saying you always need to find out more information about it. As many doctoral dissertation writers know, you will never be able to locate and review every study that has ever been conducted that has relevance for your topic. But you can easily put off actually writing that final draft by saying there's still material you need to review.

As I tried to make clear in the first chapter, it cannot be stressed enough to students that the point of critical thinking is to help people take informed action. So we have to find a way to let students know that part of being critical is (1) understanding that decisions need to be taken, and choices made, when not every piece of information we would wish for is available, and (2) there's a real possibility that the choice or decision may subsequently be viewed as wrong, or may not have the consequences we intend it to have. This is where the tradition of American pragmatism discussed in Chapter Two comes in. One of pragmatism's chief contributions to an understanding of criticality is always being open to rethinking one's position, to trying to incorporate new information and understanding into an approach that is understood as always evolving. So, for example, I am convinced by experience and analysis that the critical theory perspective on life explains what I see around me better than any other theory. But at the same time, I don't believe everything every critical theorist says. And if an argument, experience, or piece of information challenges one of my understandings, I have to be ready to rethink it. As a teacher, students' comments over the years have convinced me that modeling is something I need to do in every situation. But what that looks like and how much of it is appropriate at a particular moment are always open questions.

When teaching critical thinking, then, we have to let students know that the informed actions we take in conjunction with critical thinking will not always be 100% correct or 100% predictable. We may get the context or the action wrong, we may have misunderstood some of the information, or we may have interpreted an experience wrongly. But it's a matter of percentages. A critically thought through action has a better chance of achieving the results intended for it, than an action taken arbitrarily. I apply the same perspective to teaching; if I'm going to say that an exercise or technique works only if it always has exactly the same results, and only if those results are always good, then nothing works! Let me say again—nothing works, if we judge workability by the criterion that it always has the same good outcomes. Every teaching act is a trade-off where you know that there are going to be some drawbacks or downsides to it but where you decide that overall the potential advantages outweigh the potential disadvantages. As with teaching, so with critical thinking.

Critical Thinking Leads to Fundamental Change

In many Critical Incident Questionnaires (CIQs) over the years, one of the most frequent comments students make concerns the way I imply that critical thinking involves a major transformative change. This usually happens because the examples I choose to illustrate critical thinking involve some sort of dramatic change. I did this deliberately at the beginning of the book by using the example of how critical thinking about my own depression helped me get professional help to deal with it. My causal assumption was that a personal narrative would draw you, the reader, into the text. I also wanted to link critical thinking to a very concrete experience that every reader probably would have been touched by.

Although my assumption that starting off with an example of dramatic change would be a good way to connect with a readership that has deliberately decided to consult a text on how to teach critical thinking, it doesn't necessarily carry over to a student audience that may not even know the term or have any understanding of what the process involves. If the first thing students hear is that critical thinking will lead to dramatic changes in their lives, this can be highly threatening. Students can quickly conclude that if they think critically this means they have to challenge—even give up—many of the assumptions they've lived their life by. This is an intimidating prospect, even for the most experienced of teachers. How much more keenly will new students feel this sense of threat?

So it's important to communicate early on that just because critical thinking is occurring does not mean that change inevitably ensues. One can think critically about something and come out of the experience with a greater understanding of, and commitment to, the assumptions one began with. For example, teachers are continually improvising, or acting intuitively, in the middle of an unexpected situation in class. We do things that seem off the cuff and arbitrary, only to realize later that there was a preconscious set of understandings and assumptions that informed our seemingly random acts. When we think critically about them, we often conclude that our apparently haphazard decisions were actually rooted in assumptions that, now that we are aware of them, made good sense in the situation. So critical thinking can lead to a deepened, new, and more informed understanding of why already existing assumptions were accurate and valid, and, therefore, why assumptions—and the actions flowing from them—should stay the same.

Critical Thinking Is the Same as Problem Solving

There is almost nothing more guaranteed to ensure good career progress than gaining a reputation as someone who is good at problem solving. For example, if I'm a teacher and a head of department or dean gives me a problem to solve, I will increase my chances of getting my contract renewed, or even getting tenure, if I come back with a solution to the problem. I will become known as organizationally reliable, a troubleshooter, who can fix things. But although there are times when critical thinking and problem solving are synonymous, this is not necessarily the case. There are also many examples of problem solving that are done uncritically. How can this be so?

The first instance of uncritical problem solving occurs when the problem you are working so assiduously to solve is not the problem that really needs addressing. A critical approach to problem solving does not take the first, usually official, definition of the problem as necessarily accurate. Instead, this approach asks some hard questions of the problem such as

- In whose interests is it that this problem be solved?

- Who benefits and who is harmed by this problem being solved?

- Who initially framed the problem as a problem?

- What evidence exists that says this is the most pressing problem we need to deal with?

- What other problems would others in the organization say need to be solved?

- Is this the right problem to focus on?

So a critical approach to problem solving begins with problem posing; that is, with trying to answer the questions outlined above. Someone adopting an uncritical approach, on the other hand, immediately takes the official definition of the problem as correct and begins to work assiduously to solve it. There is no critical questioning of how the problem was framed the way it was, who did the framing, and what other problems perhaps need more attention. Most problem solving task forces are set up to solve problems defined by those high in the organizational hierarchy. That's not to say the problems are inherently wrong or that time should not be committed to solving them. For example, many diversity task forces are set up to address the problem of high attrition of students from racial minorities, or the lack of faculty of color. But we should also recognize, as critical race theory points out (Zamudio, Russell, Rios, and Bridgeman, 2010), that solving these problems benefits those in power. For example, task forces like those just mentioned ensure a smoother process through accreditation, build a good reputation among minority communities, and therefore lead to more applications.

The second way problem solving is done uncritically is when the problem solver promises a solution. This may seem a strange thing to say—after all, isn't the purpose of problem solving to come up with a solution? Well, that's true of course. But problems that are so intractable they require a task force to solve them usually don't have solutions. If they're complex enough to need a team studying them, then what they have is partial responses to them, some of which make sense at some times, and some of which make more sense at others. A complex and intractable problem is a problem simply because it has no simple solution. If it did, it wouldn't be a problem! But the authors of a report are going to have a much more positive response to their report if they come up with three, four, or five clear solutions, graded according to their utility, than if they say no clear solution exists, and that the partial responses they outline will only fit if the context has been carefully studied beforehand.

Critical Thinking Leads to a Clear and Final Outcome

To some degree, this misunderstanding arises from the one we've just discussed. Here, a student believes that applying critical thinking will allow her to discover a clear and final answer to a question that allows her put a check mark next to the question as one that's been fully dealt with. The truth is that critical thinking is more like the old cliché of peeling an onion; there's always a more complex question uncovered the deeper you go with your analysis. This is one of the most difficult and frustrating things for students to get their heads round. They want, quite legitimately, to believe that critical thinking will give them answers to questions. And sometimes this happens. But just as much, new and deeper questions are the result, or more complex understandings of the original question suggest themselves. It seems like there is no end to the process, and that the point of the exercise is to ask more questions.

It seems this way because that's the truth! There is no end point to critical thinking where you slap your hands as if to say "done and dusted" and put a line through an item as something that never needs revisiting. The truth is that we come to provisional resting places on a journey of understanding where we say to ourselves "this is as far as I can come to now in understanding this, so I need to act on what I know and to understand I may have to revisit this at a later point." This is why having a course on critical thinking—something I advocated in Chapter Seven—can backfire if it leads to the belief that by taking the course students can check off critical thinking in their minds as something they're now fully certified in, leaving them free to move on to other things.

Critically thinking isn't neatly compartmentalized that way. It's all pervasive, embedded in particular disciplines, modules, units, and situations. How it looks applied to one topic or problem will not be the same as how it looks applied to others. And the nature of learning—of constantly encountering emerging sources of new information, of having unexpected experiences that take us by surprise and lead us to come at things in a whole new way—means that critical thinking is never-ending. There will always be new questions and new ways of thinking about old questions.

Challenges to Critical Thinking

One of the problems in writing a book on critical thinking is that you can easily fall into an uncritical advocacy of the process, ignoring its contradictions and minimizing its complexities. Despite my best efforts not to do either of these things I'm sure I've fallen into each of these traps. So in this section I want to turn a critical eye on the concept of critical thinking by raising three of the most frequent challenges issued to it. These are (1) that it represents a masculine approach to knowledge that emphasizes doubting, not believing, and that ignores connected knowing, (2) that it springs from a Eurocentric intellectual heritage without acknowledging that fact, and (3) that in its search for self-awareness it is a thoroughly modernist idea that does not acknowledge the complexities of life in the postmodern era. All these critiques are well grounded, so I will deal with them in turn.

Critical Thinking as Masculine Doubting

The authors of the groundbreaking *Women's Ways of Knowing* (Belenky, Clinchy, Goldberger, and Tarule, 1986) argued that a distinctive but undervalued mode of connected knowing was evident in the women they interviewed. This connected way of knowing stood in opposition to the traditionally valued separate mode of knowing that undergirded Eurocentric conceptions of truth. The authors write "at the heart of separate knowing is critical thinking . . . the doubting game" (p. 104). Players of the doubting game "are especially suspicious of ideas that feel right" (p. 104); that is, of dominant values and beliefs that seem wholly natural, part of our structures of feeling. Belenky, Clinchy, Goldberger, and Tarule argued that "separate knowers are tough-minded. They are like doormen at exclusive clubs. They don't want to let anything in unless they are pretty sure it is good. They would rather exclude someone who belongs to the club than admit someone who does not" (p. 104). This is as good a statement of the principle of falsifiability as you can come up with—do your best to find out what's false about something, and what's left is what you can feel some confidence in.

In contrast to this exclusionary, inherently skeptical form of separate knowing, connected knowing is a form of knowing premised on playing the believing, rather than the doubting, game. Players of the believing game seek primarily to enter into, understand, and develop an empathic appreciation for, another's worldview. The *Women's Ways of Knowing* authors contended that "although it may be difficult for men, many women find it easier to believe than to doubt . . . while women frequently do experience doubting as a game, believing feels real to them, perhaps because it is founded upon genuine care and because it promises to reveal the kind of truth they value—truth that is personal, particular, and grounded in firsthand experience" (p. 113). They contrasted the competitive bull sessions in which male students played the doubting game with the conversations of women students where, in playing the believing game, no one attacked or defended positions, no one tried to prove anything, and there was no interest in converting anyone.

The idea that critical thinking inevitably emphasizes a methodology based on doubting the truth of utterances, and that this methodology is more congenial and appealing to men who have been socialized into playing this doubting game, is a serious contention and deserves far more discussion than is possible in this chapter. Certainly, the tradition of critical theory starts from a position of skepticism that assumes that ideological manipulation has ensured that the majority live unaware of their oppressed situation. By definition, ideologies are judged to be false. Their purpose is seen to be the dissemination of beliefs about the proper working of society that leave the social order unchallenged and that work for the interests of a dominant minority.

The doubting game is described as a kind of individual gladiatorial combat that pitches one against the other and where the winner is the last one left standing. Interestingly, however, this does not support what we learned in Chapter Three regarding the ways students of both genders said they learn to think critically. As we saw in that chapter, students report that critical thinking is best learned in groups in which peers serve as critical mirrors allowing students to see parts of their thinking that would otherwise remain obscured. So when a group of people asks, "What are we missing here? What have we overlooked?" or "Which assumptions haven't been checked?" the process is experienced as far more productive than when this is done in isolation. The insight from students that critical thinking is a social learning process (provided consistently by students of both genders) confirms the accuracy of the *Women's Ways of Knowing* study, but also allows for the doubting game to be played in a social learning format.

Critical Thinking as Eurocentric Rationality

The four traditions informing critical thought outlined in Chapter Two could all be traced back to the European Enlightenment. Even pragmatism was developed by European Americans and was founded on the idea that experimentation and observation of experience allowed for progress and improvement. In addition, critical thinking has often elevated a Western form of cognitive, rational knowing above other forms of comprehension. Historically there has been little attention to affect, emotion, spirituality, holistic modes of being and knowing, or to consideration of how critical thought can be triggered through aesthetic experiences, meditation, and contemplation. As the title of a popular book on critical thinking indicates, critical analysis is deemed to be *Beyond Feelings* (Ruggerio, 1990).

Given that critical thinking springs from Enlightenment rationality (a Eurocentric tradition of thought) it is easy to move to a position where it is seen as just one more manifestation of intellectual colonialism. White males, working from within a European tradition of thought, are held to claim as universal a learning process and a form of educational practice that is actually highly culturally specific. In Baudrillard's (1975) terms, although "western culture was the first to critically reflect upon itself . . . it reflected on itself also as a culture in the universal, and thus all other cultures were entered in its museum as vestiges of its own image" (p. 88). This line of criticism points out that some ethnic groups experience critical thinking as a threatening imposition of alien ways of knowing, learning, and being, a form of intellectual genocide wiping out valued components of their culture.

For example, Lee (2011) points out the influence of the Confucian tradition on East Asian students at U.S. universities. Confucius asserted that students would need a competent teacher to guide them and believed students would better spend their time absorbing ideas from experts than thinking independently. Lee quotes research (Tweed & Lehman, 2002; Pratt and Wong, 1999) indicating that East Asian learners do in fact focus on learning ideas and knowledge from the teacher, and then applying these under strict teacher supervision. A good student is deemed to be one who can properly apply the knowledge she has gained from a teacher in the exact way a teacher wishes. When told by American academics to think critically and independently—even to call into question the instructor's own reasoning—East Asian students are placed in an inescapable double-bind. To earn the respect of their teachers in the United States they have to do something deemed deeply disrespectful in their own culture.

There is no doubt that the dominant traditions of critical thinking discussed in Chapter Two represent important strands in Western intellectual thought. Does this render critical thinking inherently invalid and, by definition, irrelevant to people not living in eighteenth century Paris, nineteenth century Vienna, or twentieth century Frankfurt? No. A knee jerk rejection of all theorizing because of the unfamiliarity of the source from which it originates is anti-intellectual and shuts down the possibility of dialogue across differences. Does the historical specificity of ideology critique mean its tenets must continually be reinvented and reshaped to fit alternative times and places? Absolutely. Pragmatism itself advocates that in improving practice in any area we need to search across broader and broader terrains, and to incorporate new and inconvenient understandings. This applies just as much to critical thinking as to anything else.

There is also the point that considering anything written by dead White males as irrelevant to the complexities of a multiethnic, postmodern, fragmented society of difference thereby marginalizes a powerful stream of Neo-Marxist and Gramscian analysis that challenges dominant structures and cultural values. In this sense, it could be argued that the dismissal of Eurocentrism (which includes the Frankfurt school of critical social theory) plays straight into the hands of the ruling class. If we condemn as irrelevant anything written by dead European males then we succeed beautifully in removing a powerful tradition of revolutionary and subversive thought from our discourse and consciousness. The impact of the ideas of Marx and Gramsci is skillfully neutered. Arguing that the modernistic writings of these dead White males have no relevance to understanding the position and experiences of women and ethnic minorities today is a politically correct way of framing contemporary debate to exclude emancipatory ideas. It thus becomes possible to profess a concern for excluded groups and subjugated discourses while simultaneously and paradoxically ensuring the continuance of this exclusion and subjugation.

Critical Thinking as a Modernist Illusion

Critical thinking grounded in the four traditions explored in Chapter Two is strongly modernist. Modernism is grounded in the optimistic Enlightenment belief that people and society are ulti-mately perfectible. Modernism holds that as we increase our knowledge we can gradually rid the world of oppression and injus-tice and create a rational, just society. This optimistic, hopeful contention is central to positivism, natural science, and Marxism. Drawing on modernism, advocates of critical thinking like myself assume that students can engage in an increasingly accurate analy-sis of the world, thus coming to greater clarity and self-awareness. By learning how to surface assumptions and then subject these to critical scrutiny, people can sort out which assumptions are valid and which are distorted, unjust, and self-injurious.

Postmodernism rejects this belief that humanity's story is one of continual progress and improvement. It argues that the Holocaust and the continuing presence of genocide show the belief in prog-ress to be a comforting modernist illusion. It also questions the optimistic hope of critical theory that we can peel back the layers of ideological domination to arrive at a clear and accurate analysis of injustice. From a postmodern perspective, oppression is held to be multilayered and to shift the ways it is made manifest. The same person who is an oppressor in one context is the oppressed in the next. So from this perspective truth is local, provisional, and changing.

In particular, postmodernism questions the way in which nar-ratives of critical thinking are recounted. When people describe their critical thinking journeys, as I did in Chapter One, they are usually told in a linear and sequential manner. These tales docu-ment a move toward more accurate and valid assumptions (to use my language) or more inclusive and differentiating meaning perspectives, in Mezirow's (1991, 2000) terms. A typical shorthand narrative of a teacher's experience of critical thinking might be, "I used to teach in an unwittingly oppressive way perpetuating inequities of race, class and gender. Now—as a result of a disorienting dilemma which caused me to reflect critically on my abuse of power—I have washed my practice free of the stains of racism, classism, sexism and oppression." Or, "I used to live my life according to others' expectations. I didn't know who I was and I didn't live according to my own assumptions and beliefs. By thinking critically I've discovered who I really am—my core self—and I'm living a more authentic and integrated life."

Postmodernists, particularly Derrida (1978), Lyotard (1984), and Lacan (1979), have rejected this notion of linear progress. They contend our narratives of critical thinking and self-discovery are artifices—fictional creations in which we feature as the hero, but not to be confused with the chaotic fragmentation of daily experience. The belief that through critical analysis people come to fuller self-knowledge is held to be a necessary palliative, but essentially false. There is no core self that is waiting to be discovered. Who we are is socially negotiable. What we say and write is open to multiple interpretations or readings and our words have no core truth waiting to be discovered. There are no foundational, defining assumptions waiting to be unearthed.

The challenge of postmodernism is, in my opinion, a necessary correction to the tendency in discourse on critical thinking to assume a model of the liberatory educator as one who always has a more authentic and accurate view of the prevailing, oppressive reality, and who therefore has a duty to awaken learners from their intellectual slumbers. The critical theory approach to critical thinking envisions a dualism of oppressor and oppressed, of all-powerful, omniscient demagogues who, through a subtle manipulation of education, church, and media (or a brutal torturing of dissidents), keep the mass of people in a state of cognitive and emotional stupefaction, a culture of moral silence. This dualistic paradigm inevitably casts the educator as heroine, an activist with a line on political truth denied to mere mortals.

The confidence (some would say arrogance) regarding the apparent gullibility of working people embedded within these claims has done some damage to critical reflection. A form of triumphalism sometimes creeps in whereby critical educators portray themselves as superheroes of hegemonic analysis, the only ones who possess an accurate vision of the oppressive reality hidden from the masses. They are like heat seeking missiles, locating and penetrating ideology with a single withering glance of pure clarity. Critical educators can easily become imbued with an imperious certainty.

The postmodern challenge to critical thinking reminds us that we need to apply the same rational skepticism to our own position that we apply to analyzing how dominant cultural values serve the interests of the few over the many. A critically reflective stance toward our practice is healthily skeptical, a necessary hedge against an overconfident belief that we have captured the one universal truth about good practice. It also works against an uncritical reification of protocols of critical thinking. A postmodernist stance contends that truth is local. Struggles to teach critical thinking do not follow grand plans. They have localized scripts depending on who is involved and the contexts in which these struggles are cast. One can't take techniques and methods used in one context and simply transfer or apply them to another. One can't learn successful techniques for social change in one situation and then go back and apply them without alteration to another. These "truths" won't fit.

Risks of Critical Thinking

One of the most frequent comments made at workshops I'm running on either teaching critically or on getting students to think critically is that this is all well and wonderful, but that the risks of doing this are so great that there is no way that students can contemplate engaging with it. I have written about these risks in some detail over the years (Brookfield, 1994, 1995, 2005, 2006). In this section, I want to reprise some of the themes I have covered in this writing, and situate them within students' experience of learning to think critically. The risks I want to explore in this regard are (1) impostorship, (2) cultural suicide, (3) lost innocence, and (4) road running.

Impostorship

Impostorship is the sense learners report that at some level they possess neither the talent nor the right to become college students, and that they are doing their best not to reveal that fact to the world. Students who feel like impostors imagine that they are constantly on the verge of being found out, of being revealed as being too dumb or unprepared for college level learning. The secret they carry around inside them is that they don't deserve to be a student because they lack the intelligence or confidence to succeed. They imagine that once this secret is discovered they will be asked to leave whatever program they're enrolled in, covered in a cloud of public shame, humiliation, and embarrassment. Each week that passes without this happening only serves to increase their sense that a dramatic unmasking lies just around the corner. "Surely" the student asks herself, "sooner or later someone, somewhere is going to realize that letting me onto this campus was a big mistake. I'm not smart enough to succeed."

Not all share this feeling, it is true, but it does seem to cross lines of gender, class, and ethnicity. It is also felt at all levels, from developmental, remedial learners to participants in doctoral seminars. For example, Simon (1992) writes that when his doctoral students (who are mostly working teachers) read theoretical literature in education and its allied fields it often induces in them feelings of impostorship. The student decides "that one does not belong in this class; that one does not belong in graduate school; that one is not as smart as others think; that one is not really an 'intellectual'; that one is not as well read as one should be" (p. 85). When I spent a semester as a Visiting Professor at Harvard Graduate School of Education it was striking to me how much of an impostor I felt. Me, a Harvard professor? They must have confused this Stephen Brookfield with some other Stephen Brookfield who actually deserved the position. What was even more striking was how strongly so many of the students (all master's and doctoral candidates at a premier Ivy League school) acknowledged their own feelings of impostorship once I had introduced this concept to them. Whenever I face a class full of seemingly confident new students I have to keep telling myself that many of them are probably smitten with impostorship.

Given that feelings of impostorship are just below the surface, one of the things that usually triggers them is telling students that they have to think critically about the subject matter they are studying. Being asked to undertake a critical analysis of ideas that students read in books, or that they hear from instructors in lectures, is enormously difficult. Students feel the experts have the truth, and it's the expert's job to share this with them. If students are just beginning their studies in an area, their experience of being a student, much less of having a basic command of the subject, can be so limited that it's both brutal and confusing to tell them that they must immediately start thinking critically about it. If the student assumes that critical thinking means disclosing one's errors and owning up to one's mistakes, there's another level of emotional stress involved. A student now associates critical thinking with some sort of public humiliation. So the sense of impostorship that is already part and parcel of being a new student is now dramatically heightened because students are expected to think critically about what they are learning.

Cultural Suicide

Cultural suicide describes the process whereby students are punished by their families, peers, and communities for what appears to be an act of betrayal; that is, to be seen to be changing as a result of participating in learning. This risk forces itself onto the consciousness of students of color in high school if taking education seriously is condemned as "acting White" (Bergin and Cooks, 2002). It is felt particularly keenly by students of all racial backgrounds who are first in their family to go to college and also by many adult learners. Cultural suicide is something that affects working class students who "often become alienated from their families in direct proportion to their procurement of new ideas and attitudes" (Casey, 2005, p. 35). As a result they "feel their identities shattered, and find themselves psychologically adrift" (p. 35). Students intuitively sense from their intimates and work colleagues that if college prompts them to begin a critical questioning of conventional assumptions and beliefs shared by these peers they (the students) will risk being excluded from the culture that has defined and sustained them up to that point in their lives. The perception of this danger, and experience of its actuality, is a common theme in working class academics' autobiographies (Welsch, 2004) and was even the topic of a successful commercial feature film, *Educating Rita*. Students who take critical thinking seriously and start to question shared assumptions report that those around them start to view them with fear and loathing, with a hostility borne of incomprehension.

Learners in critical process are sometimes seen as turning into subversive troublemakers, whose raison d'etre now seems to be to make life as difficult and uncomfortable as possible for those around them. A common experience reported by first generation college students is of their rapidly being marginalized as a result of their slipping into a more critical mode in their daily lives. They find that raising critical questions regarding commonly held cultural assumptions engenders resentment and suspicion from family and friends. Those around them feel that the students concerned have somehow betrayed what the group stands for and they let them know that. Through a mix of approaches—isolation, direct confrontations, sarcasm, body language—the student is given a strong message: stop raising questions about anything the group doesn't want to talk about, and stop trying to get us to think another way.

Lost Innocence

Students often come to campus with high hopes. They think that college will turn their lives around, that now they are going to get some "truth," and that finally they'll understand how the world really works and who they really are. Going to college is viewed as a transformative marker event that's going to change their lives dramatically for the better by opening up career possibilities and helping them to self-knowledge. However, this sense of confidence is sometimes eroded almost from the first week as these students hear how their teachers emphasize the importance of thinking critically. Instructors stress that often there are no right answers and that students will have to discover their own meanings for themselves. When students ask teachers for the correct response to a dilemma or question, teachers often reply "it depends." These same teachers then go on to say that knowledge and ideas cannot be understood in starkly dualistic terms, as either right or wrong. Instead, the world of critical inquiry is painted with the gray shades of ambiguity. Students are told that the purpose of a college education is to get them to ask the right questions, not to find the right answers.

As students hear all this they sometimes feel cheated, lost, and confused. Or they just don't believe it. To them the professor is playing a sophisticated and evasive guessing game, pretending not to have the answer and testing the students to see if they have the wherewithal to push him to own up to the truth. When the penny drops and students realize their teachers mean what they say about there being no easy answers, universally correct views, or unequivocally right ways to think, they panic.

This intellectual anxiety attack is a crucial one in students' autobiographies as learners. If they can live through it they experience an epistemological transformation. Knowledge and truth become seen as contextual and open, as constantly created and recreated in a community of knowers. Students realize their lives as learners will be marked by continual inquiry, questioning of assumptions, and reframing of perspectives, just as their teachers say it will. However, if students can't face this epistemological reframing, they are at a high risk of dropping out of the whole college experience. Epistemological panic has been neglected in studies of student attrition, which focus almost exclusively on the exterior details of students' lives—their financial difficulties, problems with meeting college schedules, lack of preparedness for taking responsibility for their own learning, and so on. These factors are crucial, and their importance should never be underestimated, but the interior factor of lost innocence should also not be forgotten.

Roadrunning

As learners speak about how they experience learning to think critically they describe a rhythm that might be called incremental fluctuation. Put colloquially, this learning rhythm can be understood as one where the learner takes two steps forward, one step back, followed by four steps forward, one step back, followed by one step forward, three steps back, and so on in a series of irregular fluctuations marked by overall progress. It is a rhythm of learning that is distinguished by a gradually increased ability to learn how to hunt assumptions and consider alternative perspectives, juxtaposed with regular interruptions when this feels impossible. When these apparent regressions to earlier ways of uncritical thinking and acting take place they are felt as devastatingly final. Instead of being viewed as the inconvenient interludes they really are, they seem like the end point of the process. Learners believe they will never "get" critical thinking, that it's "beyond them." They are tempted to return to tried and trusted ways of thinking on the grounds that even if these didn't always work or make sense at least they were familiar and comfortable.

The way this halting, jagged, incrementally fluctuating rhythm of learning is spoken of reminds me of the long running Warner Brothers *Adventures of the Roadrunner* cartoon. In the cartoon the same scene is repeated endlessly. The roadrunner is hurtling along the highway, his beep-beep cry raising Wile E. Coyote's frustration to ever-higher levels. The roadrunner comes to the edge of a canyon and, because he's possessed of supernatural powers, he leaves solid ground to go out into mid air. Suspended several hundred feet above the canyon floor he turns around and makes a face at the coyote, who is himself coming to the rim of the canyon.

The coyote's adrenalin is already pumping through his veins with the thrill of the chase and he becomes even more incensed by the roadrunner's evident temerity. The coyote picks up his speed, and hurtles off the edge of the canyon into thin air in frantic pursuit of the roadrunner, his legs pedaling in space. After about three seconds, however, the coyote realizes his situation. He freezes, looks down at the canyon floor several hundred feet below, and then looks back at the camera with a goofy, quizzical, deflated expression. Realizing the nature of his situation causes an immediate existential crisis. Until he realizes where he is, he's safe. But at the moment of awareness of his situation hundreds of feet in midair, physics and perception cohere and the law of gravity takes effect. He plunges to the canyon floor and the screen is a mess of limbs and disconnected but bloodless body parts. In the next frame, of course, we see that the coyote has been magically reassembled off camera and that the chase has begun anew.

The moment when Wile E. Coyote realizes his predicament and crashes to the canyon floor has the same emotional quality as a particular moment in the incremental rhythm of critical thinking. It is the moment when students realize that the old ways of thinking and acting no longer make sense for them, but that new ones have not yet formed to take their place. This state of limbo—similar to the coyote's suspension several hundred feet above the canyon floor—is frighteningly uncertain.

Like the coyote, students experience the beginnings of college with boundless energy and an optimistic sense of how it will make their lives better. Entranced by the prospect of how critical thinking will open new employment opportunities, bring self-knowledge, or help them develop self-confidence, they embrace the prospect. As they begin struggling to discard or reformulate assumptions and understandings that now seem not to explain the world adequately, there is a sense of forward movement, of progress toward true clarity of perception. The struggle to learn, with its attendant aspects of impostorship, cultural suicide, and lost innocence, is seen as worthwhile because of the transformative fruits it will bear.

But as students leave behind the solid ground of their old ways of thinking and acting, their enthusiasm sometimes turns to terror. They realize that they have nothing that supports them. Their previously solid and stable assumptive clusters, and their familiar ways of interpreting the world, have evaporated, but no substitutes have solidified to take their place. This is the moment when their confidence drains away. They crash to the floor of their emotional canyons, resolving never to go through this experience again.

However, in the same way that the coyote is reassembled off camera to begin the chase anew in the next frame, so the quest for learning is not put off so easily. Sooner or later, students are confronted by whatever hopes and dreams, or niggling anomalies or discrepancies, that spurred them to enroll in college in the first place. Critical thinking begins anew, but this time students know that at some point they will find themselves perched precariously above the canyon floor. Out of such knowledge comes the ability to stay dangling for a few seconds longer than was formerly the case, and the forethought to bring along a parachute in the form of a supportive learning community.

The Crucial Role of Community

When I've asked students how they survive impostorship, reduce the risk of committing cultural suicide, deal with lost innocence, and create a parachute to help them float rather than crash to the canyon floor, they invariable attest to the importance of community. The importance in college of belonging to an emotionally sustaining peer learning community cannot be overstated. *Community* might seem a rather grandiose word to describe the clusters of three or four good friends that students say they value so highly. But the emphasis the members of these groups place on the emotional warmth and psychological security they provide makes the term *community* more appropriate than, say, *network*.

The important thing about these small communities is that they reassure their members that their private anxieties are commonly experienced. Through talking about their individual experiences of learning to think critically, students come to know that feeling like an impostor or being shunned by former friends is a shared reality not an idiosyncratic event. Learners lucky enough to be members of emotionally sustaining peer learning communities speak of them as "a second family" or "the only people who really know what I'm going through." These communities provide a safe haven, an emotional buttress against the lowest moments in their autobiographies as learners.

This is yet one more testimony to the importance of understanding critical thinking as a social learning process. Not only do peer groups work well on a cognitive level to encourage critical thinking—something I've argued throughout this book—they also provide the emotional support to help students keep the risks under control. If you continue to feel you're the only one feeling like an impostor, or the only one who's having problems with family or friends, the feeling of isolation can be unbearable. But if you work regularly through critical protocols with the same group of people, you inevitably start to ask them how things are going for them. When they share their own feelings of impostorship, or their own moments of cultural suicide, that's when you start to understand that it's not just you experiencing these emotional rhythms. Just knowing that your experience of impostorship, lost innocence, or road running is not idiosyncratically your own can be enormously reassuring. Peer learning communities are also good settings in which students can share tips and tactics on how to avoid cultural suicide. Below are some of the ones my own students have come up with over the years:

- If you've just come back from class the first thing you should do is ask your friend, partner, family member, or roommate what happened to him or her while you were away.

- If your time away has involved this person covering for you in any way, find some way of acknowledging that and returning the favor.

- Never talk about what happened in class until you're asked directly to do so.

- If you absolutely cannot follow rule #3 above, and you feel you really have to share what happened in class, you should make sure that you begin your sharing by disclosing moments of anxiety or insecurity. Instead of celebrating the marvelous things happening to you as a student, talk about how you feel like a fraud, how difficult you find studying, how you fear you won't make it to the end of the semester, and so on. Then, and only then, should you talk about your triumphs and the changes happening to you. This way of disclosing the details of your learning journey heartens rather than threatens.

Summary

In this chapter I've tried to clear up some common misunderstandings about critical thinking, acknowledge some of the challenges made to its discourse and practice, and briefly review some predictable risks that students run when they try to learn it. In so doing, I've ended by stressing one of the enduring themes of this book: that critical thinking should be understood primarily as a social learning process that happens best in groups. In the next chapter, the final one, I want to revisit another enduring theme—the importance of modeling critical thinking—and explore it in a few different ways from the way it has been analyzed so far.

10

Modeling Critical Thinking

In this final chapter I want to return to a theme that has been stressed throughout the book, but to examine it in a more detailed manner. This theme is the importance of teachers publicly and explicitly modeling for students their own engagement in critical thinking. The theme was explored initially in Chapter Three, where I reviewed what students said about the kinds of teaching approaches that worked best for helping them learn to think critically. In that chapter I provided some specific examples of what classroom modeling of critical thinking might look like. In this chapter I want to consider how this process can pervade a teacher's life.

Modeling is important not just for instructional reasons. Although students emphasize that they very much appreciate witnessing faculty provide examples of what it looks like to think critically about something, there is also a moral justification for modeling. It seems to me there is something essentially inauthentic about asking students to struggle with the emotional and conceptual complexities of uncovering and checking assumptions, and looking at things from very different viewpoints, if we are not willing ourselves to engage in that struggle at the outset. Given the risks and threats that the previous chapter showed that critical thinking represents for many students, we need to earn the right to ask them to do this by first modeling how we negotiate this process. We need to be willing to question some of our most deeply held assumptions, and to strive to look at ideas and practices we subscribe to from perspectives that are highly critical of them. As we do this we need to let students know that this is difficult for us but that it is also beneficial; that sometimes it leads us to make a deeper commitment to these assumptions and that sometimes it means we change them.

The key points about modeling anything are that it be public and that it be explicit. Both are necessary if the process is to have the desired effect. Private modeling, such as thinking critically about the assumptions you're making regarding students and doing your best to see your practice from multiple perspectives, may make you a better teacher but it denies students the opportunity to learn from witnessing how you struggle with critical thinking. Implicit modeling, such as using the Critical Incident Questionnaire to collect data from students without discussing with them how this data confirms or challenges the assumptions that frame how you teach the class, risks having students miss entirely how you engage in the process.

Autobiographical Disclosure

For teachers across the disciplines one of the most effective approaches to modeling critical thinking is to speak autobiographically about one's own application of critical thinking. If we consider what students across the disciplines say helps them to learn new skills and knowledge, teachers' use of autobiographical examples to explain content is mentioned consistently in all kinds of subject areas. Of course, the autobiographical examples need to be appropriate. Narrative for the sake of sharing stories may be interesting for a brief period, but it soon becomes tiresomely self-indulgent if disconnected from any broader pedagogic intent.

When it comes to the process of struggling to think critically about ideas and practices that are taken for granted, students invariably respond well to teachers' autobiographical disclosures on this topic. Let me give a personal example. In a book titled *Becoming a Critically Reflective Teacher* (Brookfield, 1995) I described my own struggle to learn how to swim, and the way that this experience challenged some of my most fundamental assumptions about how to teach effectively. I explained that it changed how I thought about the practice of peer teaching, that it confirmed my assumptions regarding the importance of creating space for students to document for me their own autobiography of learning, and that it made me doubt the usefulness of charismatic demonstration as an approach to teaching.

Of all the things I've written over a career of hundreds of articles and book chapters and fifteen books, that brief piece has generated the most responses from readers. Something about my placing my personal experience front and center connected with people in a way that outlining a model of critical reflection did not. Of course, the model was important; indeed, showing how critical reflection depended on teachers using students' and colleagues' perceptions, research and theory, and their own autobiographical experiences was the point of the book. But the model only made sense, or came alive, for readers when it was illustrated with my autobiographical experiences. The same thing has held true in workshops I run on critical thinking. When I use that example to illustrate how to do a critical analysis of personal experience, that is often the moment or action in the workshop picked out by participants as being the most engaging or helpful.

So whether you teach physics or political science, art history or astronomy, Spanish or sociology, describing to students how you try to think critically about the content of your subject is going to be one of the most effective ways to help them learn to think critically. The more contemporary your examples are, the better. Although students appreciate accounts of your own student experiences, and how you dealt with difficult material the first time you encountered it, your autobiographical disclosure is so much more effective when it deals with a problem the students face right now.

An Example: Teaching About Racism

One of the aspects of practice I struggle most with as a teacher is teaching about racism. As a White male I am a privileged member of the dominant culture and carry around all kinds of unexamined assumptions about people of different races. As part of my teaching load I regularly teach courses in educational leadership. Since, for me, being an effective leader means confronting all the "isms" (racism, sexism, ableism, homophobia, etc.) that diminish people in organizational and community settings, I feel that such courses need to prepare students how to do this. To that end I use a lot of simulations, scenarios, and case studies that attempt to ground this process in very specific situations that feel realistic. But I also intentionally and publicly try to discuss my own conflicting experiences dealing with racism as a means of engaging students with this part of the curriculum.

One of the first things I do is talk about how I have learned the racist ideology of White supremacy. By White supremacy I don't mean the ideology of Aryan superiority that holds that there is a God given racial purity that North-European peoples enjoy that marks them out as more intelligent, and that all other races are suited to menial labor that justifies enslavement or deportation. I mean instead the more subtle assumption that those best equipped to be leaders who make wise decisions on behalf of the multiracial collective are, by definition, White. Of course, the ideology of patriarchy also holds that those best equipped to make wise decisions are male.

I talk about how I have learned this ideology over the course of my life without ever being consciously aware of that happening. My skin color means that for my whole career I have been used to seeing as the gatekeepers in education people who look like me. Now I suppose I am one, continuing the unproblematized White supremacy norm. I speak about my approach to writing and how I never have to question my right to publish something. I note how White epistemology (Paxton, 2010)—the Enlightenment belief that rational, independent analysis is the apex of intellectual evolution—is something bred into my neural synapses. Racism—the structural manifestation of the ideology of White supremacy—moves in me in ways that constantly catch me by surprise. I see a Black pilot enter the cockpit of the plane on which I'm traveling and catch myself thinking, "Will this flight be safe?"—a reaction Nelson Mandela also had and which he writes about in his autobiography (Mandela, 1994), thus illustrating the all pervasive nature of ideological conditioning.

I describe how in classes I catch myself holding back from challenging students of color and realize that my so-called "concern" masks an embedded racist consciousness which says that "they" can't take a "strong" challenge from a White person. Clearly, racism moves in me. When I find myself too quickly granting paper extensions to Black students I can only assume it springs from a White supremacist judgment that because Black students are not as intelligent as White students, of course they will need more time to complete their work. It is deeply sobering, shameful, and alarming to realize how strong and enduring is the successful ideological conditioning of White supremacy.

One of my assumptions I disclose is the assumption that maintaining racism is all a matter of individual choice and I have chosen not to be racist. This assumption holds that whether or not a White person chooses to be racist is down to the moral strength or militant Christianity he or she displays in fighting the system's efforts to make them think and behave as a racist. According to this assumption Whites can choose whether or not to be racist and those with good hearts will choose not to be. If you accept this assumption then success in anti-racist work is largely a matter of individual fortitude—how assiduously you gear yourself up to detect and fight the enemy.

In class I talk about how I set ground rules, and how these can be looked at in very different ways. For example, I have already described a situation in which White students tried to convince a student of color she had not experienced racism. As a result of this I instituted a ground rule that when students of color disclose such experiences, Whites do not try to talk them out of it. This rule was welcomed by some students of color and strongly criticized by others who felt it patronizing, condescending, and paternalistic—as if only the White leader could protect them from racism since they couldn't do it themselves. I talk about the ways I have tried to engage explicitly in anti-racist practice, and how this often backfires on me, leading to accusations that I am racist.

I like to share examples of some of my most frequent missteps, such as thanking students for teaching me about their heritage and about racism. This can easily come across as condescending and underscoring the centering of Whiteness. It positions different racial traditions as exotic others, and emphasizes the "'naturalness" of White and Eurocentric perspectives. I say it's a mistake to expect colleagues of color to "teach" you about racism and White supremacy and that they have enough to do combating racism without taking you on as a learning project. I also talk about the fact that in my attempt to empathize with how it feels to be the victim of racism I have lost credibility in an instant.

Finally, I tell how in my own work I have learned to expect to be called a racist and to understand that it comes with the territory of this work. I may feel that I'm working with sensitivity and goodwill but as soon as I stir the waters with racial discussions I will inevitably inflame some people. As a White person and a representative (in the eyes of students' of color) of White supremacy I must expect to be mistrusted and not let that stop me. I must also expect White colleagues to accuse me of politically incorrect reverse racism. I say that this is not to be taken as a sign that I am somehow failing. Instead, I try to understand it as a very predictable moment that sooner or later comes to every White person engaged in this work.

As I read what I've just written I realize it might sound like I know what I'm doing. This is the opposite of how I feel. In teaching about race I constantly feel foolish and naïve. I usually end a class where race and racism has surfaced feeling like I wish I could rewind the videotape and erase all the mistakes I just made and have a second or third go at getting it "right." I try not to be too hard on myself by telling myself that in a career in its fifth decade I've really only been trying to understand how to teach about racism for the past ten years. So it shouldn't be surprising to feel like a novice. Indeed, a big part of modeling how to think critically about anti-racist work is to let people know that you're constantly questioning and changing the assumptions you operate under, and constantly being surprised by the different perspectives people have on this work. So feeling like everything's out of control and changing faster than you can appreciate is a normal state of affairs.

Modeling Critical Thinking for Colleagues

The focus of this book, and this chapter, has been on teaching students to think critically. But it would be remiss of me not to point out in this final chapter that a major element in teaching critical thinking involves us helping colleagues to do this. This is never truer than when it comes to modeling the process. If novice instructors are to learn how to teach critically, then they need to see experienced colleagues engaged in this endeavor. In this section I want to talk about ways colleagues can model critical thinking for each other.

Making Meetings Critical

One thing we can predict with total certainty as college teachers is that we will spend a good proportion of our career in meetings, many of which we will regard as totally unnecessary. It has always struck me that meetings are one of the best settings in which deans and department chairs can model critical thinking. Meetings are, after all, forums for group decision making, for taking informed action. Since the whole purpose of critical thinking articulated in Chapter One was to generate informed action, meetings seem a natural crucible for public and explicit modeling of the process.

One way to do this is to introduce some of the exercises already outlined in this book, particularly those described in Chapter Eight on making discussions critical. The Circle of Voices exercise makes sure everyone's voice is heard early on in a discussion, thus preventing the premature emergence of any dominant consensus on an issue. It seems perfect for meetings where hearing from everyone is an important foundation for discussing a particular agenda item. The Circular Response technique is helpful when the number of potential agenda items is expanding exponentially and a group needs to focus in on two or three manageable issues. Chalk Talk is a good way to generate a high level of participation and a visual record of the multiple perspectives that can be generated on an issue, along with the points of connection that connect apparently disparate items. I use this when a group has to deal with a new agenda item that has just emerged, and I want the group to have a visual depiction of where different people stand on the issue.

The Critical Incident Questionnaire (CIQ) is also a tool that lends itself to adaptation to meetings. Instead of asking questions focused on the most engaged or distanced moment in class, or the most helpful or puzzling action anyone took in class, the wording can be changed to substitute *meeting* for class. Respondents then talk about the moments in the meeting when they were most engaged or distanced, and the actions in the meeting that they found to be most helpful or confusing. The meeting CIQs are completed anonymously at the end of the meeting, and then one member of the group (not the chair) collects these. That staff

member then summarizes the main themes that came out in people's responses and prepares a summary on behalf of the group.

As the first item of business at each meeting, the results of the
previous week's CIQs are shared by whichever staff member collected and summarized them for the last meeting. All meeting
participants talk about the results and the chair of the meeting has
the chance to talk about the meaning of the responses for the new
meeting, as well as for subsequent meetings. In hearing the CIQ
responses from the previous meeting, chairs learn about the power
dynamics of the group that perhaps they were unaware of. They
see, too, how staff interpret, and misinterpret, the chair's actions.
It is chastening for a department head to realize that what she
thought were transparent and respectful ways of dealing with staff
may be experienced by those same people as duplicitous and
manipulative.

The CIQs will often yield information about frustrations and
misconceptions that are simmering below the surface but that are
never publically expressed. Just as the instrument is a good early
warning device for teachers regarding potentially destructive tensions that exist among a student group, so too it warns administrators
and leaders when something that has not been publicly addressed
risks destabilizing a department. At each meeting leaders can bring
these tensions and problems out into the open so that they can be
named and addressed before they get out of hand. Of course for
this to happen respondents must be convinced that the department chair is not able to identify the authors of particular
comments. This is why I advocate a different staff member collecting these at each meeting and summarizing their responses. This
way staff knows that the chair will never see anything anybody has
written.

Beginning the meeting with the first agenda item being "Any
Other Business" is a good way to invert the usual power dynamics
pertaining in a meeting where the chair usually sets and distributes
the agenda beforehand. Those staff members with important items

they wish to discuss typically have to wait until the end of the meeting before getting the chance to raise these. The announcement of the "Any Other Business" item signals to many that the meeting is almost over and that it's time to collect papers, gather bags, shut down laptops, and start putting jackets on. The people trying to introduce "Any Other Business" items have to do this against a background of chairs scraping on the floor, papers rustling as they're stuffed into briefcases, and computer tones signaling they are being powered down. Not surprising, those same staff members feel that their concerns are being shunted aside.

Beginning with "Any Other Business" as the first item sends three important messages from the chair to her staff. First, and maybe most important, it states that it is department members' concerns that are most important, not those of the institution as funneled through the chair. Second, it establishes an early initial sweep of departmental issues as a key moment in the meeting. This is when perspectives that have been overlooked, and that could potentially be damaging if ignored, are likely to be raised. Beginning with this item also starts the meeting off on an emotional high. Since people never know exactly what is going to be raised, it is more engaging than going straight into the first agenda item, which usually represents whatever is making life most difficult for the chair.

Another way that meetings can be turned into opportunities for critical thinking is through the adoption of Assumptions Inventories. These are used just prior to recording a major decision that has been reached in the minutes of the meeting. As a last item before this decision is logged participants are given 3×5 cards and asked to write down on their card three things:

- What's the decision we've just made?

- What's the chief piece of evidence that supports the decision?

- What results is the decision supposed to effect?

Once participants have completed their cards these are put in the middle of the table and shuffled around so no one knows who has written what. The chair then invites one of the participants to select a few of the cards and read out what people have written. If the cards document similar responses, then the decision is logged. But if major discrepancies emerge on any of the three items, another round of conversation ensues before the decision is confirmed and minuted. When I have tried this exercise it is sometimes astounding to discover that there are significant differences regarding the first item—What's the decision we've just made? When people can't even agree on what the decision is that they think they've just made, you know the group has a real communications problem.

A similar exercise to the Assumptions Inventory is the introduction of an explicit Structured Devil's Advocacy period just before a decision is logged. This is a time when the meeting participants do their best to come up with all the reasons that the decision they've made is flawed, why the assumptions it's based on are inaccurate, or what important data or perspectives have been ignored. It's a moment when a group deliberately tries to identify its own blind spots. If, at the end of this period, participants remain committed to the decision then they can minute this with a sense of confidence that it's a good decision. In a sense, utilizing a period of Structured Devil's Advocacy is the application to meetings of the principle of falsifiability, discussed in Chapter Two as a key component of the natural science model of critical thinking.

Team Teaching

If ever I was appointed the Tsar of higher education, and I was told I had unlimited resources available to me, the first thing I would do would be to mandate that all courses in higher education institutions be team taught, unless there was a very convincing reason why this should not be the case. There are several reasons that I would do this. For one, a team of teachers is more likely to be able to respond to the different learning styles, racial and cultural identities, and personalities of students. For another, a team of teachers is more likely to possess a wider repertoire of talents and skills that students can benefit from, than would be the case with a single individual. Also, as already mentioned at different points in this book, a teaching team is able to model for students, and for each other, what critical conversation looks like.

A team can model a lot of critical thinking processes in front of students. They can disagree respectfully, can point out strengths and weaknesses of each other's positions, can ask for more information, can introduce to each other perspectives that have been omitted, can point out accurate as well as potentially faulty assumptions each other is holding, can ask for evidence, and so on. Team members can also show students how to express appreciation to peers for stretching their thinking by introducing them to evidence that questions their positions. It is often also easier to create a public meta-narrative of your decisions as a teacher when you're part of a team, as your colleagues will often question you about why you did what you did in the way that you did it.

But aside from all these undoubted benefits, team teaching has another enormous advantage. It places in the classroom another pair (or pairs) of eyes that can open up classroom events to alternative interpretations. Talking to colleagues about what we do unravels the shroud of silence in which solo teaching is wrapped. Participating in critical conversation with peers opens us up to their versions of events we have experienced. Our colleagues serve as critical mirrors reflecting back to us images of our actions that often take us by surprise. As they describe their own experiences dealing with the same crises and dilemmas that we face, we are able to check, reframe, and broaden our own theories of practice.

For example, if we ask a team colleague what she thinks are the typical causes of students' resistance to learning, we will probably hear a spread of responses. Some of these we will have discovered ourselves. Others, such as how we might have made false promises, how we might be perceived as dishonest, or our underestimating students' fear of questioning previously unchallenged ways of thinking and behaving, may never have occurred to us. When we ask our colleagues how they would deal with each of these causes of resistance, we may encounter reactions that surprise us and that suggest new readings of this problem. It may never have occurred to us to apologize for anything we do, to find new ways to justify the learning we want students to consider, or to pay constant attention to our own modeling.

Talking to colleagues in our teaching team about problems we face in common and gaining their perspectives on these increases our chances of stumbling across an interpretation that fits what is happening in a particular situation. A colleague's experiences may suggest dynamics and causes that make much more sense than the explanations we have evolved. If this happens we are helped enormously in our effort to work out just what we should be doing to deal with the problem. Without an accurate reading of the causes of a problem (are these embedded in our own actions, in our students' past histories, in the wider political constraints placed on our learning and teaching, or in a particular intersection of all of these?) we are crippled in our attempts to work through it.

So checking our readings of problems, responses, assumptions, and justifications against the readings offered by colleagues is crucial if we are to claw a path to critical clarity. Doing this also provides us with a great deal of emotional sustenance. We start to see that what we thought were unique problems and idiosyncratic failings are shared by many others who work in situations like ours. Just knowing that we're not alone in our struggles can be a life-saving realization. Although critical reflection often begins alone, it is, ultimately, a collective endeavor. We need colleagues to help us know what our assumptions are and to help us change the structures of power so that democratic actions and values are rewarded within, and without, our institutions.

There is also the point that having a colleague in class with you helps you negotiate the emotional roller coaster that all teachers ride. When we're on this roller coaster we have the sense that the world is governed by chaos. Whether or not we do well seems to be largely a matter of chance. If we think this way we are powerless to control the ebbs and flows of our emotions. One day a small success causes us to blow our level of self-confidence out of all proportion. The next, an equally small failure (such as one bad evaluative comment out of twenty good ones) is taken as a devastating indictment of our inadequacy. Teachers caught on this emotional roller coaster, where every action either confirms their brilliance or underscores their failure, cannot survive intact for long. Either they withdraw from the classroom or they are forced to suppress (at their eventual peril) the emotional underpinning to their daily experiences.

From my own personal experience, I frequently leave a class session feeling frustrated at my inability to handle things as well as I might have. I obsess about the question I couldn't answer, the comment I didn't know how to respond to, or the example I used that I feel confused rather than clarified students' understanding of the material. I frequently blame myself if students are not learning and assume that I am the cause of the anger, hostility, resentment, or indifference that even the best and most energetic of students are bound to encounter from time to time.

Believing myself to be the cause of these emotions and feelings, I automatically infer that I'm also their solution. I take upon myself the responsibility for turning hostile, bored, or puzzled students into galvanized advocates for learning, brimming over with the joys of intellectual inquiry. When this doesn't happen (as is almost always the case) I sometimes become consumed with guilt for what I believe is irrefutable evidence of my pedagogic incompetence. My teaching colleagues will often help redress the imbalance in these perceptions by pointing out things that went well but that I have ignored. Or they will disclose positive elements and beneficial repercussions of my actions that I had not been aware of.

In the preceding chapter I wrote about the risks of critical thinking such as impostorship, cultural suicide, lost innocence, and road running. I applied these to students' experiences, but they are often equally present in faculty's lives. I know I constantly feel like an impostor and that in enthusiastically trying to introduce colleagues to a new idea or practice I commit cultural suicide. I know, too, that I long to discover the one manual or the one person who will solve all my pedagogic problems for me, and that I frequently fall to the floor of my emotional canyon in the way that Wile E. Coyote does. Having a colleague or colleagues on a teaching team with me helps me keep these risks manageable. Colleagues reduce my feelings of impostorship and boost my self-confidence. Even if they have no successful strategies to deal with cultural suicide, lost innocence, or road running, just knowing that I'm not alone in experiencing these is a wonderful realization. When you feel you're the only person struggling with problems, you're much more likely to give up out of embarrassment or a feeling of incompetence. When you understand that what you thought were idiosyncratic failings are in fact generally experienced realities, you breath a huge sigh of relief and stop thinking of yourself as uniquely untalented.

Modeling Critical Thinking in Online Environments

Higher education is changing at such a rapidly dazzling pace that any references I make to online platforms or tools will probably be hopelessly out of date by the time this book is published. But one thing I can say with total certainty is that the frequency of online teaching will increase, not diminish. Most face-to-face classes contain a hybrid of online technology and in-person exchange. In my own case, for example, I will often use the break in a face-to-face class to post a link on the class blackboard page to a resource that connects to a question a student asked in the first half of the class. When the class returns from break I invariably kick off the second half of the class by pulling up the blackboard page on a screen in the classroom and showing students the new resource I've just made available. Or, if a new author or researcher's name is mentioned in class, I can take a couple of seconds to pull up a link to that person's work.

As with other aspects of online teaching, many of the same dynamics pertaining to synchronous face-to-face teaching apply equally well in an asynchronous online environment. Modeling is no exception to this rule. If I am asking my students to think critically about a concept or a piece of information, then I need to model my own engagement in that same process at the outset of that learning unit. Needless to say, I don't provide a critical analysis of the exact same material I am asking students to review. The trick is to find something analogous to the content covered in the unit so students can understand the general strategies I'm using without simply copying what I've done.

When I've consulted with different organizations on how to help people think more critically, one of the things I always look at is how they conduct their meetings. For those organizations that hold meetings using computer teleconferencing tools such as *Wimba* or *Breeze*, the Circle of Voices or Circular Response exercises can easily be adapted to this environment. Even Chalk Talk can be adapted online in a meeting using the whiteboard tool available in these software platforms.

The Critical Incident Questionnaire (CIQ) tool is also easily adapted to online environments. Now that software platforms have made it much easier to post responses anonymously if so desired, students in an online environment can submit their completed forms once a week by a set time, and the instructor can summarize these and share them within 24 hours of the time of receipt. Of course in an asynchronous learning environment students will be submitting reactions to a much wider range of experiences and events than would be the case with a synchronously taught course where each student completes each classroom task simultaneously. The fact that students will be at very different stages of learning in the course makes organizing responses into clusters more complicated. It's also the case that writing up the results of a set of CIQ comments, and then writing out one's responses to these, takes longer than summarizing them verbally and speaking out load one's reactions. But essentially the CIQ dynamic online is the same as in a face-to-face classroom.

Perhaps the most important way instructors can model critical thinking online is by showing students how they assess the accuracy and validity of information available on the Web. Although informational and digital literacy are familiar concepts, they are often taught as the ability to locate and manage information. Hence, a digitally literate teacher would be one who can integrate hand held devices into classroom teaching. Where modeling critical thinking is concerned it is more appropriate to demonstrate the extent to which knowledge construction on the World Wide Web is as much a political process as is the dissemination of knowledge in books and journals. For example, although Wikipedia has five organizing principles that govern how entries are constructed, the fifth one is that there are no firm rules, while the other four are general in the extreme, such as the injunction to stay neutral and to interact in a civil and respectful manner.

A critical analysis of Wikipedia and other online information sources will draw from the different conceptions of critical thinking outlined in Chapter Two. From natural science we can focus on the notion of verifiable evidence and the emphasis on transparency that any good experimental procedure replicates. According to this conception of criticality an online source of information is judged valid to the extent that the evidence for any claims it makes is provided directly and the reasoning process behind such claims is openly described.

From analytic philosophy we can judge the degree to which common language tricks are used to establish a spurious legitimacy for claims made online. Examples of these would be repeating a distorted argument often enough in the hope that frequent repetition creates legitimacy, or representing one's argument as the will of the majority, as in prefacing a comment by saying "The American people will not stand for. . . . " or "What the American people really want is. . . . " Others are to construct an inaccurate analogy in order to discredit an opponent's argument (as in "Doing this is the first step to Nazism") or choosing one example from a general category ("I know this doctor who thinks that . . . ") and making an unwarranted generalization that represents the specifics of their behavior as the behavior of the whole.

But perhaps the most prominent critical tradition that helps us model critical literacy is that of critical theory. One of the first questions a critical theorist asks is "Who benefits from, and who is harmed by, this information?" So online information sources are analyzed as political creations that serve certain interests. Hence, one of the first things one looks for are the sponsors of a Web site. Just as traditional publishing houses have an in-house policy regarding what can and cannot be published, what is safe and what is incendiary, so too do Web masters. To this degree, a site that appears to have the stamp of official objectivity is just as much a hostage to advertising sponsors as are newspapers who rely on advertising to make a paper profitable, or TV stations that evaluate which programs to broadcast based on the degree to which companies wish to pay top dollar to run commercials during program breaks. A critical theory approach would also ask who has access to information sources available online, and it would highlight the digital divide structured by class, race, and age within a particular society and also between first and third worlds.

The clearest way a critical theory informs informational or digital literacy is to explore the degree to which online information reproduces dominant ideology. Recall that in Chapter Two critical theory was defined as assuming that inequality and exclusion are made to appear as a normal and natural state of affairs through the dissemination of dominant ideology—the set of beliefs and practices that comprise the majority way of thinking and acting. From this perspective an online information source that claims neutrality would be regarded as specious. Instead, its content would be analyzed for the degree to which it represented, as fact, perspectives and situations that supported a dominant belief. A critical race theory approach would examine the racial micro-aggressions embedded in information sources that described the characteristics of different racial groups, or the way in which notions of White supremacy went unremarked and unchallenged.

The Risks of Modeling

Although this chapter has been urging the value of modeling critical thinking, I want to draw on pragmatism's notion of criticality (also described in Chapter Two) to show that the experience of modeling is one that has all kinds of unintended consequences. Modeling should always be done experimentally. Exactly how one models criticality varies from student to student, class to class, discipline to discipline, and teacher to teacher. From student responses given on Critical Incident Questionnaires over the years it is clear that attempts to model criticality entail certain very predictable risks.

Providing a Template

The first risk is that in demonstrating how we think critically about something we provide students with a template that they copy slavishly to earn our approval and thereby gain the A grade they desire. The challenge for a teacher is to provide enough scaffolding in terms of a general strategy that can be applied to the analysis of a problem, but not to choose a problem that is too close to the one the students will be examining. In a sense the whole of Chapter Six deals with this issue in that it offers questions, exercises, and strategies to help students conduct a critical review of literature, but it leaves them at a general level of applicability. This means that the questions can be asked, and the strategies applied, with no clearly predetermined response being expected.

This is the most important rule to follow in modeling any approach to critical thinking. There should never be a predetermined response implied in whatever techniques or exercise you demonstrate. So while students have the reassurance of a specific strategy or activity that you've applied, they have no way of knowing in advance where using this approach will take them. Hence, the exercises described in Chapter Eight such as Circle of Voices, Circular Response, or Chalk Talk all provide very specific instructions to be followed, but in none of them is there any implicit suggestion that a certain response is expected. This is another way in which discussion and critical thinking intersect; in both processes the end point is never specified in advance. You literally do not know where you will end up as you begin the process.

Modeling with Intimidating Ease and a Level of Excellence

This risk emerges when the modeling is done publicly and explicitly, but seems to the students to be both seamless and attaining a level of excellence far beyond them. I well remember a seminar I attended in graduate school where the instructor showed us how to undertake a critical deconstruction of a text. He did a line by line analysis of a couple of pages that seemed so natural and obvious to him that I was left convinced I'd never be able to replicate anything like the dazzling display of intellectual dexterity I'd just witnessed. So, far from preparing me to undertake an independent critical analysis of a text (which was the point of his demonstration) I was left only with a conviction that I was intellectually inadequate for the task.

What would have made his modeling more effective? Well, if he had begun the process by emphasizing that this was something he had been trained to do, and that he had then successfully implemented for the last ten years, I would have had a better sense that this apparently seamless display was actually the result of years of disciplined application and trial and error. It would also have been helpful if he had stressed at the outset some of the typical difficulties he had faced when first trying to conduct this kind of textual deconstruction. If he had shared some of his early anxieties, disclosed potential missteps, or talked about his early feelings of impostorship, I would have felt more at ease with the prospect of beginning this intellectual journey myself. But because he did none of these things I experienced his modeling as an intimidating form of showing off how brilliant he was at this process.

Modeling Skepticism and Self-Doubt Creates Anxiety for Students Regarding Your Competence

This risk emerges when your attempt to model the self-questioning inherent in critical thinking leads you to admit publicly that your earlier assumptions about something were wrong, or that you are unsure about your response to a question. In the attempt to demonstrate that critical thinking entails always being open to the possibility that your analysis is wrong, or your convictions misplaced, you communicate to students the sense that you are unsure about what you are doing. Instead of this being interpreted the way you want it to be—as a reminder to students that all genuine intellectual inquiry carries with it the prospect that at some later stage you will be found out to have been wrong—students take it to mean you are not competent to be their teacher. In this case the early disclosure of self-doubt induces anxiety in students who are already intimidated by the prospect of having to question their assumptions and look at things differently.

In this aspect of modeling, as in so much of teaching, timing is everything. When students have already developed a confidence in your essential credibility, the disclosure of self-doubt and the application of critical analysis to one's own reasoning works well. So if you have provided helpful directions and instructions for exercises, provided examples and illustrations that have made sense to students, and answered questions about critical thinking processes in a helpful and convincing way, then your credibility is sufficiently established for you to engage in modeling self-doubt. But beginning a first encounter with students with a disclosure of how you're undecided on something, or by describing how you've already changed your thinking on an issue several times, and of how you may well change it again in the future as new facts or experiences emerge, risks increasing the anxiety they already feel to breaking point.

As with so many aspects of teaching critical thinking, the Critical Incident Questionnaire (CIQ) is enormously helpful here. Students' anonymous responses to questions about engaging and distancing moments in the class, or helpful and confusing actions that anyone in class has taken, can help you "read" their readiness to hear self-disclosures from you regarding your own critical journeys. If it's clear from responses that classroom activities are perceived as helpful, and if examples and illustrations you provide of critical thinking are experienced as engaging, then you can model self-doubt with a realistic confidence it will be perceived how you wish it to be. However, if the CIQs are full of responses documenting students' confusion about what the course is trying to achieve, then it's better to step back, regroup, and provide some more reassuring scaffolding (teacher presentations, clearer directions and explanations, or directed activities) before moving into a disclosure that self-questioning and changing one's mind are integral to the process.

Modeling Engagement with Multiple Perspectives Creates Confusion

This difficulty arises when your attempt at fostering intersubjective understanding—showing students how you can move in and out of multiple worldviews or theoretical paradigms—leaves them bewildered and confused regarding what you actually think. One of the things we can expect critical thinking activities to do is to loosen up students' rigid perspectives so they can consider different viewpoints on a topic or issue. We want them to be able to leave their familiar and well thought out cognitive homes and travel to unfamiliar intellectual destinations. This is the cognitive equivalent of cross-cultural experiences where the result of having to understand and adapt to a very different culture helps visitors understand that what they thought was normal and universal (their own culture's values) are but one of many legitimate possibilities. To adapt Vygotsky's (1978) notion of the zone of proximal development, critical experiences move students out of their familiar ways of thinking and acting into realms that are challenging in their newness.

But it is easy to misjudge when instead of jogging students out of a rut in a productively troubling way, this attempt to explore multiple perspectives only sows the seeds of disorientation and confusion. Team teaching helps keep this possibility in check to some degree. If different members of a team can make it clear that for the next 15 or 20 minutes in a discussion they are going to be speaking in a certain theoretical voice, students are better able to understand the different perspectives that can be brought to bear when analyzing a problem. It's much harder for a solo teacher to say "Now I'm speaking from viewpoint A, now I'm speaking from viewpoint B, now I'm speaking from C," and so on. If you do have to teach solo there are visual aids you can use. My favorite (which may sound contrived) is to use baseball hats. Hence, when I wear my Minnesota Twins hat I'm speaking as if I subscribed to perspective A, when I wear my LA Dodgers hat I'm speaking as if it were perspective B, and when I wear my Boston Red Sox hat it's perspective C.

Another exercise I use is an adaptation of the Speaking in Tongues mentioned in Chapter Three. Here I post signs for three or four stations around the room, each of which represents a different theoretical paradigm or analytical standpoint. I give an analysis of an issue, or explanation of some content, from each of these stations, speaking each time as if I found the argument represented at each station to be completely accurate. I then ask students to go and stand at the station that they feel represents the most compelling argument. In groups I ask them to compare reasons why they chose the station they did, and then to summarize—on newsprint, or in a small group report—what was most convincing to them about that paradigm or standpoint. After each group has reported out, students are then offered the opportunity to switch their vote and move to a different position because they find the arguments they've just heard to be even more compelling. The exercise ends with students explaining to the whole class why they made the switch they did.

Giving an Honest Answer Prematurely

One of the classroom moments a lot of us dread is the question from students—"but what do *you* think professor?" If we are trying to get them to think critically about their own and others' assumptions about a topic, and if we are encouraging them to take responsibility for developing their own independent intellectual judgments, then we may feel that the last thing we want to do is tell them what our thinking is on the question that's been raised. The danger of doing this, of course, is that students will then take your response as gospel truth, as the "correct" way to think about a topic or problem. However, if we wish to model for students what we're asking them to do, it seems fundamentally contradictory not to be able to give our views on something. After all, we're asking students to tell us their emerging thinking—shouldn't students expect us to tell them ours?

My way through this is slightly convoluted, but it is one I use a lot and it has got me out of a lot of these "What do *you* think professor?" situations. Basically, I tell the students I will give them two or three answers to the question. One of them represents my true reasoning on the topic; the other two are plausible viewpoints but they don't represent my own thinking. I briefly explain my two or three responses and then ask students to vote on which answer they feel really represents my own views. Students then form into groups based on which of the three answers they believe represents my own. I give them a few minutes to share with each other the reasons they have for believing my view was (a), (b), or (c).

The whole class then reconvenes and I ask each group to tell me what were the main reasons why they thought view (a), (b), or (c) represented my own thinking. I ask them particularly to talk about the assumptions they think I hold that causes me to believe (a), (b), or (c), and to provide the evidence that prompted their choice. This is where students will refer back to previous classes I've taught in the course and the evidence I quoted there, or they'll point to the correspondence between one of my answers and what they've read in the textbook.

I like this exercise because I am meeting them halfway and showing them that I'm not playing a guessing game where I hide my own opinions and then pounce on someone who asks a question or makes a discussion contribution that contradicts these. So they are finding out what I believe, but they have to work to do this. Instead of the student's question being met by a straight answer from me that will then probably determine all future conversation on the topic, students have to do some intellectual work, to trawl my past comments or what the textbook says, before deciding what they think are my opinions. And then of course, they have to provide reasons, assumptions, and evidence to support their choice. To me this exercise strikes a nice balance between telling people immediately what you think (which is consistent with modeling for students what you are asking *them* to do but runs the risk of providing template for students' own views) and avoiding their question entirely (which would force them to think it out for themselves, but which is inconsistent with the conviction that you should be willing to model, first, whatever you're asking students to do).

Summary

This chapter has tried to reaffirm, and to explore more deeply, the commitment teachers need to make to model critical thinking—publicly and explicitly—in front of students. It is a necessary but also a complicated dynamic. The chances of understanding and negotiating this dynamic are raised considerably if we have some information about how students perceive our actions. This is why I have emphasized the importance of the Critical Incident Questionnaire (CIQ) throughout the book. The CIQ is the instrument I find to be most helpful for me in collecting reliable data about how students are experiencing my teaching. But other classroom assessments are available for this purpose (Anderson, 2002; Brookhart, 2000; Butler and McMunn, 2006). The particular instrument you use is much less important than the general principle that making good decisions as a teacher depends on your knowing how your students are learning.

Although I have tried to give general advice throughout this book, and to provide as many practical examples of exercises, techniques, and methods, as I could, I should end with a caution about my own project. Learning to think critically is an enormously complex process that manifests itself in unlimited ways across different disciplines, different students, and with different teachers. I can't walk in your shoes, know your students, or inhabit your classrooms and staffrooms. So don't feel any compunction about stealing an idea here, a technique there, from these pages and then reshaping them to fit your practice. Skillful teachers are like good cat burglars; they can enter someone else's house, do a quick scan of its contents, and decide in an instant what is most important to take away (I don't speak from personal experience of criminality here!). So if you find something in these chapters that looks like it might be helpful, feel free to change or adapt it in any way you think fit to make it more usable in your classroom, community, or organization. After all, you're the person who knows your work context better than anyone else.

Finally, I should come clean and say that I am still trying to figure out the apparently endless permutations and variations of my own practice. Needless to say, I feel permanently like an impostor and view myself as a novice, even though I've been doing this for over forty years. But there are some things I know as truth:

- I know that with each new course I teach, and each new group of people I work with, I'm going to learn something that will change how I think about the dynamics of learning and teaching critical thinking.

- I know that, given the accelerating pace of technological change, I will have learned some new techniques by the time this book is published.

- I know that no matter what the context, being able to think critically is crucial to your survival and to helping you make choices that are in your best interests.

- I know that there will always be people who will try to squelch your critical thinking because it makes it harder for them to control you.

- I know that although dominant ideology celebrates thinking critically, and that every organization argues that it should be part of learning and working, actually doing it is risky.

- I know that the struggle to live this way is worth it.

References

Adams, K. L. "The Critical Incident Questionnaire: A Critical Reflective Teaching Tool." In *Exchanges: The Online Journal of Teaching and Learning in the CSU*, 2001. Retrieved on Feb. 22 from http://www .exchangesjournal.org/classroom/ciq_pg1.html

Allman, P. *Revolutionary Social Transformation: Democratic Hopes, Political Possibilities and Critical Education.* Westport, CT: Bergin and Garvey, 2000.

Allman, P. *Critical Education Against Global Capitalism: Karl Marx and Revolutionary Critical Education.* Westport, CT: Bergin and Garvey, 2001.

Anderson, L. W. *Classroom Assessment: Enhancing the Quality of Teacher Decision Making.* Mahwah, NJ: Lawrence Erlbaum Associates, 2002.

Andolina, N. *Critical Thinking for Working Students.* Albany, NY: Delmar/ Thomson Learning. 2000.

Andolina, M. *Practical Guide to Critical Thinking.* Albany, NY: Delmar/Thomson Learning. 2002.

Argyris, C. *Organizational Traps: Leadership, Culture, Organizational Design.* New York: Oxford University Press, 2010.

Barnet, S., and Bedau, H. *Critical Thinking, Reading, and Writing: A Brief Guide to Argument.* Boston: Bedford/St. Martin's, 2005.

Bassham, G., Irwin, W., Nardone, H., and Wallace, J. M. *Critical Thinking: A Student's Introduction.* (3rd ed.) New York: McGraw-Hill, 2007.

Baudrillard, J. *The Mirror of Production.* New York: Telos Press, 1975.

Belenky, M. F., Clinchy, B. M., Goldberger, N. R., and Tarule, J. M. *Women's Ways of Knowing: The Development of Self, Voice, and Mind.* New York: Basic Books, 1986.

Bergin, D. A., and Cooks, H. C. "High School Students of Color Talk About Accusations of 'Acting White'." *Urban Review*, 2002, 34(2), 13–34.

Bronner, S. E. *Critical Theory: A Very Short Introduction.* New York: Oxford University Press, 2011.

Bronner, S. E., and Kellner, D. M. (eds.). *Critical Theory and Society: A Reader*. New York: Routledge, 1989.

Brookfield, S. D. "Tales from the Dark Side: A Phenomenograhy of Adult Critical Reflection." *International Journal of Lifelong Education*, 1994, *13*(3), 203–216.

Brookfield, S. D. *Becoming a Critically Reflective Teacher*. San Francisco: Jossey-Bass, 1995.

Brookfield, S. D. *The Power of Critical Theory: Liberating Adult Learning and Teaching*. San Francisco: Jossey-Bass, 2004.

Brookfield, S. D. "Overcoming Impostorship, Cultural Suicide and Lost Innocence: Implications for Teaching Critical Thinking in the Community College." In C. McMahon (ed.), *Critical Thinking: Unfinished Business*. San Francisco: Jossey-Bass, 2005.

Brookfield, S. D. *The Skillful Teacher: On Trust, Risk and Responsiveness in the Classroom*. (2nd ed.) San Francisco: Jossey-Bass, 2006.

Brookfield, S. D. "When the Black Dog Barks: Adult Learning in and on Clinical Depression." In T. Rocco (ed.), *Challenging Ableism, Understanding Disability: Including Adults with Disabilities in Workplaces and Learning Spaces*. San Francisco: Jossey-Bass, 2011.

Brookfield, S. D., and Holst, J. D. *Radicalizing Learning: Adult Education for a Just World*. San Francisco: Jossey-Bass, 2010.

Brookfield, S. D., and Preskill, S. *Discussion as a Way of Teaching: Tools and Techniques for Democratic Classrooms*. (2nd ed.) San Francisco: Jossey-Bass, 2005.

Brookhart, S. M. *The Art and Science of Classroom Assessment: The Missing Part of Pedagogy*. ASHE-ERIC Higher Education Report Series, Vol. 27, No. 1. San Francisco: Jossey-Bass, 2000.

Browne, M. N., and Keeley, S. M. *Asking the Right Questions: A Guide to Critical Thinking*. (8th ed.) Upper Saddle River, NJ: Pearson/Prentice Hall, 2007.

Bruff, D. *Teaching with Classroom Response Systems: Creating Active Learning Environments*. San Francisco: Jossey-Bass, 2009.

Butler, S. M., and McMunn, N. D. *A Teacher's Guide to Classroom Assessment*. San Francisco: Jossey-Bass, 2006.

Calderon, J. "Perspective Taking as a Tool for Building Democratic Societies." *Diversity and Democracy*, Vol. 14, No. 1. Retrieved on February 24, 2011, from: http://www.diversityweb.org/DiversityDemocracy/vol14no1/calderon.cfm?utm_source=news&utm_medium=blast&utm_campaign=divdemvol14no1

Casey, J. G. "Diversity, Discourse, and the Working-Class Student." *Academe*, 2005, 91(4), 33–36.

Chaffee. J. *Thinking Critically.* (8th ed.) Boston: Houghton Mifflin, 2006.

Chaffee, J. *The Philosopher's Way: Thinking Critically About Profound Ideas.* (2nd ed.) Upper Saddle River, NJ: Pearson/Prentice Hall, 2008.

Cherryholmes, C. H. *Reading Pragmatism.* New York: Teachers College Press, 1999.

Conrad, M. F. *How to Stop Assumicide: How to Think Critically About What You Believe Without Destroying Your Faith.* Tallahassee, FL: The Learning Doctor, 2008.

Cooper, S., and Patton, R. *Writing Logically, Thinking Critically.* (6th ed.) New York: Pearson/Longman, 2009.

Derrida, J. *Writing and Difference.* New York: Routledge, 1978.

Diestler, S. *Becoming a Critical Thinker: A User Friendly Manual.* (5th ed.) Upper Saddle River, NJ: Pearson/Prentice Hall, 2009.

Eagleton, T. *Ideology: An Introduction.* London: Verso Press, 2007.

Elder, L., and Paul, R. W. *The Miniature Guide to the Art of Asking Essential Questions.* Tomales, CA: Foundation for Critical Thinking, 2006.

Elder, L., and Paul, R. W. *The Thinker's Guide to Analytic Thinking.* Tomales, CA: Foundation for Critical Thinking, 2010.

Evans, C. "Historicism, Chronology and Straw Men: Situating Hawkes' 'Ladder of Inference'." *Antiquity*, 1998, 72, 398–404.

Finkel, D. L. *Teaching with Your Mouth Shut.* Portsmouth, NH: Heinemann, 2000.

Fisher, A. *Critical Thinking: An Introduction.* New York: Cambridge University Press, 2001.

Flew, A. *How to Think Straight: An Introduction to Critical Reasoning.* (2nd ed.) Amherst, NY: Prometheus, 1998.

Foucault, M. *Power/Knowledge: Selected Interviews and Other Writings, 1972–1977.* New York: Pantheon Books, 1980.

Freire, P. *Education for Critical Consciousness.* New York: Continuum, 2005.

Fromm, E. *Escape from Freedom.* New York: Holt, Rinehart and Winston, 1941.

Fromm, E. *Marx's Concept of Man.* New York: Ungar, 1961.

Gay, G. *Culturally Responsive Teaching: Theory, Research, and Practice.* (2nd ed.) New York: Teachers College Press, 2010.

Ginsberg, M. B., and Wlodkowski, R. J. *Diversity and Motivation: Culturally Responsive Teaching in College.* (2nd ed.) San Francisco: Jossey-Bass, 2009.

Glowacki-Dudka, M., and Barnett, N. "Connecting Critical Reflection and Group Development in Online Adult Education Classrooms." *International Journal of Teaching and Learning in Higher Education*, 2007, *19*(1), 43–52.

Gould, R. "The Therapeutic Learning Program." In J. Mezirow and Associates, *Fostering Critical Reflection in Adulthood: A Guide to Transformative and Emancipatory Learning*. San Francisco: Jossey-Bass, 1990.

Gramsci, A. *Selections from the Prison Notebooks*, ed. Q. Hoare and G. N. Smith. London: Lawrence and Wishart, 1971.

Gramsci, A. *The Antonio Gramsci Reader*, ed. D. Forgacs. New York: New York University Press, 1988.

Habermas, J. *The Theory of Communicative Action: Volume Two, Lifeworld and System—A Critique of Functionalist Reason*. Boston: Beacon Press, 1987.

Hagstrom, D. *From Outrageous to Inspired: How to Build a Community of Leaders in Our Schools*. San Francisco: Jossey-Bass, 2004.

Herrera, S. *Biography-Driven Culturally Responsive Teaching*. New York: Teachers College Press, 2010.

Hooks, B., and West, C. *Breaking Bread: Insurgent Black Intellectual Life*. Boston: South End Press, 1991.

Horkheimer, M., and Adorno, T. *Dialectic of Enlightenment*. New York: Seabury Press, 1972.

Horton, M. *The Myles Horton Reader: Education for Social Change*. Knoxville, TN: University of Tennessee Press, 2003.

Janis, I. L. *Groupthink: Psychological Studies of Policy Decisions and Fiascoes*. Boston: Houghton Mifflin, 1982.

Keefer, J. "The Critical Incident Questionnaire: From Research to Practice and Back Again." In *Proceedings of the 2009 Adult Education Research Conference*. Chicago: Dept. of Adult and Continuing Education, National Louis University, 2009, pp.177–182.

Kuhn, T. S. *The Structure of Scientific Revolutions*. Chicago: University of Chicago Press, 1962.

Lacan, J. *The Four Fundamental Concepts of Psychoanalysis*. London: Penguin, 1979.

Laing, R. *The Divided Self: A Study of Sanity and Madness*. London: Tavistock Publications, 1960.

Lee, H. J. "Thrust into Leaning and Thinking Critically: East Asian Doctoral Students' Experience, Meaning, and Process of Engaging in Critical Reflection at U.S. Universities." *Proceedings of the Transnational Migration and Adult Education Conference: Global Issues and Debates*. Toronto: Dept.

of Adult Education, Ontario Institute for Studies in Adult Education, 2011.

Lindeman, E. C. L. *The Meaning of Adult Education*. Montreal: Harvest House, 1961. (First published by New Republic, 1926.)

Loach, K. *Family Life*. London: Kestrel Films, 1971.

Lyotard, J. *The Postmodern Condition: A Report on Knowledge*. Minneapolis: University of Minnesota Press, 1984.

Mandela, N. *Long Walk to Freedom: The Autobiography of Nelson Mandela*. Boston: Little Brown and Company, 1994.

Marcuse, H. *One Dimensional Man*. Boston: Beacon, 1964.

Marcuse, H. "Repressive Tolerance." In R. P. Wolff, B. Moore, and H. Marcuse. *A Critique of Pure Tolerance*. Boston: Beacon Press, 1965.

Marcuse, H. "Philosophy and Critical Theory." In S. E. Bronner and D. M. Kellner (eds.), *Critical Theory and Society: A Reader*. New York: Routledge, 1989.

McInerny, D. Q. *Being Logical: A Guide to Good Thinking*. New York: Random House, 2005.

McKinley, J. *Raising Black Students Achievement Through Culturally Responsive Teaching*. Alexandria, VA: American Society for Curriculum and Development, 2010.

McWhorter, K. T. *Study and Critical Thinking Skills in College*. (6th ed.) New York: Pearson/Longman, 2008.

Mezirow, J. "A Critical Theory of Adult Learning and Education." *Adult Education*, 1981, *32*(1), 3–27.

Mezirow, J. *Transformative Dimensions of Adult Learning*. San Francisco: Jossey-Bass, 1991.

Mezirow, J., and Associates. *Learning as Transformation: Critical Perspectives on a Theory in Progress*. San Francisco: Jossey-Bass, 2000.

Mezirow, J., and Taylor E. (eds.). *Transformative Learning in Practice: Insights from Community, Workplace, and Higher Education*. San Francisco: Jossey-Bass, 2009.

Mills, C. W. *The Sociological Imagination*. New York: Oxford University Press, 1959.

Mills, C. W. *The Marxists*. New York: Dell, 1962.

Nosich, G. M. *Learning to Think Things Through: A Guide to Critical Thinking Across the Curriculum*. (3rd ed.) Upper Saddle River, NJ: Pearson/Prentice Hall, 2009.

Orwell, G. "Politics and the English Language." In G. Orwell (ed.), *A Collection of Essays*. New York: Doubleday, 1946.

Palmer, P. *A Hidden Wholeness: The Journey Toward an Undivided Life*. San Francisco: Jossey-Bass, 2008.

Pari, C., and Shor I. (eds.). *Education Is Politics: Critical Teaching Across Differences, Postsecondary*. Portsmouth, NH: Boynton Cook, 2000.

Paul, R. W., and Elder, L. *Critical Thinking: Tools for Taking Charge of Your Professional and Personal Life*. (3rd ed.) Upper Saddle River, NJ: Pearson/Prentice Hall, 2005.

Paul, R. W., and Elder, L. *The Thinker's Guide to Fallacies: The Art of Mental Trickery*. Tomales, CA: Foundation for Critical Thinking, 2006a.

Paul, R. W., and Elder, L. *The Thinker's Guide for Conscientious Citizens on How to Detect Media Bias and Propaganda*. Tomales, CA: Foundation for Critical Thinking, 2006b.

Paul, R. W., and Elder, L. *The Thinker's Guide to the Art of Socratic Questioning*. Tomales, CA: Foundation for Critical Thinking, 2007a.

Paul, R. W., and Elder, L. *The Thinker's Guide to How to Write a Paragraph*. Tomales, CA: Foundation for Critical Thinking, 2007b.

Paul, R. W., and Elder, L. *The Thinker's Guide for Students on How to Study and Learn a Discipline*. Tomales, CA: Foundation for Critical Thinking, 2007c.

Paul, R. W., and Elder, L. *The Thinker's Guide to How to Read a Paragraph*. Tomales, CA: Foundation for Critical Thinking, 2008.

Paxton, D. "Transforming White Consciousness." In V. Sheared, J. Johnson-Bailey, S. A. J. Colin Jr., E. Peterson, and S. D. Brookfield (eds.). *Handbook of Race and Adult Education: A Resource for Dialogue on Racism*. San Francisco: Jossey-Bass, 2010, pp. 119–132.

Peters, R. S. *The Philosophy of Education*. New York: Oxford University Press, 1973.

Popper, K. R. *The Open Society and Its Enemies*, Vol. 1: *The Spell of Plato*. Princeton, NJ: Princeton University Press (Revised edition), 1971a.

Popper, K. R. *The Open Society and Its Enemies*, Vol. 2: *Hegel, Marx, and the Aftermath*. Princeton, NJ: Princeton University Press (Revised ed.), 1971b.

Popper, K. R. *The Logic of Scientific Discovery*. (2nd ed.) New York: Routledge, 2002. Originally published 1959.

Popper, K. R. *The Poverty of Historicism*. (2nd ed.) New York: Routledge, 2002. Originally published 1957.

Pratt, D. D., and Wong, W. "Chinese Conceptions of 'Effective Teaching' in Hong Kong: Towards Culturally Sensitive Evaluation of Teaching." *International Journal of Lifelong Education*, 1999, *18*(4), 241–258.

Reason, R. "Encouraging Perspective-Taking Among College Students." *Diversity and Democracy*, Vol. 14, No. 1. Retrieved on February 24th, 2011, from: http://www.diversityweb.org/DiversityDemocracy/vol14no1/calderon.cfm?utm_source=news&utm_medium=blast&utm_campaign=divdemvol14no1

Rogers, C. R. *On Becoming a Person: A Therapist's View of Psychotherapy.* Boston: Houghton Mifflin, 1961.

Rogers, C. R. *A Way of Being.* Boston: Houghton Mifflin, 1980.

Ruggerio, V. R. *Beyond Feelings: A Guide to Critical Thinking.* Mountain View, CA: Mayfield, 1990.

Ruggerio, V. R. *Becoming a Critical Thinker: A Master Student Text.* (6th ed.) Belmont, CA: Wadsworth, 2008.

Schick, T. Jr., and Vaughn, L. *How to Think About Weird Things: Critical Thinking for a New Age.* (3rd ed.) New York: McGraw-Hill, 2002.

Searle, J. *The Construction of Social Reality.* New York: Simon and Schuster, 1995.

Senge, P. *The Fifth Discipline: The Art and Practice of the Learning Organization.* (revised ed.) New York: New York: Doubleday, 2006.

Shor, I. (ed.). *Freire for the Classroom: A Sourcebook for Liberatory Teaching.* Portsmouth, NH: Boynton Cook, 1987.

Shor, I., and Pari, C. (eds.). *Education Is Politics: Critical Teaching Across Differences, K–12.* Portsmouth, NH: Boynton Cook, 1999.

Simon, R. I. *Teaching Against the Grain: Texts for a Pedagogy of Possibility.* Westport, CT: Bergin and Garvey, 1992.

Sinnott, J. D. *The Development of Logic in Adulthood: Postformal Thought and Its Applications.* New York: Plenum, 2010.

Smith, H. "The Foxfire Approach to Student and Community Interaction." In L. Shumow (ed.), *Promising Practices for Family and Community Involvement During High School.* Charlotte, NC: Information Age Publishing, 2009.

Souto-Manning, M., Ayers, W. A., and Shor, I. *Freire, Teaching, and Learning.* New York: Peter Lang, 2010.

Sternberg, R. J., Forsyth, G. B., Hedlund, J., Horvath, J. A., Wagner, R. K., Williams, W. M., Snook, S. A., and Grigorenko, E. *Practical Intelligence in Everyday Life.* New York: Cambridge University Press, 2000.

Storr, A. *The Integrity of the Personality.* New York: Ballantine Books, 1992. (First published in 1961.)

Taylor, E., and Cranton, P. (eds.). *The Handbook of Transformative Learning Theory.* San Francisco: Jossey-Bass, forthcoming.

Thomson, A. *Critical Reasoning: A Practical Introduction.* (3rd ed.) New York: Routledge, 2008.

Tweed, R. G., and Lehman, D. R. "Learning Considered Within a Cultural Context: Confucian and Socratic Approaches." *American Psychologist,* 2002, *57*(2), 89–99.

Vaughn, L. *The Power of Critical Thinking: Effective Reasoning About Ordinary and Extraordinary Claims.* (3rd ed.) New York: Oxford University Press, 2009.

Vygotsky, L. S. *Mind and Society: The Development of Higher Psychological Processes.* Cambridge, MA: Harvard University Press, 1978.

Wall, T. F. *Thinking Critically and Moral Problems.* Belmont, CA: Wadsworth/ Thompson Learning, 2003.

Waller, B. *Critical Thinking: Consider the Verdict.* (5th ed.) Upper Saddle River, NJ: Pearson/Prentice Hall, 2004.

Welsch, K. A. (ed.). *Those Working Sundays: Female Academics and Their Working Class Parents.* Lanham, MD: University Press of America, 2004.

West, C. *Prophesy Deliverance: An Afro-American Revolutionary Christianity.* Philadelphia: The Westminster Press, 1982.

West, C. *Prophetic Thought in Postmodern Times.* Monroe, ME: Common Courage Press, 1993.

Willingham, D. "Critical Thinking: Why Is It So Hard to Teach?" *American Educator,* 2007, *31*(2), 8–19.

Wittgenstein, L. *Philosophical Investigations.* (4th ed.) Malden, MA: Blackwell-Wiley, 2009.

Zamudio, M., Russell, C., Rios, F., and Bridgeman, J. L. *Critical Race Theory Matters: Education and Ideology.* New York: Routledge, 2010.

Index